Radical Abundance

'Degrowth or ecomodernism? This book offers a compelling alternative. More than a utopian ideal, radical abundance is the guiding principle of a socialist revolution already in action.'

—Kohei Saito, author of *Slow Down: How Degrowth Communism Can Save the Earth*

'The crises we face – mass deprivation and ecological breakdown – cannot be resolved within capitalism. We need a pathway out. *Radical Abundance* delivers exactly that. If you're looking for practical steps to a post-capitalist future, don't miss this book.'

—Jason Hickel, author of *Less is More: How Degrowth Will Save the World*

'*Radical Abundance* resets the terms of left debate. With its concrete, compelling, and creative embrace of class struggle as a politics of transition, it is indispensable to anyone committed to building popular power on a rapidly heating planet.'

Jodi Dean, author of *Capital's Grave: Neofeudalism and the New Class Struggle*

'This is the book that many of us were waiting for: a breath of fresh air out of the false choice between the bullshit abundance of neoliberal capitalism and the artificial scarcity of austerity policies. Building on Marx's view of communal abundance, and on different experiences where it has been put into practice, this book gives a new meaning to the politics of transition.'

—Stefania Barca, author of *Workers of the Earth: Labour, Ecology and Reproduction in the Age of Climate Change*

'A rigorously argued and radically hopeful book, which exposes the gross inefficiency of modern capitalism and shows precisely how we can begin to build societies that guarantee a good life for all.'

—Grace Blakeley, author of *Vulture Capitalism: How to Survive in an Age of Corporate Greed*

Radical Abundance

How to Win a Green Democratic Future

Kai Heron, Keir Milburn
and Bertie Russell

PLUTO PRESS

First published 2025 by Pluto Press
New Wing, Somerset House, Strand, London WC2R 1LA
and Pluto Press, Inc.
1930 Village Center Circle, 3-834, Las Vegas, NV 89134

www.plutobooks.com

Copyright © Kai Heron, Keir Milburn and Bertie Russell 2025

The right of Kai Heron, Keir Milburn and Bertie Russell to be identified as the authors of this work has been asserted in accordance with the Copyright, Designs and Patents Act 1988.

British Library Cataloguing in Publication Data
A catalogue record for this book is available from the British Library

ISBN 978 0 7453 5135 3 Paperback
ISBN 978 0 7453 5138 4 PDF
ISBN 978 0 7453 5137 7 EPUB

This book is printed on paper suitable for recycling and made from fully managed and sustained forest sources. Logging, pulping and manufacturing processes are expected to conform to the environmental standards of the country of origin.

Typeset by Stanford DTP Services, Northampton, England

Simultaneously printed in the United Kingdom and United States of America

EU GPSR Authorised Representative
LOGOS EUROPE, 9 rue Nicolas Poussin, 17000, LA ROCHELLE, France
Email: Contact@logoseurope.eu

Contents

For Amy, Mathilde, Phoebe, Sara, Ayla, Alice, and Mae.
We hope you get to live in a world of radical abundance.

List of Figures

Acknowledgements

This book is a coming to fruition of what is now approaching two decades of collaboration and friendship. It is a product of our individual and shared political histories, an uncountable number of experiences, debates, and disagreements, and the wealth of relationships we've each built along the way. It also reflects the broader shifting political coordinates of the past 25 years, how we've perceived this from within the UK in particular, and the broad failure (at least within imperial core countries) to develop any tangible response to the compounding social and ecological crises we face. In this respect, the book is a collective outcome that far exceeds the thoughts of the named authors, and we hope others might see their own experiences and analysis reflected throughout.

Yet this book is also the result of a more specific collaboration that began in 2018, which led to the development of the UK-based organisation, Abundance (in-abundance.org). In many ways this book can be read as the underpinning hypothesis of that organisation which, along with our comrades and co-directors Frances Northrop and Ben Beach, is committed to advancing a politics of commoning and common ownership, or what we call public-common strategies for ecosocial transition. If this book is our theory of change, Abundance is one way we're trying to put a politics of transition into practice. Indeed the latter three chapters of the book — in which we focus specifically on urban development, pharmaceuticals, and agroecological food sovereignty — draw on some of the past and ongoing work of Abundance. It's by telling a short story of how this organisation came into being that we can acknowledge some of the fellow travellers and supporters of this project.

The particular significance of 2018 was that it marked an affectively unfamiliar moment of political optimism. Irrespective of the wider shortcomings, the Jeremy Corbyn and John McDonnell leadership of the UK Labour Party opened a window where it was possible to think seriously about the prospect of fundamental transformations in how we organise our lives. What Joe Guinan and Martin O'Neill* called the 'institutional turn' in the UK Labour Party was not so much about the machinations of party politics, but rather a renewed focus on the importance of ownership. Who owns our collective wealth? How do they own it? And with what political consequences? The 2017 *Alternative Models of Ownership* report commissioned by the then shadow chancellor McDonnell was emblematic of this institutional turn, serving as a clarion call for new thinking on how we might push beyond simplistic understandings of 'public ownership'. In some respects, this book is an ongoing meditation on the central role that institutions will play in an ecosocialist transition.

This moment of optimism gave birth to a number of important organisations on the British left, not least Common Wealth, whose founder and director Mathew Lawrence asked us to write the organisation's first report — *Building Public-Common Partnerships: Building New Circuits of Collective Ownership*. Latterly incubated under its wings, we received particular support from Bonnie Hewson, Christine Berry, and Miriam Brett, who encouraged us to move from conceptual proposition to exploring the development and implementation of PCPs in practice. Many of those we have subsequently met and collaborated with — including Daniel Fernández Pascual, Alon Schwabe, Shona Cameron, Carlos Burgos, Vicky Alvarez, Frédéric Sultan, Gaelle Krikorian, Gareth Brown, David McEwen, and Jamie Hignett — have been integral to pushing our work forward both concretely and conceptually.

It is through this work that we eventually turned to the prospect of writing this book. After a number of years focusing on practical challenges and organisational mechanics — along with participating in US anti-pipeline and anti-imperialist movements, Europe's 'new municipalist movement', and broader European commoning initiatives — our intention was to return to the development of a

* See Guinan & O'Neill, 2018, and our response Russell & Milburn, 2018.

more systematic and coherent account of how an 'organisational turn' would play a fundamental role within a broader politics of ecosocial transition. Our analysis would also come to incorporate lessons from global working-class and peasant movements fighting for common ownership or participating in communal institutional forms from Venezuela, to Kerala, to Berlin. Here a number of broader personal and collective discussions were particularly supportive and informative to our work, including (but by no means limited to) Max Ajl, Iolanda Bianchi, Patrick Bresnihan, Mauro Castro, Jodi Dean, Chris Gilbert, Andoni Egia, Iker Eizagirre, Rodrigo Nunes, Alejandro Pedregal, Boštjan Remic, Isaac Rose, Laura Roth, Matthew Thompson, Jess Thorne, and Project REAL's politics circle at Universidad Autónoma de Barcelona and the University of Lausanne.

In particular, we want to thank a number of people who read and provided critical feedback on various chapter drafts, or who pointed us towards essential resources, including Emma Cardwell, Amy Clancy, Jodi Dean, Sam Deboise, James Fraser, Simona Getova, Chris Gilbert, Alex Heffron, Jason Hickel, Inea Lehner, Charles Stevenson, Hilary Wainwright, and Lancaster's Political Ecology of Agrarian Transitions research group. Their feedback has been invaluable.

We would also like to thank Naira Antoun for her close edits and suggestions, and the team at Pluto including David Shulman, David Castle, Sophie O'Reirdan, James Kelly, and Jonila Krasniqi for their editing, encouragement, and support.

This work was supported by the European Union's Horizon Europe research and innovation programme under the Marie Skłodowska-Curie Grant Agreement No. 101026892.

Thanks also to Arby Hisenaj and Amy Clancy, who developed our conceptual sketches into the original versions of Figures 1–5.

1

Introduction: From Bullshit Abundance to Radical Abundance

We live in a world of bullshit abundance. A world where we have too much of what we don't need and too little of what we do. Even worse, there are people who want to keep it this way. As you read this, for example, microplastics are coursing through your bloodstream, contributing to potential changes in your immune system, and building up in your organs.[1] If you've had a child in recent years, they will have been born with microplastics already in their system. If you are thinking of having children in the future, there's next to nothing you can do to protect them. Microplastics are now considered a constituent part of every rain cloud and every raindrop.[2] The health and ecological effects of microplastics are not yet entirely understood, but studies show that they contribute to heart attacks, cancer, low fertility, and strokes in humans, and that they toxify soils and disrupt ocean carbon storage and nitrogen cycles.[3] While some efforts have been made to address the crisis of accumulating microplastics — including research to develop microplastic-consuming bacteria and giant hoover-like machines that suck microplastics from the ocean — far too little has been done to stop the use of plastics at source. The fossil fuel companies that extract the oil and gas used to manufacture plastics and the largest corporate users of plastic in the world, such as the Coca-Cola company, have vociferously resisted regulatory changes that would hurt their bottom lines.[4] In the name of protecting the profits of the few, the world suffers the bullshit effects of an abundance of microplastics.[5]

Though it isn't often thought about in these terms, the world also suffers from a bullshit abundance of greenhouse gas emissions. Centuries of burning fossil fuels have increased carbon parts per million (ppm) in the atmosphere from 280 ppm prior to the industrial revolution to around 421ppm today. Because of these ever-increasing emissions, the agreement made at COP21 in Paris back in 2016 to keep global warming to 1.5C above pre-industrial levels is dead. On our current path, limiting warming to a catastrophic 2C seems almost fantastical. In a poll of senior climate scientists conducted by the UK's *Guardian* newspaper, almost 80 percent expected average global temperatures to blast past 2.5C causing untold social and ecological destruction.[6] The fossil fuel industry has known it has been destroying the support systems for life on earth as we know it since the 1950s, and has lied about the dangers of the industry for decades. Western governments have similarly known that they need to take immediate action on their emissions for over half a century,[7] and yet responses to the crisis have been constrained by the prioritisation of bullshit abundance: massive accumulations of wealth for the capitalist and political classes, and massive accumulations of atmospheric CO_2 emissions at the expense of the conditions needed for human and non-human life as we know it.

Then there's the bullshit abundance of low-quality mass-produced consumer goods. We are all familiar with the idea of planned obsolescence: the practice of intentionally designing products that break or become quickly outdated to compel consumers to buy more stuff. From lightbulbs, to smartphones, to fast fashion, to kitchen appliances, manufacturers cut the lifetime of commodities short to guarantee maximum profits. In fact, business sustainability scholar Mansoor Soomro finds that common household appliances have 20–30 percent shorter lives than they did even a decade ago.[8] This practice causes chaos up and downstream from the consumer. Upstream, it means more and more material must be mined, grown, processed, and manufactured into consumables, placing pressure on planetary resources and requiring huge amounts of energy. Downstream, it results in an abundance of waste. Products that have unnecessarily come to the end of their lives languish in landfills because it costs more to recycle or refurbish them than to toss them aside where they contaminate soil and water systems. Right in the middle, there's the consumer, who is compelled to buy an only slightly updated version of their phone after the battery stopped charging, or another household appliance after the last one quickly gave up the ghost. Things are getting worse so that profits can get better.

Our lived experience of bullshit abundance isn't only caused by waste and pollution. It's also caused by a proliferation of bullshit that makes our lives harder, less satisfying, and more precarious. To give one example of what we mean, a recent global traffic analysis of almost 1,000 cities from 37 countries found that in 2023 the average New Yorker spent 101 hours sitting in traffic jams. Car dependency is particularly acute in the US, but the top ten most congested cities also included Mexico City, London, Paris, Istanbul, Cape Town, and Jakarta. In the UK, the average worker wastes 61 hours a year — almost two whole working weeks — sitting in a bullshit abundance of traffic.[9] And even then, traffic jams are only a fraction of the total time we spend commuting each year. Research conducted by the Trades Union Congress in 2019 found that annual commuting time in the UK had risen by 21 hours over the previous decade, with the average worker spending 221 hours — more than *an entire month* of workdays — dealing with the infuriating bullshit of travelling to and from work.[10]

Many of us are painfully familiar with this bullshit. We hate that plastics are killing us, our loved ones, and non-human nature. We've felt the depths of despair and the highs of righteous anger thinking about the world's many ecological crises. We resent the time spent sitting in traffic, literally wasting our lives away. The problem is that we feel pretty much powerless to do anything about it. In fact, unless we act collectively, *we are* powerless to do anything about it. This is by design. As we'll argue throughout this book, under capitalism our lives are diminished and our access to the fruits of our collective labour restricted, because it is the profit motive and not the world's working classes that decide what is produced, how, and who by. We might vote every few years, but our vote has little impact; whichever party we choose, our entire social system still prioritises gross domestic product (GDP) over social and ecological needs.

Instead of having a say over what matters most to us, we are increasingly given a bullshit abundance of choice over things we have no interest in choosing. In his book *The Paradox of Choice: Why More is Less*, US psychologist Barry Schwartz shows that while choice has increased precipitously in capitalist societies, consumer satisfaction hasn't increased as much as conventional economic theories predict.[11] The titular paradox at the heart of Schwartz's book is that very often in modern life, the more choices we have, the *less happy* we are with our decisions. Maybe we chose the wrong thing. Maybe the other cereal would have tasted better, would have been healthier, would have saved us money, and so on. A bullshit abundance of choice can also mask a worsening of quality. The UK's Health and Social Care Act 2012, for example, implemented new duties for parts of the NHS to 'offer more patient choice', ostensibly to extend our rights to access the healthcare we need.[12] Again, more freedom of choice might sound good, but in practice the policy has entrenched market mechanisms into the healthcare system, deteriorating standards of care and paving the way for privatisation. Behind our power to 'choose' lies a single, forced, choice: the organisation of healthcare around a bullshit abundance of profits for the few at our collective expense. Similarly, anyone who has tried to travel by train in the UK in the past two decades will have experienced the irony of being thanked 'for choosing to travel' with a monopolised privatised train operator while services are overpriced and chronically delayed, and billions in profit are delivered to shareholders.

ARTIFICIAL SCARCITY

We have pointed above to just a few examples of how bullshit abundance makes our lives harder, shorter, and less enjoyable today. Once you start looking for it, you'll find instances everywhere. One peculiar feature of bullshit abundance, though, is its inseparability from what may at first seem its opposite: scarcity. The scarcity we have in mind isn't the kind experienced when there just isn't enough of something to go around, but when scarcity is *imposed* on some for the economic and political benefit of others. It is an *artificial scarcity*.[13]

The British Conservative Party's austerity agenda after the 2008 financial crash is an obvious example. Along with organisations like the International Monetary Fund and the European Central Bank, Britain adopted the seemingly contradictory doctrine of expansionary austerity, whereby deep cuts to public services and welfare systems would stimulate private investment which had been 'crowded out' by state provision. A 2010 research paper by Carmen Reinhart and Kenneth Rogoff seemed to provide support for this argument. They found statistical evidence that economic growth slows dramatically if government borrowing reaches 90 percent of GDP. Governments across the world implemented deep public spending cuts, causing great hardship and suffering, yet the promised growth never arrived. At the same time that the British government was telling the public that cuts must be made, government borrowing grew, subsidies for fossil fuels continued unabated, and military expenditure carried on as usual. In 2013, a PhD student discovered basic spreadsheet errors in Reinhart and Rogoff's paper which discredited their findings. Of course, the UK government didn't change course despite the disproof of the flimsy evidence they were hiding behind. The fiasco underlines that austerity is always a political choice, a decision to impose artificial scarcity in order to create opportunities for a bullshit abundance of private profits.

The notion of artificial scarcity is not just useful for understanding the spheres of politics and economics. We can think of artificial scarcity as reaching into our bodies, even. A growing body of research shows that the so-called 'Western diet's' bullshit abundance of foods low in fibre but high in saturated fat, refined sugars, salts, and sweeteners is contributing to dramatic declines in gut microbiome diversity. In 2018, a large cohort study found that a reduction in the diversity, function, and composition of the gut microbiome was strongly correlated with immigration to the United States, with diet likely being a contributing factor alongside issues such as wider prevalence of antibiotic use.[14] Why does an artificial scarcity in our microbial diversity matter? Because it's directly associated with an increased risk of diabetes,[15] obesity and cardiovascular diseases, inflammatory bowel diseases,[16] asthma,[17] and a wide range of allergies.[18] The artificial scarcity in our gut microbiome — in part the product of the mass produced and ultra-processed Western food economy, which comprises over half of the average diet in both the US and UK — is making us sick, while making the food and beverage industry, privatised healthcare systems, and private healthcare insurers hundreds of billions in profits each year.

Then there are the more surprising ways that artificial scarcity insinuates itself into our lives. While it might seem like we have an abundance of cultural experiences today, we're actually in the midst of a quite rapid decline in diversity, and hence an artificial scarcity of opportunities to experience things that are radically new and interesting. Take music streaming services. From a quick look at their apps it might seem like we have more choice and more personalised music preferences than ever, yet research into megatrends in the music industry suggests the opposite.[19] A recent study of over 350,000 English-language songs found that, over the past five decades, both the lexical complexity of lyrics (such as the richness of the vocabulary) and the overall structural complexity has decreased. Earlier research had already highlighted a general tendency towards a reduction in the variety of pitch transitions (harmonic content of the piece, including its chords, melody, and tonal arrangements) and the overall homogenisation of the timbre palette (essentially associated with instrument types, recording techniques, and some expressive performance resources).[20] A separate study on the instrumentational complexity of music found that genres become increasingly formulaic in terms of instrumentation once commercial or mainstream success sets in, demonstrating an overall decline in complexity.[21] The music industry's pursuit of profits, in other words, imposes an artificial scarcity on the kinds of musical forms that you are likely to be exposed to.

Artificial scarcity is also created in non-human nature. Since 1970, UK species have declined by around 19 percent and nearly one in six are threatened with extinction.[22] Globally, conservationists and ecologists have warned of a 'sixth great extinction'. Wildlife populations have plummeted by an average of 73 percent in 50 years as capital's pursuit of profits at the expense of non-human nature pushes ecosystems beyond their limits.[23] The UN's Food and Agriculture Organization (FAO), on the other hand, found that the global rate of deforestation had slowed in the three decades up to 2020.[24] This is seemingly good news, but the slowdown is in part caused by the planting of 131 million hectares of cash crops such as palm oil, timber, or rubber to deliver carbon-offsetting programmes. An incredible 45 percent of this new tree cover is composed of just one or two species. This dramatic reduction in the variety of trees makes it impossible for many species to survive. Where once there was a rich diversity of life, there stands row after row of the same crops or supposedly carbon-offsetting trees. One meta-study of the effects of palm oil plantations on biodiversity found that only 15 percent of species recorded in primary forests were latterly found in new plantations, with vertebrae species declining by more than 50 percent.[25] Separate research has found that commercial pine, eucalyptus, and teak plantations, all of which are popular in carbon-offsetting schemes, are driving soil acidification, depleting groundwater, and increasing the risk and intensity of wildfires.[26] Mainstream economists like to speak of these things as 'negative externalities'. It would be better to think of them as the active generation of an artificial scarcity of the conditions needed for a socially, culturally, and ecologically biodiverse life.

WHOSE BULLSHIT? WHOSE SCARCITY?

Bullshit abundance and artificial scarcity are two sides of the same coin. More properly speaking, they're dialectically related, which means that a bullshit abundance of profits for some — landlord and capitalist classes — cannot be produced without imposing artificial scarcity on the human and non-human majority. But capitalism's dialectics of bullshit abundance and artificial scarcity are not experienced equally by everyone. The world's working classes, by which we mean waged and unwaged workers, peasants, and Indigenous peoples are differentially exposed to the violence that is capitalist "business as usual". Not everyone has the dubious pleasure of accessing a bullshit abundance of increasingly shoddy consumables. Not everyone is equally suffering a decline in their microbiome. Neither is everyone experiencing the loss of biodiverse forests that their culture and livelihood relies on.

Capitalism generates bullshit abundance in some parts of the world by imposing artificial scarcity on others. The cheap consumables and cheap food that some have access to in the Global North — or, more accurately, the imperial core, since the US, Western Europe, and their imperial allies are today's hegemonic powers — are made possible by imposing various kinds of artificial scarcity on workers and ecosystems in the Global South — or, more accurately, the periphery.[27] Through a process known as labour arbitration, multinational companies registered in the imperial core hire subcontractors to employ labour with low wages and poor working conditions in the periphery. Keeping wages and welfare to a minimum, while limiting international freedom of movement of workers, means commodities can be manufactured at a low enough price in the periphery to be affordable to most in the core. Through this bullshit process, which divides the global working class against itself, profits are made for the world's capitalist classes.

The political economist John Smith has shown how the process of labour arbitration that is at work in everyday commodities, from coffee to clothing to smart phones, has deleterious effects for workers — usually racialised, usually women — in the periphery.[28] Development scholars Utsa and Prabhat Patnaik show that tropical foods and flowers are similarly produced through the super-exploitation of lands, seas, and labour in the periphery to ensure the core has an abundance of tropical foodstuffs in and out of season, even as hunger and malnutrition increase among the very people growing our food.[29]

And even this can't secure a good life for everyone in the core. Labourers and non-labourers of 'advanced' capitalist countries are often the relative beneficiaries of this global division of labour, but the key word here is relative. Access to cheap consumer goods and ultra-processed food, while only possible through the super-exploitation of the periphery, does not secure a good life for all in the imperial core. These countries are themselves riddled with inequalities structured along class, racialised, gendered, and urban/rural divides. If farmworkers living near the lithium mines on Chile's Salar de Atacama face dire water shortages, chemical pollution, and low wages, it's also the fate of the majority-Black communities drinking lead-contaminated water in Flint, Michigan. If racialised women are those who work in dire conditions in the 400 garment factories located in the Savar district of Dhaka, it is also racialised women who work in the hundreds of fast-fashion factories in Leicester. And as the so-called 'cost of living' rises in the core, as secure well-paid employment becomes harder to find, and as affordable housing becomes harder to source, more and more workers in the core — including within formerly reasonably safe and well-paid jobs such as teaching or secretarial work — are experiencing an artificially imposed scarcity that generates a bullshit abundance of profits for energy companies, landlords, asset managers, and shareholders. The *absolute* beneficiaries of all of this, as always under capitalism, are the capitalist, landlord, and asset-holding classes.

This polarisation of bullshit abundance and artificial scarcity also plays out in non-human nature. Toxic and polluting by-products of manufacturing are routinely disposed of into water systems, soils, and the atmosphere. Under capitalism, the manufacture and disposal of by-products associated with everything from solar panels to clothing, from hamburgers to vegan sausages, are dumped into landfills, released into the atmosphere, or otherwise improperly disposed of to reduce costs. These practices negatively affect biodiversity in critical ecosystems across the planet, creating an artificial scarcity of life where once there was human and non-human abundance. Although these practices are global, they are especially pronounced in the world-system's peripheries, where through a process known as 'ecologically unequal exchange' the ecological costs of bullshit abundance are thrown onto human and non-human lives in the imperial core's colonies and neo-colonies, which are locked into a situation of dependence and underdevelopment that constrains the life opportunities of its working classes.[30] Studies into ecologically unequal exchange show that countries in the core are not only net importers of embodied materials, energy, and land but that they gain a monetary trade surplus while peripheral nations suffer monetary trade deficits. Many supposedly British-reared beef cattle, for example, are fed on soy grown in regions of Latin America including Argentina, Brazil, and Paraguay.[31] By using an area of land the size of Wales overseas, Britain can sustain a level of meat consumption that is not only ecologically destructive in its own right but that is two times higher than the global average. Here, the dialectics of generating bullshit abundance in one part of the world-system by imposing artificial scarcity of wealth, land, and resources on another are on full display.[32]

These dialectics also play out in ecosystems in the imperial core. In the UK, for-profit water companies have preferred to pay large dividends to investors rather than repair or update deteriorating sewage systems. As a result, they have little 'choice' but to pour untreated human waste into our rivers and seas. The practice is catastrophic for water-based ecosystems. A bullshit abundance of effluence leads to eutrophication and algae blooms that deprive water-based life of the conditions they need to survive, producing ecological dead zones. These ecological effects loop back around to have social ramifications. Whereas once it was possible to freely swim in the UK's seas and many lakes, streams, and rivers, today the majority are so heavily polluted as to be unsafe. Once again, an artificial scarcity of non-human life and possibilities for human self-expression are the accompaniment of a bullshit abundance of profits for capitalists. Or as Marx puts it, the 'accumulation of wealth at one pole is, therefore, at the same time accumulation of misery, agony of toil, slavery, ignorance, brutality, [and] mental degradation, at the opposite pole'.[33] This is the violent dialectic of bullshit abundance and artificial scarcity that lies at capitalism's rotten core.

WHY NOT GIVE CAPITALISM A CHANCE?

Some may argue that the examples cited above are unfair. Capitalism's proponents would say that they are bugs, not features, of the capitalist system and that technological and regulatory fixes are just around the corner. Capitalism, they say, has lifted millions out of poverty and destitution. Yes, babies are born with microplastics in their circulatory systems, but capitalism has dramatically reduced child and infant mortality rates. Yes, capitalism has deteriorated ecosystems and superheated the planet, but it has also unleashed the collective productive potential of humanity in ways that could not even have been imagined a few generations ago. And yes, many people are still desperately poor, and change has been frustratingly slow, but capitalism is alleviating poverty. Capitalism has so far been a net good for the world and now, with a green transition under way, capitalism will manage to keep the good and get rid of the bad. Material abundance for all is possible, capitalism's proponents say, only by and through capitalist production.

On the surface these arguments may seem persuasive but dig a little deeper and it quickly becomes apparent that they rely on a kind of circular reasoning. For every problem capitalism creates, the same solution is prescribed: more capitalism. This requires ignoring capitalism's intrinsically violent, exploitative, and anti-ecological character. In *Enlightenment Now* the cognitive psychologist Steven Pinker writes that 'those who condemn capitalist societies for callousness towards the poor are probably unaware of how little the pre-capitalist societies of the past spent on poor relief.'[34] One need not idealise pre-capitalist societies — an excessively broad category of analysis by any account — to see the flaw in this logic. Pinker critiques pre-capitalist social formations from capitalism's perspective, forgetting that only under capitalism is poverty as we know it possible.[35] Poverty isn't first and foremost living on a low-income, as some might think. Rather, its precondition is that of having been violently and continually separated from what one needs to live and flourish. Poverty exists because under capitalism most of us — the world's working classes, waged and unwaged — are forced to 'work for a living' or face destitution.

To a keen ear, the phrase 'work for a living' should indicate the degree of structural violence entailed in our situation. The choice is simple: work or die. Without this threat, without what Marx calls the 'wage relation' established between those who must sell their labour power to survive and those who receive profits through the work of others, poverty as we know it simply could not exist. The separation of the working class from the resources and social relationships which would otherwise enable it to reproduce itself *without* a wage — the means of *re*production — is therefore the most fundamental form of artificial scarcity that capitalism imposes on the world's working classes, and so it is no surprise that it is flagrantly and systematically ignored by capitalism's defenders. From the working classes' alienation from the means of reproduction, capitalists the world over generate their profits while bullshitting us that they're 'job creators' and 'innovators'. Yet even on its own terms, the claim that capitalism has lifted people out of poverty is a lie, just another instance of bullshitting to conceal capitalism's true nature. The scholars Jason Hickel and Dylan Sullivan have shown that poverty *increased* in the majority of the world as a result of capitalism's violent expansion, which robbed people of the means to live outside of the wage relation[36] — which is to say that they have been robbed of the power to democratically determine what is produced, how, and by whom.

For those of us who have only ever known what it is like to live under capitalism, it can be hard to imagine that poverty hasn't been a constant in human history, but there is plenty of evidence that societies can exist without it. In *The Dawn of Everything*, anthropologists David Graeber and David Wengrow describe how some early European settlers in the Americas who spent time living with Indigenous communities were reluctant to return to European settlements. The Indigenous peoples they encountered could not understand how anyone could be left hungry or homeless. This wasn't because they were worried that by a stroke of bad luck or misfortune they may themselves become poor, but because 'they found life infinitely more pleasant in a society where no one was in a position of abject misery'.[37] A good life for one depended on the good life for all. Poverty was so confounding to early Indigenous commentators that upon seeing homeless people in European settlements they wondered 'why the homeless did not burn down the mansions of the rich.'[38] Given the choice between European and Indigenous ways of living, some settlers simply opted for the latter. Those who did gave numerous reasons for their decision, but Graeber and Wengrow explain that 'by far the most commons reasons... had to do with the intensity of social bonds they experienced in Native American communities: qualities of mutual care, love, and above all happiness which they found impossible to replicate back in European settings.' Qualities, as we'll see shortly, of what we call radical abundance.

One might hope that as capitalist technology advances, we would have more time for this kind of mutual care, love, and happiness. After all, if jobs that previously required human labour are automated, surely this means we can work fewer hours a week, job-share, or go part-time? Almost a century ago, the economist John Meynard Keynes predicted that productivity gains were large enough that no one would need to work more than 15 hours a week in the not-too-distant future.[39] We are living in Keynes' future in terms of productivity gains, but many low-income workers in the imperial core are forced to work outrageously long hours or hold multiple jobs in an attempt to make ends meet. More than 60 percent of the world's working classes are 'informally employed', not because they don't need to work to make a living, but rather workers are forced to compete with one another for the right to be exploited at all.[40] This is because, as capital harnesses technology to dispense with human labour, it creates an artificial scarcity of employment opportunities with the effect that workers must compete for jobs and therefore accept lower wages and poorer working conditions. Mainstream economists call the percentage of people kept out of work in a 'healthy' economy the 'natural rate of unemployment', but there's nothing natural about it. It is, in truth, a product of *the* fundamental form of artificial scarcity imposed on workers to maximise a bullshit abundance for the few at social and ecological expense. Deprived of access to the things and relationships we need to reproduce ourselves, we are forced to sell our labour power to survive.

It's on this point that we diverge from David Graeber's thesis on 'bullshit jobs', from which we take the theme of capitalism's bullshit. For Graeber, a job is only considered bullshit if it is perceived as such by the individual who works it, if, that is, the employee knows deep down that their job is societally pointless. For Graeber, 'there can be no objective measure of social value' and so a job is only bullshit if it is 'so completely pointless, unnecessary, or pernicious that even the employee cannot justify its existence even though the employee feels obliged to pretend that this is not the case.'[41] This is what we would call a subjective account of bullshit. From our perspective, however, capitalism's bullshit is an *objective* feature of the capitalist system derived first and foremost from the global working classes' separation from the means and instruments of their own survival. Bullshit abundance exists because capital exploits waged and unwaged labour and non-human nature to realise a bullshit abundance of profits for the few. Bullshit jobs in Graeber's sense certainly exist in this system, but they presuppose the more fundamental, objective, violent dialectics of bullshit abundance and artificial scarcity. Today, the social and ecological effects of bullshit abundance and artificial scarcity are piling up. Something has to change, and it has to change quickly. Contrary to capitalism's defenders, a genuine alternative requires a break with capitalist business as usual, with the dialectics of bullshit abundance and artificial scarcity. This means a reorganisation of social life around the pursuit of radical abundance.

TOWARDS RADICAL ABUNDANCE

So far we've argued that we live in a world of bullshit abundance and artificial scarcity: a world where we have too much of what we don't need and too little of what we do. Under capitalism, for the sake of generating a bullshit abundance of privatised wealth for the few, our collective freedom and capacity to flourish is constrained. Our horizons are limited. Our lives are diminished and foreshortened. Most of us, in other words, experience an artificial scarcity of *time* to do as we please; to shape our own futures and the futures of those we love and care for.

This is where the pursuit of radical abundance comes in. We can get some way towards defining radical abundance by approaching it as the mirror image of capitalism's bullshit abundance. Where bullshit abundance delivers profits for the few by imposing artificial scarcity on the many, radical abundance names a world where everyone has what they need to live and flourish. Instead of a bullshit abundance of pollutants, traffic jams, and greenhouse gases that accumulate in the atmosphere, radical abundance regenerates ecosystems and pursues reparations for peoples — usually racialised, Indigenous, and working class — who have had their lands stolen, polluted, or turned into zones of extraction. Where bullshit abundance is linked to an artificial scarcity of options to democratically determine the things that matter most to us, radical abundance is created through collective democratic participation. Where bullshit abundance measures human betterment through the quantitative metric of GDP, radical abundance aims at qualitative improvements to human and non-human life. More free time, ecologically regenerative food systems, more diverse ecosystems, and healthcare, free education, and transport for people not profit.

In all these respects and more, radical abundance is the antithesis of bullshit abundance. It's the product of society organised not to realise profits for the capitalist, rentier, and asset holding classes, but to maximise the capacity for human and non-human life to flourish. Because of this, and unlike the so-called 'abundance' proffered by the liberal commentators Ezra Klein and Derek Thompson in their book *Abundance: How We Build a Better Future*, radical abundance can never be delivered by capitalist means.[42] Instead, through processes of democratic social and ecological planning, and through the common ownership of the things we need to forge enriching lives, workers and their communities can ensure that everyone has everything they need to live, love, care, and maximise their time on this earth. The pursuit of radical abundance, then, is about producing more of what we need and less of what we don't: more free time, more accessible housing and commonly owned services, more biodiverse landscapes, more control over our lives, communities, and environments, less polluted landscapes, and fewer parts per million of greenhouse gases in the atmosphere.

But radical abundance is also more than this. It's that something extra that becomes possible when we no longer need to sell our labour to survive, because our collective wellbeing is under our democratic control. Radical abundance is what we get up to not because we must, but simply because we can. In his enigmatic book *The Grasshopper*, philosopher Bernard Suits offers one way to think about this. What, he asks, would we all do if we were freed from the daily grind of capitalist necessity? His answer is that we would play games, which he defines as 'the voluntary attempt to overcome unnecessary obstacles'.[43] Perhaps this means using one's free time to learn an instrument or language, to play sports, or learn a new craft. Or perhaps it means organising great festivals, parties, and gatherings. Or perhaps it means inventing new technologies and new systems of production to make work faster or more enjoyable. We can imagine all of this and more, but if we follow Suits' definition, the full dimensions of a world of radical abundance can't be predicted in advance. They must be played into existence.

We are far from the first to talk about radical abundance in these terms. In fact, the pursuit of radical abundance lies at the heart of the communist tradition. As the Hungarian philosopher István Mészáros summarises 'Marx envisages as the material basis of the emancipated society a world of "abundance", i.e. conditions under which the struggle for the necessarily iniquitous appropriation of scarce resources no longer determines the life-activity of individuals'.[44] For his part, anthropologist Jason Hickel argues that 'capitalism transforms even the most spectacular productivity gains not into abundance and human freedom, but into new forms of artificial scarcity.'[45] Philosopher Kohei Saito proposes that the way to radical abundance is through the establishment of a commons — or collective ownership of what we need to live and flourish — in and against capitalism's privatised and nationalised forms of ownership.[46] Recent research has suggested that such a vision is *technically* possible. In a hypothetical 'post-transformation' economy, the needs of up to 10.4 billion people (current population is estimated at around 8.2 billion) might be met — which is to say everything from food and water to housing, healthcare, and education — without transgressing various planetary boundaries such as ozone depletion, biodiversity loss, soil erosion, and of course CO_2 equivalent emissions.[47] Radical abundance is materially possible if we want it.

While this literature is illustrative, it has surprisingly little to say about how to go from a world of bullshit abundance to one defined by radical abundance — which is to say that it is almost silent on what a transition looks like today. It has even less to say about the kinds of institutional forms that can sustain and expand a transition, or that will enable the world's working classes to democratically and sustainably govern their metabolic exchanges with non-human nature. It is here that we make our intervention. Drawing on the anti-imperialist Marxist tradition, Europe's new municipalism movement, and Latin American projects of socialist construction such as Venezuela's experiments with communal self-governance, this book is laser-focused on the problem of transition and the institutional forms that sustain it. Learning lessons from the limitations of the sometimes-termed 'horizontalist' movements of the early 2010s and the defeat of the electoral turn in the late 2010s, we propose that the cell-form of socialist construction today must be a network of institutions that can empower workers to democratically deliberate about how to use the social surplus generated by their collective labour. The name for this cell-form at its most advanced is the commune, but for reasons that will be explained as this book progresses, our focus here is on an institutional form that is not quite a commune but that could serve as the basis for the construction of communes. We call this institutional form a public-common partnership, or PCP for short. The PCP, we argue, is a useful strategic wager for those of us in the imperial core who wish to wrest control over our lives from capitalism's profit motive, and who wish to stand in solidarity with struggles to do the same the world over.

BOOK OVERVIEW

As its subtitle indicates, this is a book about how to win a green and democratic future. But don't mistake us. By green, we don't mean the same thing as capitalist marketeers and public relations firms. Nor do we mean the same thing as social democrats and progressives, who falsely imagine a 'Green New Deal' and abundance are possible within capitalism. Rather than applying a thin veneer of concern for the non-human world to business as usual, we have in mind a revolutionary transformation in how we relate to one another and non-human nature. And by democracy we don't mean today's moribund bourgeois system of representative democracy. What we have in mind is a future where we collectively and democratically plan our collective reproduction; where capital's control over what is produced, where, and by whom is dismantled and replaced with a new communal system of production. As we'll show, only in this way is it possible to put an end to capital's bullshit abundance and maximise radical abundance for all. This book asks what it takes to make this scenario a reality and aims to contribute, albeit modestly, to the answer by presenting public-common partnerships (PCPs) as one institutional form, among several, that could support the necessary transition.

Though this book is in part about PCPs, we do not want to imply that they are the only, or even necessarily the best, way to fight for a green and democratic future in every context. PCPs are what, following the Brazilian philosopher Rodrigo Nunes, we call a political wager. By this we mean a strategically calculated bet, a gamble, on a specific course of collective action. As with any wager, there are no guarantees that this one will pay off. Nevertheless, we have made a wager on PCPs because we are reasonably confident that they can contribute to the struggle for a green and democratic future for all. This confidence stems from several years organising for PCPs with communities in the UK and France and from conversations with comrades across Europe, the US, and elsewhere, all of whom are trying to imagine institutional forms that can build what we call, following Marta Harnecker, 'popular protagonism', or the capacity for workers to build a collective consciousness and act on it.[48] There are many institutional forms that *might* do this, each appropriate to different contexts and conjunctures: trade unions, revolutionary parties, and communes to name just a few. Our hope is that the institutional form we present in this book adds to our collective repertoire of possible institutional wagers.

We have divided the book's arguments into two parts. After this introductory chapter, Chapters Two to Four form the first part, where we present the theoretical and historical context that has led us to believe that PCPs are a useful strategic wager today. Chapter Two theorises in abstract terms what *must* happen for there to be a transition away from capitalism and towards radical abundance. The chapter begins by explaining how the problem of transition has been avoided or overlooked in recent years, before introducing what we consider the invariant features of any revolutionary transition irrespective of context. For these we draw from the Hungarian Marxist philosopher István Mészáros (who the late Venezuelan leader Hugo Chavez once referred to as 'the pathfinder of twenty-first century socialism'), the Chilean radical intellectual and journalist Marta Harnecker, and the Canadian Marxist Michael Lebowitz. This chapter introduces several concepts that will return throughout the book, the most important of which are 'capital's metabolic control', 'contested reproduction', and 'popular protagonism'. The complexity of these categories means that this is arguably the book's most challenging chapter. We think this is unavoidable if we are to have the tools we need to think about the messy, protracted, and always provisional nature of transition.

Chapter Three follows by giving a broad overview of the post-2008 sequence of struggle in the imperial core. This sequence is generally narrated as a shift from a wave of 'horizontalist' struggles exemplified by the Occupy Movement towards an electoral turn around 2015. We argue that this narrative does a disservice to a series of global struggles and wagers aimed at building popular power through new institutions of common democratic ownership and planning. It also results in the marginalisation of many different theoretical perspectives that *are* trying to grapple with the problem of transition. The chapter introduces five inspirational examples: Hernani's strategies for territorial sovereignty in the Basque Country; Berlin's Deutsche Wohnen & Co. Enteignen campaign, which is seeking to socialise the city's housing stock; Jackson, Mississippi's Jackson-Kush Plan, a strategy aimed at achieving self-determination, economic democracy, and social liberation; Kerala's experimentation with participatory planning; and Venezuela's commune system. Though these initiatives are variant and distinct, we think they all embody the invariant features of transition to a greater or lesser degree and can therefore serve as inspiration for new efforts to build institutions of common ownership and planning today.

The ability to outline the invariant features of transition and find them at work in specific contexts is important, but neither of these things tell us how to act in the here and now. What is appropriate and effective in the Bolivian altiplano is, perhaps quite evidently, unlikely to offer a blueprint for those in the deindustrialised outskirts of Oldham, UK, or vice versa. To enact the invariant features of transition appropriately requires a strategic analysis of how we can apply our limited collective capacities to achieve the greatest possible social change in any given time and place. In Chapter Four, we follow Antonio Gramsci in calling this procedure a conjunctural analysis. Here, we argue that global capitalism is struck by two intractable, accelerating crises: secular stagnation and global heating. Rather than tackle these issues at the source, liberal and reactionary approaches to denying the need for a revolutionary departure from capital have emerged across countries in the imperial core, each providing different opportunities for a politics of radical abundance. This brings the book's first part to a close.

Chapter Five opens the book's second part by introducing the formal structure of PCPs, and in particular what we hold to be most significant about them: the capacity to set in motion a 'self-expansion of the commons' that can contest capital's own self-expansionary dynamics. Chapter Six shows how PCPs can intervene in processes of urban development, drawing from our experience organising for a PCP with communities in North London, UK. The chapter is especially attuned to how PCPs can create new kinds of political consciousness. Chapter Seven shows how PCPs can intervene in one of the most powerful sectors of the global economy — pharmaceuticals — and builds from our experience organising with French trade unionists and campaigners. Chapter Eight is more speculative in nature and shows how PCPs could support a transition towards agroecological food sovereignty in the UK through a repurposing of England's publicly owned council farm estate. The book's conclusion reiterates our central argument and explains how PCPs can support the global struggle to win a world of radical abundance for all. Taken together, these chapters provide a detailed study of how PCPs can transform three sectors: urban development, pharmaceuticals, and agriculture. We focus on these sectors both because of their importance to systemic transformation, and because it is where we have practical experience organising to implement communal alternatives. This does not mean that the PCP model would not be appropriate for other sectors that are critical to winning a world of radical abundance including energy, landscape conservation, transportation, and more besides.

As this summary may suggest, this book is best read linearly. It applies a certain method. Chapter Two uses theory to find the invariant features of transition. Chapter Three casts around for inspirational examples of this theory in practice. Chapter Four thinks about how to apply theory and practice in our own times and within conjunctural constraints. Chapters Five to Eight make a wager on a specific answer — public-common partnerships — in the sectors of urban development, pharmaceuticals, and food systems.

A WORD ON REAL UTOPIAN SOCIOLOGY

Finally, a few words are in order about this book's approach to the problem of transition. Our thinking on this subject has been influenced to some extent by Erik Olin Wright's vision of a 'real utopian sociology'. This approach to thinking about socialist transition emphasises the role of popular institutions and the task of 'identifying the contours of a politics of the here and now that can be fundamentally transformative'.[49] In the way we interpret it, real utopian sociology incorporates two related procedures. The first identifies and researches actually existing institutions and social struggles that have liberatory potential, with the goal of understanding how and why they can contribute to a broader socialist trajectory. The aim here is to produce 'accounts of empirical cases that are neither gullible nor cynical, but try to fully recognize the complexity and dilemmas as well as the real potential of practical efforts at social empowerment'.[50] For researchers associated with the Real Utopias Project, the experiences of Participatory Budgeting in Porto Alegre or the Mondragon cooperative federation were emblematic cases of institutions that might play a role in helping to 'erode capitalism'. For us, Chris Gilbert's book *Communes or Nothing!* is an excellent contemporary example of real utopian sociology. Beginning with Venezuela's communal system, Gilbert seeks to understand how lessons learned in Venezuela might be translated into new contexts.[51]

The lessons from this research informs the second procedure of real utopian sociology, which extrapolates from real-world examples to construct 'theoretical models of new institutional designs that are not represented by any real world cases' but that nevertheless engage with the dilemmas, limits, and problems associated with existing projects. This procedure is done both abstractly in terms of how institutions might function, and concretely in terms of the challenges associated with their implementation. There are two traps associated with this second procedure that must be avoided: abstract utopianism and reformism. Avoiding abstract utopianism means ensuring that our designs are responsive to, and make sense within, the broad, practical, judicial, and ideological contexts in which our movements operate. There is no point making a flawless plan for communal production, or perfectly describing a communist society, if these plans and descriptions do not help movements make this desired future a reality. To avoid reformism, our institutional designs must contain a revolutionary logic and dynamism that can't be contained or accommodated by capital or the capitalist state. They must work to change the boundaries of social possibility, progressively shifting the balance of forces in our favour.

Given the global scale and the sheer severity of the crises the world faces today, it might appear wildly out of touch to write a book advocating for the patient work of institution-building. The target of 1.5C of global warming above pre-industrial levels is dead. The far right is everywhere on the rise. Economic growth is stalling globally. Genocides, from Palestine to Sudan, are perpetrated with impunity.

And as the US's status as the world's foremost imperial power declines, it is preparing for a new and vicious phase of confrontation with its 'enemies' the world over. To put the problem paradoxically, now isn't the time to propose the slow, difficult, and at times boring work of building institutions, and yet in many cases this is precisely what must be done. There is no doubt that we must leave capitalism's violent dialectics of bullshit abundance and artificial scarcity behind if we are to survive and flourish in this wounded world. But in the absence of both mass revolutionary parties and pre-existing communal forms that can sustain our political energies while reproducing us outside of capital's circuits of accumulation — even if partially at first — we have little choice but to build the institutions we need, and to build them from within our imperfect conditions. Building the kind of institutions we describe in this book isn't the only task before us. We still need mass street mobilisations, party-building efforts, national liberation struggles, trade union activity, and electoral interventions where these strategies make sense. We must also keep struggling against patriarchal, racist, ableist, and imperialist structures wherever they appear. The institutional forms we describe in these pages are not an alternative to these struggles. Their goal is to support and amplify them.

After reading this book, you might agree with our description of the invariant features of transition, you might similarly find inspiration in the struggles we draw from in Venezuela, Germany, Euskal Herria, Brazil, India, Mississippi, and elsewhere. You might agree with our assessment of the strategic opportunities created in our current conjuncture. You might even agree that we need to build institutions for transition. And yet, for whatever reason you might conclude that public-common partnerships are a strategic dead end. To the extent that it is part of the pursuit for alternative transitional institutional forms, we welcome such critical engagement. Above all else, what we hope to present across this book's pages is a way of thinking and acting that takes the problems of transition seriously, because only by tackling the challenge of transition can we win a green and democratic future for all.

PART I

2
The Necessity of Transition

The world of bullshit abundance we inhabit may be morally objectionable to many — even to the majority — but those who benefit from the system are in no rush to change it. As long as their interests are defended and as long as there are profits to be made, they will exploit waged and unwaged labour and non-human nature to the greatest extent possible. Similarly, capitalist states, whose role it is to sustain the capitalist world-system, will uphold the laws and ideological formations necessary to defend it.[1]

The good and bad news is that things cannot carry on as they are for much longer. Almost everywhere you look, the violent dialectics of bullshit abundance and artificial scarcity have unleashed decisive social and ecological upheaval. Global heating, ecological deterioration, geopolitical conflagrations, zoonotic spillovers, and economic uncertainty converge and compound one another to create a highly combustible political landscape. Any one of these issues alone would pose a significant challenge; together they become greater than the sum of their parts, calling into question the capitalist system as we know it and forcing the problem of transition upon the victims and beneficiaries of bullshit abundance alike.

It isn't difficult to find evidence that the 'catastrophic convergence' of these phenomena is precipitating the question of transition.[2] One of the clearest signs is the rise of a host of concepts seeking to give name and shape to the unsettled and unsettling world we inhabit. In 2020, Deutsche Bank published a report entitled 'The Age of Disorder', in which they proposed that the convergence of geopolitical tensions, economic crises, ecological deterioration, and Covid-19 has forever destabilised the neoliberal global order that had been favourable to Deutsche Bank and global finance capital more generally.[3] In 2022, the Collins English Dictionary chose 'permacrisis' as its word of the year. A permacrisis, as the dictionary has it, is 'an extended period of instability and insecurity resulting from a series of catastrophic events'.[4] Around the same time, the economic historian Adam Tooze popularised the term 'polycrisis' to describe the convergence and mutual amplification of multiple crisis tendencies.[5] The term has since been widely used by social movements, UN bodies, reinsurance companies, and critical academics alike.

Whatever name we want to give to this moment, it seems practically everyone — from finance capital, to international organisations, to progressive social movements — agrees that things cannot carry on as they are. The Global Economic Forum's Global Risks Report for 2024 surveyed 1,500 global experts from academia, business, government, and civil society, concluding that there is a 'pessimistic global outlook'. Within the next two years (that is, until 2026), 54 percent of respondents anticipated 'some instability' and 'moderate risk of global catastrophe', while 30 percent anticipated an even greater risk of 'global catastrophes'. Expanding the view to the next 10 years, 17 percent saw 'global catastrophic risks looming', while a further 46 percent predicted 'upheavals and elevated risks of global catastrophes' led by 'extreme weather events', 'critical change to earth systems', 'biodiversity loss and ecosystem collapse', and 'natural resource shortages'.[6] Bullshit abundance, in other words, is not just morally objectionable. Unless we want to pile global catastrophe upon global catastrophe, the end of bullshit abundance is a social and ecological necessity.

It's because of this that a transition — of some sort, to somewhere — has become the problem of our times. In 2021 the Intergovernmental Science-Policy Platform on Biodiversity and Ecosystem Services (IPBES) called for a 'fundamental, system-wide reorganisation across technological, economic and social factors, including paradigms, goals and values.'[7] The IPCC's Sixth Assessment Report, published in 2023 and widely referred to as the organisation's 'final warning' on global heating, called for a 'transition' from 'incremental to transformational adaptation'.[8] For the IPCC's authors, gradual reductions in emissions and fossil fuel-reliant food systems and infrastructure would no longer cut it. Nothing short of a rapid and far-reaching transformation in how our lives are organised would do.

This, believe it or not, is a conservative estimation. As climate scientist Kevin Anderson argues, the methodologies used by intergovernmental bodies like the IBES and IPCC mean that their findings commonly understate the severity of our situation.[9] Add to this that the IPCC has a dirty habit of including ineffective or non-existent technologies such as carbon capture and storage in its transition pathways, and calls for a practical social revolution become even more imperative.

The problem is that just because things must change doesn't dictate how they will change. While most agree that a transition of some kind to somewhere is needed, there is little agreement about the destination or how we get there. This is where the struggle lies, yet unfortunately, as we'll show in this chapter, those who would fight for and win a world of radical abundance in the imperial core have broadly neglected the theoretical challenge of transition. In contrast, those who have benefitted from this world of bullshit abundance *have* constructed a theory and practice of transition that ensures nothing will fundamentally change. In this chapter we aim to theorise transition on its own terms with the help of the Hungarian Marxist philosopher Istvan Mészáros, Chilean intellectual Marta Harnecker, and Canadian Marxist economist Michael Lebowitz.

CAPITALIST TRANSITIONS

One of the greatest injustices of our time is that those who have benefitted the most from the generation of bullshit abundance are best placed to lead our collective response to its ill effects. In research papers produced by bourgeois academics and think tanks, knowledge is produced and policies concocted that play around the edges of the capitalist system, refusing to tackle the root causes of our predicament. Similarly, behind closed doors, in boardrooms, conference rooms, and parliamentary chambers far removed from the world's working classes, transition plans are laid down that, as the saying goes, put profits before people and planet.

As a result of these machinations, some politicians and sectors of capital in the imperial core have promised that our social, economic, and ecological crises can be remedied through a capitalist green transition. Through what is often referred to as 'green growth', market-based mechanisms will supposedly facilitate an 'orderly transition' from a fossil fuel-based economy to a renewable one,[10] lifting global capitalism out of its period of 'great stagnation' in the process.[11] Plans like the US Green New Deal proposed by Senator Ed Markey and state representative Alexandria Ocasio-Cortez in 2019, or the UK's Green New Deal proposed by members of the UK Labour Party, also in 2019, sought to combine decarbonising the economy with public sector-led reindustrialisation in the imperial core. This, they claimed, would also bring back the kind of good-quality unionised jobs that were once the mainstay of the imperial core's industrial economies.

Left-wing critics of these proposals pointed out that they were predicated on the exploitation of the periphery's lands, seas, and labour.[12] A green transition for some would be secured by perpetuating the now centuries-old relation of uneven ecological exchange between the core and its neo-colonies.[13] More than this, colonies and former colonies would be required to borrow from imperial powers to fund their own green transitions, which would only deepen the neo-colonial global system and expose peoples in the periphery to the worst effects of ecological deterioration.[14] In this way, these supposedly progressive transition plans would limit the freedom and self-determination of peoples in the periphery, thereby imposing an artificial scarcity of development options on the global majority. For right-wing critics of these proposals, they were simply too costly, by which they meant that they imposed too many limits on private capital. Or in the terms we've been introducing in this book, their reliance on state-led investment meant they struck a blow against the private sector's unconstrained production of bullshit abundance.

More mainstream proposals for a green transition, such as former President Joe Biden's Inflation Reduction Act and the European Union's Green Deal, also propose to combine a green transition with productivity gains and greater employment. Here, as we'll discuss in

Chapter Four, the transition wouldn't be led directly by the public sector but rather through the public sector's derisking of private sector investment and profit-making. These proposals have had a rocky reception among the imperial core's electorate, who rightly intuit that if the private sector stands to gain from such a transition, its various social and ecological costs will be carried by workers themselves. As a result, protests against green policies that put the burden of transition on urban commuters, petit bourgeois small business owners, and agricultural workers have intermittently flared up across the imperial core. Think, for example, of the French Gilets Jaunes protests of 2018, the wave of European farmers' protests that began in 2019, or opposition to ultra-low emission zones in London in 2023. Put plainly, this opposition exists because the green transition plans offered by mainstream political parties are technocratic solutions decided upon behind closed doors in the interests of capital, and not workers. Such anti-democratic — dare we say authoritarian — policymaking is only possible because under capitalism the global working class has an artificial scarcity of opportunities to exercise collective agency over how we live our lives, and over what is produced, who produces it, and how. We live, as Lenin would say, under the dictatorship of capital.[15]

So while a green transition of some kind is essential, none of those on offer in the electoral manifestos of the imperial core even try to overcome capitalism's violent dialectics of bullshit abundance and artificial scarcity. Some, such as those proposed by Europe's resurgent far right, even promise to radically exacerbate this dialectic so as to defend a minority of the world's working classes from the worst of capitalism's ill effects, at the expense of workers and ecosystems elsewhere. Militarising borders, leaving refugees to drown in Europe's seas, pursuing energy-intensive green transitions that place pressure on the lands, seas, and labour of people in the periphery, lifting agricultural land out of productive use to plant monocultural 'carbon sequestering' forests, rolling back women's reproductive rights, and increasing policing among racialised communities are a recipe for what some have called 'eco-apartheid'.[16]

Solutions to the world's problems don't lie in this direction. Neither do they rest with 'sensible' centrist politicians, many of whom are starting to borrow from the far right's agenda on everything from immigration and policing to imperial foreign policy. Unwilling to break with the socially and ecologically destructive system they've benefitted from, these so-called plans for transition tweak legislation here and adjust energy mixes there, refusing to confront the root cause of our collective woes: capital itself. A genuine alternative requires a break with capitalist business as usual. It requires a reorganisation of life around the pursuit of radical abundance.

ANTI-CAPITALIST TRANSITIONS?

To go from a world of bullshit abundance to one of radical abundance takes a plan. We need a way to link together short-term tactical interventions, longer-term strategic thinking, and *institutions of transition.* Whereas capitalist theorists of transition like to think about transition as a strictly technocratic and thus apolitical problem, we need to understand transition as an irrepressibly political project. The transition, in the Marxist sociologist and former Bolivian vice president Álvaro García Linera's words, is a 'battlefield between capitalism in crisis and the tendencies, potentialities and efforts to bring production under community ownership and control'.[17] Transition is an act of class struggle, a process of extricating ourselves from capitalist social relations so that we might democratically plan our collective reproduction and the survival of non-human nature. It is, for this reason, a *proactive* and *future-facing* endeavour: a collective wager on the promise of radical abundance in a world that has denied it from us.

For the most part, this understanding of transition has receded from view among left-wing movements and intellectuals today. This isn't a personal or collective failing, but rather the intended effect of decades of concerted counter-revolutionary organisation by the beneficiaries of bullshit abundance: the incapacitation of unions, the assassination of anti-colonial leaders, the imposition of sanctions, the waging of wars, and the erasure of radical histories and traditions have all been used to crush the forces of radical abundance. As a result, as Marxist scholar Isabelle Garo puts it, 'historical episodes that attest to [a] culture of self-government by workers have been forgotten; reflections on the forms and instruments of the transition from capitalism to communism have been excommunicated, as have those on democratic planning of the economy and the redefinition of production and labour accompanying them'.[18] In lieu of these lines of thought, the challenge of transition is today overlooked by the Left in two ways. The first is to deny the importance of thinking about transition as a political project that takes us from capitalism's bullshit abundance to a world defined by radical abundance. The second is to jump over the problem of transition by describing desirable postcapitalist futures without addressing the realities of how to get there.

Despite their differences, proponents of a wide range of perspectives, from prefigurative politics to communisation theory take the first approach.[19] Rather than understanding transition as a distinct political project replete with its own challenges and uncertainties, immediate acts of living beyond or outside of capital are pursued in the 'cracks' of capital's circuits of accumulation,[20] or else they're said to emerge 'immediately' wherever capital's social relations are attenuated by class struggle.[21] With its emphasis on immediacy — literally meaning without mediation, without transition — these theories of change deny the importance of thinking transition on its own terms. The point here isn't that these theories don't imagine that it will take time for a new social order to emerge, but that they deny the necessity of conceiving of transition as a definite and discrete social project.

The most sophisticated justification for this perspective in the communist tradition comes from groups like Théorie Communiste, Troploin, Endnotes, and other proponents of the political tendency known as communisation theory.[22] For these groups and thinkers, any strategy of transition is misplaced today for two reasons. First, because the phase of capitalism's development in which 'the proletariat' could assert itself as a collective subject against capitalism is over. Today, the social function of being a worker is experienced by most as an imposition, and not something to be affirmed as a political identity. Because of this, the figure of the proletariat no longer carries a political charge, and the interests of the working class no longer necessarily arc towards communism. Workers may fight for higher wages within capitalism, as trade unions do, or they may even align with reactionary movements. The time of revolutionary programmes for transition is therefore over. Second, communisation theorists argue that capitalism is increasingly failing to reproduce the world's working classes and so growing numbers are in informal work, unemployed, or otherwise exposed to capitalism's violence and turmoil. As capitalism's contradictions escalate, workers will be forced to find ways to sustain themselves outside of capital and — according to communisation theorists — these ways are likely to be communist.[23] From this perspective, there's no need to theorise transition, and no need to plan for a transitionary period, because the workers themselves will introduce immediate 'communist measures' when and where they are needed.[24]

If communism is to become a reality it will indeed emerge through the self-activity of the world's working classes, but communisation theory's denial of the problem of transition is misguided. As Alberto Toscano argues, there is no guarantee that capitalism's crises will lead to immediate communising measures.[25] They could, as Jodi Dean has proposed, lead to something far worse.[26] This means that those of us who are already convinced of the need to depart from capitalism in the name of something better should generate knowledge about the messy realities of struggling to implement an enduring alternative to capitalism's endless production of bullshit abundance. We should also experiment with tactics, strategies, and organisational forms of transition. As Toscano argues, these should be 'advanced as the inevitably truncated, imperfect and embryonic testing out of certain practices, whose role in future struggles may be undefined, but which at the very least begins to explore the creation of collective organs of opposition.'[27] This is how we understand the role of public-common partnerships and similar communal forms today.

Many versions of prefigurative politics also overlook the problem of transition. As Ted Trainer, an influential thinker on the subject of postcapitalist transitions, says in a critique of transition towns, community gardens, and food co-ops that applies more generally, many prefigurative cooperative and green movements 'assume that if we just work at establishing more and more of these things then in time this will have created a new society'. This, as Trainer says, is a 'serious mistake'.[28] The first reason Trainer gives is that small efforts to live differently are easily accommodated within a larger capitalist system and appeal to too few people to feasibly replace business as usual. Arguably, this critique applies even to the most successful acts of autonomous self-governance and counter-cultural living, such as Metelkova in Ljubljana, Slovenia, Christiana in Copenhagen, Denmark, or the *zones à defendre*, otherwise known as ZADs in France. Trainer's second reason is that such 'alternatives' don't establish a long-term self-sustaining replacement for what we have been calling the world of bullshit abundance, but only some respite from it — to which we would add that were these initiatives to seriously call the capitalist system into question they would be swiftly repressed. The ZAD in Notre-Dame-des-Landes, for example, has been continuously limited in scope and ambition by violent interventions from the French state. It now exists as an important, but limited, island of autonomy in a sea of bullshit abundance.

Trainer's critique is correct, but his alternative is little better. According to Trainer, the solution lies in organising self-sustaining local economies, or what he calls 'the simpler way'.[29] For Trainer, the fact that 'the simpler way' envisions a systematic transformation of local social and economic activity is what separates it from the reformist tendencies of transition towns and similar projects he criticises. This, however, is a distinction without a difference. It's not clear how small, localised initiatives of living otherwise can reach beyond themselves to transform society at large, which is after all what must be done. Nor is it necessarily self-evident that the solutions to the world's problems require localisation and simplicity. As we'll show time and again in later chapters, it's not the complexity or global scope of the capitalist system that is undermining the conditions for life on earth as we know it. The problem is capital's 'metabolic control' over what is produced, who produces it, and how.[30] Indeed, to solve many of the problems caused by capital's generation of bullshit abundance — not least the global ecological crisis — will require complex political coordination at multiple scales, including the global.

This brings us to the second way that the problem of transition is avoided: simply jumping over it entirely to imagine and describe desirable postcapitalist futures. This tendency is found among movements and authors depicting radical versions of the Green New Deal,[31] a Red Deal,[32] degrowth economies,[33] half-earth socialism,[34] and fully automated luxury communism,[35] among others. Here, the problem of transition is eschewed in favour of presenting desirable visions of the future, presumably in the hope of inspiring a social base in the present. Though we agree with the authors of *Half-Earth Socialism* that such 'speculation is a vital political act', these visions invariably overlook, or implicitly presuppose answers to, the indispensable questions of transition: how is a social base galvanised?[36] Who is it composed of? What institutional forms strengthen and sustain it? And *how, through struggle and collective planning of production, can capital be abolished once and for all*?

Despite the avowedly utopian and speculative nature of *Half-Earth Socialism*, for instance, the book's authors occasionally hint at what might seem like a theory of transition. 'How could an eco-socialist coalition take power?'[37] they ask, or 'How such a Half-Earth socialist coalition might come to power we cannot say' they caveat.[38] Such phrasing contains an implicit theory of transition: the 'Left' — whose specific class composition goes unelaborated — *first* takes control over the state *then* implements a programme.

The authors of the book *A Planet to Win: Why We Need a Green New Deal* similarly deploy a thin and unelaborated theory of transition: 'Radical change only happens when millions of people are organising, striking, and marching, shaping politics and the economy from below.'[39] True enough, but *how* do they shape politics and the economy? According to the authors, 'tackling the climate crisis will require action from unions, social movements, Indigenous peoples, racial justice groups and others to take back public power from the elites who've presided over the climate emergency.'[40] Here again it is assumed, rather than argued, that transition is a matter of taking state power through elections before implementing climate crisis-mitigating state policies.

As we'll show shortly, however, the seizure of state power isn't in itself a positive theory of transition. Taking over the state might be an important part of a strategy of transition, but even if we were successful in this endeavour, the questions of how to abolish capital and how to organise a new system of collective social reproduction would persist. In fact, the history of revolutionary struggles from Russia and China, to Cuba, Guinea-Bissau, and Venezuela tell us that these questions become all the more urgent. This means that the challenges of transition today must be confronted on their own terms. If they're not, we doom ourselves to either unwittingly repeating theories of transition that don't respond to the current conditions of struggle, or to projecting our imaginations into far-flung utopian futures with no sense of how to get there.

A THEORY OF TRANSITION

By this point in our argument, we hope to have established the need for a theorisation of transition on its own terms, one that lingers in the messy realities of struggling to bring about a green and democratic future. Transition, however, isn't an easy thing to theorise. In John Bellamy Foster's estimations it is even 'the most difficult problem of socialist theory and practice'.[41] In the words of Michael Lebowitz, the very term itself can introduce 'more than a hint of teleology' into our theorising and our strategising.[42]

For most people, transition implies a period of passing from Point A to Point B without vestige or remainder. Autumn is a period of transition from summer into winter in which deciduous trees go from having leaves to not having leaves, such that winter has no trace of summer. Transition words in sentences are used to link one self-contained clause or idea to another: however, furthermore, besides. In a more socio-historical key, transition is the passage from feudalism to capitalism, which for bourgeois historians marks the realisation of our collective freedom and which for teleological Marxists must in turn be followed by a further transition to a classless communist society. In these renderings of transition the contested, mutable, variegated, plural, and under-determined character of capitalism's expansion and reproduction on a world scale recedes from view, as does the potential for transitions to reverse and fall back into the old order from which they departed.[43] Mechanistic approaches to transition like these are a barrier to implementing a transition because they replace the concrete, messy, and contingent realities of struggling to bring about a world of radical abundance with abstract linear ideas of change. Autumn is indeed a period in which deciduous trees lose their leaves between summer and winter, but when it comes to social transitions it is as if some trees might lose their leaves as others blossom, or as if autumn could fall back into summer, or indeed never arrive at all.

Transition doesn't have to imply teleology. For the remainder of this chapter, we draw from three Marxist theorists who have thought deeply about the non-linear and contingent nature of transition: Istvan Mészáros, Marta Harnecker, and Michael Lebowitz. These thinkers are notable for having developed their ideas about transition through intellectual exchanges with actually existing revolutionary struggles in Venezuela, Cuba, Kerala, and elsewhere. Together with a reading of Marx and Engels themselves, we can use them to elaborate the invariant features of a transition away from capital's world of bullshit abundance towards one of radical abundance.

Though we use the concept somewhat differently, we take the idea of 'invariant' features of transition from the Italian communist Amadeo Bordiga. For Bordiga, Marxism has certain unchanging 'invariant' features that must be applied irrespective of time or place, lest the communist movement slide into reformism.[44] In a similar way, our goal in the following is to outline on an abstract level what it takes to break with what Mészáros calls capital's 'metabolic control', or capital's domination over our social and ecological interactions within the global economy and beyond.[45] We think these invariant elements *must* be present in any revolution or transition away from capitalism, irrespective of the tactics or strategies applied. In the following two chapters, we'll move down a level of abstraction. In the chapter immediately following this one, we'll look at how the theory of transition we outline already takes many concrete forms in necessarily provisional and imperfect ways across the world. Then, in Chapter Four, we'll undertake a conjunctural analysis of contemporary capital's tendencies towards contradiction and crisis, mapping how and where we can intervene to bring about a green and democratic future.

To move from the abstract to the concrete in this way is to temporally brush aside the messiness of the present so we can better understand what makes it tick, before returning to comprehend the present anew in its rich complexity. In the *Grundrisse*, Marx describes this method as a process of ascending from the abstract to the concrete. The concrete — the problem of how to transition away from fossil fuels and industrialised agriculture, for instance — is for Marx concrete because, as he puts it, 'it is the concentration of many determinations'.[46] The need to decarbonise energy and food systems is a brute empirical fact, a necessity, that we cannot respond to appropriately until we comprehend how capital's underlying dynamic forces, or 'laws of motion', shape the capitalist system's antagonistic structure and our collective capacities to win something better. Once we grasp how bullshit abundance and artificial scarcity are generated by capital's metabolic control in the abstract, we can theorise — and strategise — more effectively about how to leave them behind once and for all.

TRANSITION: FROM CAPITAL'S METABOLIC CONTROL TO COMMUNAL CONTROL

Capital is the motor force behind the dialectics of bullshit abundance and artificial scarcity, which means that to do away with both we must dismantle capital's grip over human and non-human life. This is what transition must be about in our wounded and warming world. In his 1995 work *Beyond Capital: Toward a Theory of Transition*, the Hungarian Marxist philosopher Istvan Mészáros makes one of the most important contributions to theorising transition.[47] Mészáros' theory relies on two conceptual innovations, drawn from

Marx and extended in new directions in response to the advances and defeats experienced by projects of socialist construction in the twentieth century. As we will see, the first innovation is Mészáros' understanding of capital as a historically specific 'second order' metabolic system, one that commandeers and transforms a transhistorical 'primary mediation' of metabolic exchanges between humans and between humans and non-humans. The second innovation, which builds on the first, is Mészáros' distinction between capital and capitalism.

Mészáros' use of the language of exchange, mediation, and metabolism stem from Marx's observation that it is the material relations among people and non-human nature, or how people organise the work needed to secure their collective reproduction, that defines a social order. Irrespective of the kind of society people live in — nomadic, city-state, feudal, capitalist, communist, and so on — Marx observed that they must necessarily enter into interactions with one another and with non-human nature to meet essential needs, as well as culturally specific interests and desires. Borrowing from leading natural scientists of his time, Marx named this process a metabolism (*Stoffwechsel* in the original German) to indicate that our collective reproduction is a process constantly enlisting flows of matter and energy across multiple scales of human and non-human existence.[48] Though somewhat broad, the language of metabolism draws our attention to how capital is far more than just an economic process. It is an *ecological* process from the start. Capital, as Jason Moore puts it, is a way 'of organising nature', of using, carving up, moving around, transforming, disrupting, repairing, building, destroying, and more besides.[49]

Importantly, these metabolic interactions, or mediations, between people and non-human nature don't leave those who labour or non-human nature untouched. As Marx explains:

> Labour is, first of all, a process between man and nature, a process by which man, through his own actions, mediates, regulates and controls the metabolism between himself and nature. He sets in motion the natural forces which belong to his own body, his

> arms, legs, head and hands, in order to appropriate the materials of nature in a form adapted to his own needs. Through this movement he acts upon external nature and changes it, and in this way he simultaneously changes his own nature... [Labour] is the universal condition for metabolic interaction between man and nature, the everlasting nature-imposed condition of human existence.[50]

Those who do a certain kind of work, who take on specific functions in a given society, are themselves transformed by it. Their ideas, habits, and skills are moulded by the social fabric they inhabit and which they help to reproduce. Similarly, as humans work upon non-human nature they *produce* a specific kind of nature, which in turn rebounds back on and shapes social relations.[51] A society that meets its needs for energy by burning fossil fuels, for example, produces a different kind of non-human nature than one organised around wind and tidal energy, which in turn has serious consequences for society as a whole.

Labour, whether waged or unwaged, free or unfree, is what *mediates* humanity's interaction with non-human nature in a *transhistorical* way. All social formations we can possibly imagine *must* work to reproduce themselves and distribute the proceeds of labour, and they must do this work through their mediation with, or in metabolic interaction with, non-human nature. This base level fact of human existence is what Mészáros calls humanity's 'primary mediation'.[52] Critically, this level of abstraction tells us nothing about the who, where, why, or how of production. People ploughed fields in the 1300s and they plough fields today, but the who, where, why, and how has changed substantially. As Marx writes, 'the taste of porridge does not tell us who grew the oats, and the process we have presented [of producing oats] does not reveal the conditions under which it takes place, whether it is happening under the slave-owner's brutal lash or the anxious eye of the capitalist'.[53]

Extrapolating from Marx's observation of a transhistorical metabolism between non-human nature and human labour, Mészáros outlines six features of this primary mediation: i) the biological reproduction of human populations; ii) the 'production of goods required for human gratification' including the tools, industry, and knowledge needed to produce them; iii) a means to optimise available 'natural and productive — including culturally productive — resources'; iv) the 'co-coordination and control of a multiplicity of activities through which the material and cultural requirements can be secured and safeguarded'; v) the 'rational allocation of the available material and human resources'; and vi) 'the enactment and administration of the rules and regulations of the given society as a whole'.[54]

For Mészáros, as for Marx, what is of critical importance is that 'none of these primary mediatory imperatives' require 'the establishment of structural hierarchies of domination and subordination as the necessary framework of social metabolic reproduction'.[55] As the anthropologists David Wengrow and David Graeber show, the fact that most of us live under a deeply unjust capitalist system in which wealth and power are unevenly distributed and in which bullshit abundance piles up as people live in misery is a contingent fact of history, of *class struggle*, and not a natural fact of so-called 'human nature'.[56] It follows that if there is nothing natural about this state of affairs, if the reasons for injustice are social all the way down, then they can be changed. We can create, in Mészáros' terms, a different system of 'second order' mediations.

We find ourselves up to our necks in bullshit abundance today because through violent imposition, capital has become the reigning second order mediation. Capital's ceaseless drive to accumulate at human and non-human expense dictates what is produced, who by, where, and how. We are thus subject to what Mészáros calls capital's 'metabolic control', or the 'capital system'. Mészáros proposes that capital's metabolic control is present in any society featuring the following characteristics. First: a labouring class who are dispossessed of the instruments, machines, and apparatus needed to reproduce themselves. This alienated status can be upheld by law (private property), violence (police, military), ideology (education, media), or more abstract forms of coercion (the coercive fact that we must all 'work for a living'). Second: where the separation of the working class from the means of production is used to compel workers to produce a surplus that they don't directly control. Under capitalism, for example, this surplus is controlled by the capitalist class, by those who receive rents, and by the state through various forms of taxation. Third: a division of labour exists that subordinates some in society to the whims and inclinations of others. If, for instance, only some in society grow food, do care and reproductive work, or plan what is produced and how, this establishes a division of labour that is susceptible to manipulation and the formation of social hierarchies.[57]

As might be clear from this description, for Mészáros, capital is far more than an economic system. As a mode of metabolic control, capital is a kind of power that inflects itself through and inflects our day-to-day interactions with one another and with non-human nature. It mediates our everyday dealings, our metabolic exchanges, and thus our collective reproduction. Under capital's metabolic control, the production of everything we need to survive and flourish is *not* the primary goal of production. The goal is the extraction of surplus labour — waged and unwaged work in excess of what's needed for social reproduction — from the working classes. Only secondarily are our needs met, if at all, and only insofar as meeting them ensures that we keep contributing to the production of an alienated surplus. Because of this, in all spheres of life our individual and collective potential is subordinated to, and diminished by, a coercive force beyond our immediate control: the law of capital accumulation. It is this law that guarantees an endless production of bullshit abundance and artificial scarcity.

Overthrowing Capitalism Isn't Enough

A keen-eyed reader may have noticed that so far in this section we have been primarily writing about *capital* rather than *capitalism*. The reason for this can again be traced to Mészáros, who makes a novel and indispensable distinction between the two. To put it simply, for Mészáros, one can depart from capitalism without departing from capital, and this is because capitalism is but one form that capital's metabolic control over social and ecological systems can take. As Mészáros explains, 'you can overthrow the capitalist but the factory system remains, the division of labour remains, nothing has changed in the metabolic functions of society. Indeed, sooner or later you find the need for reassigning those forms of control to personalities, and that's how the bureaucracy comes into existence'.[58] Hence the 'overthrow of capitalism can hardly even scratch the surface of the problem', which is the 'complete eradication of capital from the social metabolic process'.[59]

The Soviet Union serves as Mészáros' primary example to understand the distinction between capital and capitalism. At various moments in its existence, the Soviet Union succeeded, to a greater or lesser degree, in abolishing capitalist class relations and the capitalist state-form, but it did not succeed in dismantling the alienated character of capital's metabolic control over production driven by the need to accumulate the products of surplus labour. As Mészáros explains, 'capital is a command system whose mode of functioning is accumulation-oriented, and the accumulation can be secured in a number of different ways'. In the Soviet Union, he proposes, 'surplus labour was extracted in a political way', whereas under Western capitalism, the 'economically regulated extraction of surplus labour and surplus value' prevails. It follows that 'the Soviet Union was not capitalist, not even state capitalist. But the Soviet system was very much dominated by the power of capital: the division of labour remained intact, the hierarchical command structure of capital remained'.[60] In Marx's words, under capital's coercive effects 'wage labourers cooperate, moreover, only because a mass of capital puts them to work simultaneously. The cohesiveness of their functions and their unity as a total productive organism reside outside them in the capital that brings them together and holds them together'.[61] Because the Soviet Union did not challenge the alienation of workers from the means of production, from themselves, and from one another, because it used political force to extract surplus labour in the name of socialist development, Mészáros says it failed 'to attack the social economic foundation [of capital] and devise an alternative way of regulating the metabolic process of society in such a way that the power of capital is at first curtailed and is of course in the end done away with altogether'.[62]

Today, for the majority of the world's working classes, the challenge before us is the dismantling of the capitalist variant of capital's metabolic control, which, as Mészáros notes, operates chiefly (though not exclusively) through the 'economically regulated extraction of surplus labour and surplus value'.[63] This poses certain problems. Since surplus is extracted economically rather than politically, it follows that simply overthrowing those in political power will not abolish capital's metabolic control. In fact, as ongoing projects of socialist construction like those in Cuba and Venezuela or alternative systems of economic production like cooperatives demonstrate, even worker control of the state or means of production isn't enough to end capital's metabolic control. Marx usefully describes capital's metabolic control as an 'inhuman power' that holds everything in its sway.[64] By this, Marx aims to capture how under capitalism it is capital itself and not the possessors of capital that determines that production must take place for 'accumulation for the sake of accumulation' instead of to meet immediate social and ecological needs.[65] As Marx explains, 'capital is thus the governing power over labour and its products. The capitalist possesses this power, not on account of his personal or human qualities, but inasmuch as he is an owner of capital.'[66]

The possessors of capital — or capital's personifications as both Marx and Mészáros call them — are therefore also subject to capital's metabolic control. One way this is evident is the presence of competition between different possessors of capital. Competition, as Marx argues, 'subordinates every individual capitalist to the immanent laws of capitalist production, as external and coercive laws. It compels him to keep extending his capital, so as to preserve it, and he can only extend it by means of progressive accumulation'.[67] Competing capitals — such as different manufacturers of smart phones — must, in other words, continually accumulate, must constantly reinvest in their operation, to stay ahead of the competition or to force them out of the market entirely so as to gain monopoly control. Even if they wish to be 'ethical', they can only be so within the bounds of profitability. If the choice is to be ethical or make a profit, the 'coercive laws' of capital force the unethical path of profit-making every time.

Another, maybe less expected, place where capital's metabolic control dictates production is in worker-owned sites of production like cooperatives. As Rosa Luxemburg explains in her essay 'Reform or Revolution', 'Co-operatives, especially co-operatives in the field of production, constitute a hybrid form in the midst of capitalism. They can be described as small units of socialised production within capitalist exchange.'[68] But precisely because cooperatives exist under capital's metabolic control, workers organised as cooperatives must function as *both* workers and capitalists. They must constantly self-exploit to produce enough profit to reinvest in the cooperative and they must keep prices competitive with private enterprises. Or as Marx argues, while 'the opposition between capital and labour' is abolished in the cooperative form, it is nevertheless the case that 'workers in association become their own capitalists, i.e, they use the means of production to valorise their labour.'[69] For Luxemburg, this means that workers' cooperatives

> are thus faced with the contradictory necessity of governing themselves with the utmost absolutism. They are obliged to take toward themselves the role of capitalist entrepreneur — a contradiction that accounts for the usual failure of production co-operatives which either become pure capitalist enterprises or, if the workers' interests continue to predominate, end by dissolving.[70]

Capital's 'inhuman power' governs over the cooperative, dictating what is produced and how, rather than the workers being able to fully govern and plan production themselves.

Mészáros' insistence that it isn't enough to 'overthrow' the capitalist state or expropriate the expropriators is key to what makes him so useful for theorising transition today. For Mészáros, these are negative acts which must be accompanied by a positive project of building an alternative 'second order' system of metabolic control that is democratically governed by the associated producers. This 'positive dimension of the socialist alternative', Mészáros explains, 'cannot be turned into reality without finding a rationally controllable and humanly rewarding equivalent to all those vital functions of social reproduction which must be fulfilled — in one form or another — by all conceivable systems of productive mediatory interchange'.[71]

'The real objective of socialist transformation', of winning a world of radical abundance, is therefore 'the establishment of a self-sustaining alternative metabolic order' which entails 'the positive appropriation and ongoing improvement of the vital functions of metabolic interchange with nature among members of society by the self-determining individuals themselves'.[72] In practice this means diminishing capital's metabolic control while establishing a new, enduring, communal, second order metabolism. It means the creation of an entirely different social reality — an entirely different social metabolism — that must, for now, run alongside and be in unavoidable contestation with capital's metabolic system. In an organisational sense, rather than being mediated by prices in a market system, or by the alienated command structure as in the Soviet model, this alternative social metabolic order will require decisions about our collective social reproduction to be mediated by the conscious democratic planning of what Marx calls the 'associated producers'. As Mészáros argues, 'the sustainability of a global order of socio-metabolic reproduction is inconceivable without an adequate planning system, administered on the basis of substantive democracy by freely associated producers'.[73] Or as Marx puts it in *Capital: Volume III*, it requires 'that socialized man, the associated producers, govern the human metabolism with nature in a rational way, bringing it under their collective control' and 'accomplishing it with the least expenditure of energy and in conditions most worthy and appropriate for their human nature'.[74] This is the essential precondition for a world of radical abundance.

THE INVARIANT FEATURES OF TRANSITION

The task before us is nothing less than that of dismantling capital's metabolic control and constructing a new richly democratic and ecologically reparative way of mediating our metabolism with one another and with non-human nature. This means finding practical ways to 'suppress' capital's second order metabolic control by 'consciously and persistently reducing capital's power of regulating the social metabolism itself'.[75] As we'll argue in later chapters, this complex political project must be attuned to its specific circumstances from which workers struggle. Even so, a reading of Mészáros, Harnecker, and Lebowitz suggests there are at least two aspects that are indispensable to the task of reducing and eventually ending capital's metabolic control, whatever the context and conjuncture: the generation of 'popular protagonism' and the creation of a situation of 'contested reproduction'.

Popular Protagonism

Speaking at the Cologne Communist Trial in 1852, Marx argued that the global working class would have to 'go through 15, 20, 50 years of civil wars and national struggles not only to bring about a change in society but also to change yourselves and prepare yourselves for political power'.[76] Marx's observations about the need for the working classes to prepare themselves for power are no less true today. As anyone who has engaged in protests, rallies, riots, strikes, and occupations will know, the people who engage in struggles are themselves transformed by them. Social struggles enable and compose new collectives, new modes of consciousness, and new capacities. We learn practical skills like how to hold a well-attended rally, how to get out the vote among union members, or how to lock-on to fossil fuel infrastructure. We also acquire intangible skills and deepen our political understandings about the need to act collectively to achieve our goals, the necessity of putting the interests of the majority before our own, and how to understand that our actions are part of an ongoing global class struggle. Or, as Marta Harnecker says, 'realising that there are many of us who are in the same struggle is what makes us strong; it is what radicalises us'.[77]

In her studies of socialist construction projects in Venezuela, Kerala, and Cuba, Harnecker observes that those who participate in certain forms of democratic planning and deliberation are transformed by the experience. Participation thus constructs a new, powerful, collective agent of social transformation. She calls this agent, and the process of building and sustaining it, 'popular protagonism'. Popular, because it is exercised by the working classes, or the popular classes, in their differentiated unity: industrial workers, service workers, care workers, unwaged workers, peasants, and so on. Protagonism, because through collective action the popular classes become the 'main characters' of social transformation. For Harnecker, transitions organised through the exercise of popular protagonism should be contrasted with those that entrust a bourgeois state or bourgeois political party to act paternalistically on the popular classes' behalf. As Harnecker says, a world of radical abundance cannot 'be decreed from on high, it has to be built with the people'.[78] The working classes themselves must foster the institutional means and capacities 'to make decisions, and through struggles get results.' The institutional means can take many forms, from revolutionary parties, to assemblies, to communes. What matters, as Marx puts it, is that 'the emancipation of the working classes must be conquered by the working classes themselves'.[79]

For popular protagonism to develop, or become stronger where it already exists, two things must happen simultaneously. First, the associated producers must learn through acting collectively they have the power to change the world, which is to say they must become conscious of themselves as a collective political subject. Second, the associated producers must build institutional forms that empower them to act in their collective interest both at the site of production and in broader practices of social reproduction.

On the first of these, Michael Lebowitz has shown that for capital's metabolic control to endure, it must not only reproduce the capital-wage relation but also, in Marx's words, 'the advance of capitalist production develops a working class which by education, tradition and habit looks upon the requirements of that mode of production as self-evident natural laws'.[80] For capital to exist, in other words, workers must be convinced that there is simply no other way of doing things. It follows that a transition towards radical abundance must *denaturalise* capital's metabolic control by creating a situation in which a new communal metabolic order becomes self-evidently necessary to a new and always developing collective political subject.[81] Through struggle, capital's metabolic order must be shown to be what it always was: a barrier to our collective pursuit of radical abundance.

On the second of these, this new political subject must inhabit institutional forms that sustain and strengthen class consciousness and popular protagonism. As Louis Althusser writes, 'ideology exists in institutions and the practices specific to them', meaning among other things that the institutions we live in shape our understanding of what is necessary, realistic, or proper.[82] For Althusser, various capitalist 'state apparatus' — the police, schools, prisons, media, parliament, and hospitals — normalise capital's metabolic control and train us in specific rituals, habits, and practices. In a similar way, then, the popular classes must construct institutional forms with the power to shift the boundaries of what is politically possible and inculcate new collective habits, practices, and cultures. These institutions of democratic planning and popular protagonism hold the promise of becoming the cell-form of a new communal regime of metabolic control.

It is often argued that alternative socio-economic forms like cooperatives and mutual aid networks can play a critical role in 'forging the new subjectivities and social relations that would be needed to sustain a long-term revolutionary transformation'.[83] Even so, cooperatives, mutual aid networks, and similar initiatives are frequently constrained by the fact that their expressions of solidarity and scope of action do 'not necessarily extend beyond the geographical bounds of the community in question nor to individuals who are not viewed as members of that community'. Lebowitz calls this the problem of 'collective atomism'.[84] People organise together, but they do so in isolation from other groups organising together in different contexts, and sometimes even the same context. To overcome collective atomism and build popular protagonism requires institutional forms that foster a universal class consciousness and the institutional means to facilitate strategic coordination and economic planning at scale. 'Small spaces for protagonism are not the goal; nor is it a confederation of freely associated communities', but a new and eventually global communal system of metabolic control.[85] The Argentinian revolutionary Che Guevara called this aspiration the 'institutionalisation of the revolution'. As he explained in a speech delivered in 1965:

> We are looking for something new that will permit a complete identification between the government and the community in its entirety, something appropriate to the special conditions of the building of socialism, while avoiding at all costs transplanting the commonplaces of bourgeois democracy — such as legislative chambers, for example — into the society in formation.[86]

For Guevara the democratic practices associated with radical abundance are not the same as our bourgeois system, where each of us gets to put a cross in a box every four or six years before having no further say in what happens in our communities and other areas of concern, let alone what our workplaces do and how they're managed. Nor is it about the pretensions of 'participation' that are sometimes entertained by the bourgeois system, such as citizen assemblies, which often amount to little more than technocratic consultation exercises. Instead, as Harnecker explains, a 'participatory and protagonistic democracy... is a democracy for the great majority of the people. Within it, the common citizen can participate in a variety of matters, not only in formulating demands and supervision, but more fundamentally in making decisions and ensuring they are carried out'.[87] This entails a different kind of democracy, and a different kind of political subjectivity, to what most of us are familiar with. It is 'democracy in *practice*, democracy *as* practice, and *democracy as protagonism*' and can therefore only be sustained by new, richly democratic, working-class institutions that have exorcised capital's metabolic control from their functioning.[88] Popular protagonism is thus the first invariant feature of transition.

Contested Reproduction

The mistaken idea that revolutions exist as ruptural events — moments in which a new social order bursts forth ready-formed from the carcass of the old — looms large in contemporary anti-capitalist thought. As Vincent Bevins writes in his recent journalistic account of the 'movement of the squares', 'many people in my generation...thought that if you simply gave the thing a kick, it would come unstuck and move in the right direction', something akin to a Hollywood narrative in which 'once Sauron falls, all the dark magic in the universe simply dissipates, and the forces of evil disappear'.[89] This comparison with Tolkien is well-chosen. The idea of a decisive rupture makes for an exciting narrative arc, but it does not reflect the history of past and present projects in socialist construction. Overemphasising the symbolic and heroic moment in which power appears to transfer from one class to another — or where one metabolic order begins to dominate over another — underplays the messy, patient, and protracted realities of transition. To properly theorise what it takes to establish a 'self-sustaining alternative social metabolic order' to capital, the idea of revolution as rupture must take a backseat to the notion of transition as an enduring period of struggle for supremacy between two metabolic systems: capital and a communal system.[90]

This, however, isn't to say that all meanings of rupture — or indeed, revolution — are irrelevant to thinking about transition. Nor is it to endorse an 'organic', reformist, and gradualist theory of change that eschews class conflict or forecloses contestation over the state. Marx and Engels understood that the overthrow of capital would be a protracted process and that it would, in all likelihood, require the working classes to impose their will on the defenders of capital. Even so, they retained a very specific, and important, understanding of rupture. Arguing against those they call 'bourgeois socialists' in the *Communist Manifesto* who *did* endorse a reformist theory of change, Marx and Engels write that 'the communist revolution is the most radical rupture with traditional property relations'.[91] By this they mean that communism is not in continuity with bourgeois society. It is a *qualitatively different* mode of metabolic control that for a time will necessarily co-exist with capital's metabolism until the class forces mobilised around one order finally defeats the other.

Transition is therefore a period in which incompatible and antagonistic social metabolisms 'coexist and interpenetrate'.[92] Taking inspiration from the Soviet political economist Evgenii Preobrazhensky, Lebowitz calls this phenomenon 'contested reproduction'. For Lebowitz, thinking the challenge of transition through the concept of contested reproduction helps to understand that 'the central question' for revolutionaries is 'how to create the conditions in which elements of capitalism can be subordinated to the system of community', the latter being Lebowitz's term for a world of radical abundance.[93] In Preobrazhensky's words, what is needed is 'the ousting of other economic forms, the subordination of these forms to the new form, and their gradual elimination'.[94] Or in the language we've introduced so far in this chapter, revolutionary transition is a protracted process of replacing capital's metabolic control with democratically planned production determined by the associated producers.

Preobrazhensky's context was post-revolutionary Russia, so the period of contested reproduction with which he was concerned came after a revolutionary party had taken control of the state. It was a response to a series of novel challenges that the newly formed workers' state encountered. Preobrazhensky proposed that since the Russian Revolution had taken place in a context where the agricultural sector was broadly capitalist and capitalist industry was immature, the post-revolutionary workers' state would have to enact a process of 'primitive socialist accumulation', generating a surplus from state-owned industry and agriculture, to eventually squeeze out capitalist sectors and influences entirely. As he explained in 1927, 'the enormous preponderance of petty commodity production, combined with the relative weakness of the state sector, forces the state economy into an uninterrupted economic war with the tendencies of capitalist development, with the tendencies of capitalist restoration'.[95] The advance towards socialism therefore 'takes place in the form of the antagonistic development of contradictions and the struggle between the law of primitive socialist accumulation and the law of value'.[96]

During the historical period in which these antagonistic metabolic systems overlap, Russia's social metabolism would be defined by a situation of contested reproduction where neither the capitalist nor state-planned system would dominate, but each would struggle against and interpenetrate with the other. As Preobrazhensky writes, 'the unity of the whole system in a certain sense rests on the coexistence of these two economic formations in our economy, but the equilibrium of that system is achieved on the basis of a struggle along the whole front'.[97]

Preobrazhensky saw contested reproduction as a problem to be resolved by party cadres and intellectuals, who, due to the tragic situation of capitalist encirclement and underdevelopment in which the Soviet Union found itself, had to extract surplus labour from peasants and workers until capitalism had been replaced by state socialism. Whether this was an accurate appraisal of the Bolsheviks's situation is irrelevant to our purposes. What matters is Preobrazhensky's indispensable insight that during a transitionary period it is essential to 'oust' capital's metabolic control. Revolutionary transitions can take many forms, but whatever the form, there will inevitably be a period of antagonism between capital's metabolic system, with its endless bullshit, and a new communal system defined by radical abundance.

As significant as this contribution is, Preobrazhensky's theory isn't without its problems. With Mészáros' distinction between capital and capitalism we can see that Preobrazhensky is involved in a struggle to replace one form of capital's metabolic control with another. Since the working classes would still be subjected to a power over and beyond themselves — the alienated power of the state — they would *still be subject to capital's metabolic control*. Moreover, we can see with Harnecker's help that since for Preobrazhensky the party and state were to act paternalistically on behalf of the peasantry and working classes, there was no space for direct democratic control over production. Or in our terms: No space for popular protagonism.

The way out of this impasse is found in a return to Marx. In 1871, the working classes of Paris took control of the city and installed a worker's government, the Paris Commune. In the commune, those who governed over society were themselves workers. Bourgeois systems of representation were removed and, in their place, the working classes installed recallable representatives paid no more than the average worker. Watching these proceedings with great interest from London, Marx claimed that the Parisian working classes had discovered the 'political form' of their 'social emancipation'.[98] For Marx, the discovery of the communal form demonstrated that 'the working class cannot simply lay hold of ready-made state machinery, and wield it for their own purposes'.[99] Instead, there must be a 'reabsorption of the state power by society as its own living forces instead of as forces controlling and subduing it, by the popular masses themselves, forming their own force instead of the organised force of their suppression'.[100]

To truly oust capital's metabolic control, in other words, power over the collective reproduction of the working classes and non-human nature cannot be achieved by passing control from the private managers of capital to the organs of the state but must, in one way or another, be passed directly to the associated producers. Contested reproduction must therefore exist not between two different forms of capital's metabolic control but between capital's bullshit abundance and the nascent, provisional, and at first deeply vulnerable cell-forms of a world of radical abundance. Transition becomes a period, in Hugo Chavez' words, of 'deconstructing on the one hand and constructing on the other'.[101] Capital's metabolic control is dismantled, and a new communal metabolism is installed in its place.

As we'll show with examples from across the world in the next chapter, understanding contested reproduction in this way invites us to think strategically about how to set a transition in motion by producing and expanding spaces of social property — property owned by everyone in contrast to private property or state-owned property — and popular protagonism. During the transition, these spaces coincide with and struggle against capital's metabolic control. Thinking transition in this way means acting within our existing capacities and constraints to diminish capital's metabolic control over institutions of democratically planned production. As Mészáros puts this point:

> the very process of radical restructuring — the crucial condition of success of the socialist project — can only make progress if the strategy aims at the radical suppression of capital as such, consciously and persistently reducing capital's power of regulating the social metabolism itself... This can be accomplished by locating neutralizable and adaptable mechanisms and processes which favour the required complex transformation.[102]

Critically, though state support in this endeavour is highly advantageous, there is no need to wait until the working class takes state power. The transition can begin by proliferating spaces of popular protagonism and contested reproduction within and across partial and provisional communal experiments. In this way a new communal-based logic of social control can be embedded and sustained by 'ousting' or contesting the logic of capital from spheres of social production on multiple simultaneous fronts. One of the wagers made in this book is that if these projects can connect and amplify one another, if they can support and defend the development of new institutions of social reproduction that are to a limited extent liberated from capital's metabolic control, then it is feasible to weaken capital's *overall* metabolic control and begin to tip the balance of forces in favour of radical abundance.

We are under no illusions that this is an easy task. Those who benefit from capital's metabolic control will resist at every turn. Yet by building communal institutions, the associated producers can put themselves in the best possible position to withstand inevitable attacks from the capitalist, landlord, and rentier classes. If as much of our collective reproduction is in our own hands as possible, then we are less dependent on capital to reproduce ourselves day-to-day and more capable of sustaining the fight to win a world of radical abundance for all. Labour strikes are eminently more winnable, for example, if the strike can be prolonged because workers have their immediate collective needs met, even if only in part, outside of the individualised and individualising wage relation. Revolutionary parties, meanwhile, can find a wellspring of support among those participating in the development of communal institutions. And if popular sympathies are with the emerging communal system, then the capitalist classes' inevitable backlash against them will only drain capital's metabolic control of any remaining legitimacy. Capital will be exposed as the undemocratic, violent, system of metabolic control that it always has been. For all these reasons, the struggle to build communal institutions brings a full transition towards a world of radical abundance that little bit closer.

PUTTING THEORY INTO PRACTICE

This chapter has sought to understand, at a high level of abstraction, what it takes to transition towards a world of radical abundance for all. With Istvan Mészáros we have argued that capital's metabolic control is something far more expansive than simply the capitalist economy. In today's world, capital insinuates itself into and structures nearly all metabolic exchanges between humans and non-humans, pressing them into the service of capital accumulation. This sounds abstract, and often in this chapter we have stayed at a high level of abstraction, but it has very concrete effects. When we do reproductive work at home like cooking meals, washing clothes, or cleaning, we feed ourselves and our loved ones but we also reproduce our ability to go to work and be exploited to create surplus value. When we relax on weekends or days off, we enjoy ourselves but we are also resting our bodies, so we are able to work and create more surplus value. When we raise children, we also raise future workers whose labour will be exploited, or capitalists who will exploit others. When we buy something as a gift for a friend, we express our love and appreciation, but we also valorise capital. To the extent that society conserves and protects nature, it also reproduces the climactic and ecological conditions of possibility for capital accumulation. And all of these practices are conducted, generally speaking, within the limits of what capital's metabolic control will tolerate. If we challenge them too much, the state will intervene on capital's behalf.

Crucially, capital's metabolic control is at play even in spaces that some have mistakenly thought are outside of the worker/capitalist relation. Cooperatives and other worker-owned forms of production are just as subject to capital's metabolic control as private capitalist industry. Nationalising industry may indeed be part of a revolutionary transition, but not if it simply replaces private ownership and control of production with state ownership and state-managed processes of capital accumulation. State planning meanwhile, as Mészáros argues, might end *capitalism* but it's not enough to end *capital*'s metabolic control. What is needed to transition away from capital's production of bullshit abundance and towards a world of radical abundance for all, is a way to support what Marx calls the 'reabsorption of state power by society as its own living force', a way for the freely associated producers to control their own metabolic interactions with one another and with non-human nature.

In this chapter we propose that a transition of this kind requires two things, which we have called 'invariant features'. First, the development of popular protagonism in worker-controlled democratic institutions. In and through collective deliberation and organisation, new kinds of political consciousness and new skills are developed. Second, the fostering of situations of contested reproduction through which capital's metabolic control over our collective reproduction is curtailed, constrained, and diminished, enabling a new communal form of metabolic control to take root. We are under no illusion that these by themselves are enough to put an end to capital's bullshit, but they *are* essential, and once these processes are underway the associated producers are in a stronger position to fight against capital and its proponents until they finally win a world of radical abundance for all.

Understanding capital's metabolic control and the invariant features of transition at this abstract level is crucial but insufficient. In *Capital: Volume I*, Marx rightly spends considerable time elaborating how the capitalist value-form structures production, but there is very little about the value-form as such that can tell us how to act in the here and now. Similarly, knowing that we must build institutions that foster and expand spaces of popular protagonism tells us nothing about the form these institutions ought to take, or how they might position themselves in relation to the state and capital during the inevitable period of contested reproduction. For this, we must move down a level of abstraction. As Lenin argued, 'the very gist, the living soul' of Marxism is a 'concrete analysis of a concrete situation.'[103] The next two chapters conduct this concrete analysis.

3

Instituting Popular Protagonism

Writing in the immediate aftermath of the 2010 UK election, Mike Rustin — who along with Doreen Massey and Stuart Hall was a founding editor of the progressive journal *Soundings* — opined that 'the uncertainties of the conjuncture brought about by the implosion of the neo-liberal regime' provided 'opportunities for decisive political action, leading to radical changes in a social system' for those 'who grasp the needs and opportunities that the crisis has opened up'.[1] This apparent implosion of the 'neo-liberal regime' stretched far beyond Britain's shores, reverberating across the imperial core. Countries including Ireland, Italy, Spain, Portugal, Finland, Denmark, and Japan all reported a contraction of their economy between 2007 and 2012. Though the crisis manifested differently and with various intensities across time and place, the dominant political response was one of austerity — whether this was imposed by the Troika (the European Commission, the European Central Bank, and the International Monetary Fund) as part of a structural readjustment policy or willingly embraced as in the UK with the Conservative Party's 'Big Society' agenda. Rustin's remarks nicely captured the political mood on the Left. The idea that the crisis was a moment which demanded (and was perhaps ripe for) radical change was felt deeply. And yet it was altogether less clear what 'radical changes in a social system' would actually look like, or what type of 'decisive political action' could precipitate such changes.

The 2010s thus became a decade of political experimentation in which a series of wagers would be made by social movements about how to exploit the 'uncertainties of the conjuncture' to bring about radical — perhaps even socialist — transformation. Two political tendencies appeared to dominate in this period: the movement of the squares and the emergence of left populism. For all their differences, the wave of street occupations and mass protests — from Gezi Park to Occupy Wall Street, and from Tahrir Square to the Spanish Indignados — signified a huge conflagration of discontent that resonated across the periphery before spreading to the imperial core, sometimes bringing down governments in the process. The second was a populist electoral turn that saw significant efforts to constitute some form of progressive alternative via the ballot box. With a certain degree of precedence in Latin America's 'pink tide', the first of these electoral waves in was in 2012 when Syriza became the official opposition to Greece's coalition government and was subsequently elected to government in 2015. From 2014 onwards this electoral wave travelled from Podemos in Spain, to Bernie Sanders in the US, to Jeremy Corbyn's surprise leadership of the UK Labour Party, and to the formation of La France Insoumise by Jean-Luc Mélenchon.

These two tendencies reflected a tension which, in some shape, has long-dominated radical-left and socialist strategy: would radical change be achieved by gaining control of the legislative and executive branches of the state, or would it come about by trying to 'change the world without taking power'?[2] These two broad philosophical orientations, nominally in opposition to one another, each have a whole series of implications for how to organise and how change may happen. Yet, as we'll argue in this chapter neither of these broad tendencies demonstrated (in theory or practice) the two invariant features of transition we outlined in the previous chapter: building popular protagonism and contested reproduction. If the post-2008 conjuncture did indeed provide opportunities for a transformative socialist politics to develop within the countries of the imperial core, any sober assessment would find those opportunities to have been largely squandered.

Yet there was a third and altogether less commented on set of socialist political practices that had already begun to take root, some of which emerged in the same period whilst others had a longer history. While less visible and not yet clearly articulated into a common project, a series of largely disconnected political wagers have emerged in both the imperial core and the periphery that are driven by the shared intuition that we need an entirely different form of socialist practice. The theoretical inspirations and political traditions underpinning these initiatives are diverse, drawing variously on autonomous theories of commoning, certain strains of Latin American Marxism, communal socialism, radical municipalism, Marxist feminism, agroecology, the social-solidarity or transformative economy, and certain traditions of US Black radicalism. Yet whatever terms they use to frame their projects, their focus is on struggling to directly create enduring institutions that deepen and extend the role of collective democratic processes in mediating the work we do to reproduce ourselves (from food and housing, to machine tools and waste collection) while working to restrict or subordinate capital's role in mediating that activity. In other words, they are building popular protagonism and contested reproduction.

These wagers are embryonic and diverse. Each has a distinct character and composition of class forces, meaning that we can't impose a single reading of their aims and strategic direction. Yet to recall Michael Lebowitz, 'small spaces for protagonism are not the goal; nor is it a confederation of freely associated communities'[3] that temporarily sustain themselves in the interstices of capital. The reason we are interested in these wagers, and why we consider them to represent an important socialist tendency, is precisely because of their potential to do more than offer some temporary respite to capital's bullshit imperative to 'accumulate, accumulate!'.[4] Whatever their differences, they are all finding contextually specific strategies to develop the cell-forms of an alternative socio-metabolic order. Working within the confines of their uniquely hostile conditions, and yet building territorial outposts from which to keep expanding, these are the initiatives that we see the need to act in solidarity with, to draw lessons from, and to translate into our own situation.

FROM THE SQUARES TO THE BALLOT BOXES

Mohamed Bouazizi's self-immolation in Tunisia on 17 December 2010 is widely understood to be what sparked a sequence of more-

or-much-less connected political upheavals in the early 2010s. The ensuing protests led to the collapse of Tunisia's government in January 2011 which, along with a wave of mass demonstrations and political unrest in Libya, Egypt, Yemen, Syria and Bahrain, were collectively dubbed by Western commentators the 'Arab Spring'. If the extent to which these political conflagrations were connected is open to interrogation, the links to a wider set of mass street mobilisations and occupations — from Gezi Park in Istanbul and Syntagma Square in Athens, to Occupy Wall Street in New York and the 15-M occupations across Spain — is even more ambiguous. Many words have been written trying to identify some common narrative that might be told about these diverse street mobilisations, ranging from the proliferation of communication technologies through to the failure of governments to address the structural underpinnings of the 2008 financial crisis.[5] Perhaps one of the most enduring stories told about this period was that it marked the emergence of the 'leaderless revolution',[6] where instead of vanguard parties calling the shots about how to organise for socialism, politics was now associated with leaderless organisation and spontaneity.

The consequences of this development have been widely contested. For writers such as Michael Hardt and Antonio Negri, these experiences indicated the discovery through practice, of forms of organising and organisation that are appropriate to the current conditions of struggle and composition of class forces in the imperial core.[7] For Jodi Dean, by contrast, their refusal of the party-form undermined their ability to build collective power.[8] Similarly, for Vincent Bevins, in his retrospective of this decade entitled *If We Burn: The Mass Protest Decade and the Missing Revolution,* even though these waves of protest reflected 'a huge amount of desire for changes to the structures that comprise our global system', the channelling of this desire into the political forms of the 'assembly' and the 'occupation of the squares' ultimately meant that movements were poorly equipped to offer a substantive alternative to extant regimes. Bevins attributes this failure to the legacy of 'horizontalism', a very loosely defined philosophical orientation initially associated with the alter-globalisation movement, and more latterly with the prospects for spontaneous or leaderless social transformation.[9]

Without losing ourselves in the specifics of these debates, what matters from our perspective is that the turn towards horizontalist organising was an attempt to resolve perceived issues with historical modes of socialist organising including the party, hierarchical decision-making, the role of the state in revolutionary processes, and — more distantly — the trade union. Horizontalism means immediacy; it means a politics without representation, and therefore a politics without the risk of a minority acting against the majority's interests while *claiming* to speak or act on their behalf.[10] At least in the US and much of Europe, the belief that this was the way to bring about social transformation marked a turn towards a politics of prefiguration that in fact has its roots in the 1960s.[11] This strategy refuses to wait until 'after' a revolution has been won through the seizure of state power and aims instead to demonstrate that other-ways-of-being-together are possible in the here and now. Strong influences came from Latin America's experience following a wave of structural readjustment policies and economic crisis in the 1990s. An explosion of factory occupations in Argentina and the Zapatista's infamous declarations of the Lacandon Jungle offered a timely intellectual and political impetus for a global Left looking for new forms of political praxis.[12]

Horizontalism infused a series of campaigns and organising efforts including the World Social Forum and alter-globalisation summit protests, forms of environmental direct action, media projects, and social centres. As Hurricane Sandy hit the north-eastern coast of the United States in 2012, the latent networks formed through the Occupy movement were mobilised into mutual aid relief networks that 'proved more effective than FEMA in bringing aid to the most distressed communities'.[13] Others formed projects like the Strike Debt collective, which organised an innovative Rolling Jubilee that purchased cheap medical and student loan debt on secondary markets, only to cancel it anonymously for the debtors. There is no question that these horizontalist movements produced inspiring forms of social-political action which, at times, helped to shape popular discourse and deliver concrete outcomes. The limited successes of the Sunrise Movement, Extinction Rebellion, and Fridays for Future are especially notable examples in the climate movement.

Yet for all that has been learned from these experiments, the potential for horizontalist movements to transform the world is limited by the fact their strategies don't embody the invariant features of transition, precisely because the problem of transition is collapsed into the immediacy of living and being otherwise. This weakness was perhaps most acutely illustrated during Occupy Wall Street, where the occupation found itself unable to articulate political demands that might build popular power or curtail capital's metabolic control, instead focusing on the 'prefigurative' nature of the crowd. As one protestor put it: "I don't think we should issue a list of demands at all. That's not what this is about. It's about creating a new kind of community, of showing people a new way of relating to one another".[14] Occupy was held together by a negation, by a clear *no* to the existent, but it lacked what Meszaros calls a 'positive alternative' that could transcend the immediacy of being together, of the tactic of occupation itself.[15] Indeed, in general, the intrinsically ephemeral nature of horizontalist initiatives was reflective of the tendency to jump over the problem of transition and to hope instead that a proliferation of interstitial transformations or 'nowtopias'[16] would *somehow* add up to a serious counter-project to capital's metabolic regime.

But the story of the 2010s isn't just one of mass protest and innovative forms of mutual aid. It is also a story about a wave of electoral initiatives that were in many cases strongly influenced by the limitations of the 'horizontalist' organising that preceded them. Indeed, the most conspicuous omission from Bevins' account of the decade is the Spanish Indignados movement, also known as the 15-M movement on account of the major demonstrations and square occupations that began on 15 May 2011. Although these demonstrations may not have directly brought down a government, they led to an explosion of political experimentation and a significant change in Spain's electoral calculus. Successfully gaining over 20 percent of the vote in both the 2015 and 2016 general elections,

Podemos, as the movement's electoral party was called, was notable for its attempt to create a party rooted in its organisational circles that were envisioned as spaces of participation. Podemos internalised many of the 15-M movement's organisational practices, from consensus decision-making to open membership. In this respect, Podemos was less a rejection of the political insights and desires of those that had flooded Spain's squares than a wager that the horizontalist practices and revolutionary desires that had circulated in the squares must find institutional form or else dissipate. It was a wager that a national electoral vehicle, built on local participatory spaces, might help to consolidate movement energy while opening new avenues for strategic intervention. In this sense, Podemos grasped the need for institutions that could foster popular protagonism, but this popular protagonism took a limited political form that ultimately came to focus only on the state. There remains a slim possibility that Podemos will come to have some bearing on Spain's future electoral arithmetic. Yet as an experiment in mass democratic participation the project has more or less come to an end, without tackling the challenge of contested reproduction, and without methods for articulating popular protagonism outside of formal political institutions.

Often surprisingly, perhaps especially for those who were participating, this electoral turn became a significant factor in a number of countries that had not seen anything like a left wing in decades. Unlike the rise of Podemos, for instance, Jeremy Corbyn's election as the leader of the UK Labour Party in 2015 wasn't the result of long-term organising by a concerted mass left-wing movement. Instead, a change to Labour Party policy meant that new party members could vote immediately for their preferred party leader. Corbyn's candidacy for leader of the party went from an implausible proposition to reality, in part because many who had lived experience of the limits of horizontalist strategies saw an opportunity to reshape the Labour Party into a progressive force. Under Corbyn's leadership, Labour Party membership surged, almost tripling between 2015 and the 2017 election. The establishment of Momentum was the most notable attempt to create a political vehicle to support and direct the energies of this membership surge, yet despite commitments to 'scale up political education' and 'support struggles in our communities and our workplaces', Momentum became increasingly focused on internal lobbying and generating support in future leadership contests. Here, the need for institutions to develop our collective power was rightly intuited, but the movements around Corbyn failed to transform the Labour Party into a vehicle for the expansion of popular protagonism, either in the 'political' sense attempted by Podemos or in a popular 'social' sense that might exercise power outside of the state, and hence the project never came close to the problem of contested reproduction.

A comparable electoral turn emerged in the US with Bernie Sanders' improbable campaigns to be the Democratic Party's presidential candidate for the 2016 and 2020 elections. Like in the UK, this resulted in a surge in membership of the Democratic Socialists of America (DSA), which reported a 15-fold increase up to 2021, bolstered by the 2018 election of DSA member Alexandria Ocasio-Cortez to the House of Representatives. DSA is a broad church, and while many branches and caucuses have done important organisational work — such as New York city's Build Public Renewables Act which grants local authorities the power to build and own renewable energy systems[17] — their successes are often achieved *in spite of* the Democratic Party rather than because of it. Of the three electoral experiments summarised here, DSA has perhaps struggled the most to build transformative institutions for the development of popular protagonism and contested reproduction. Of the three, it is also the only substantially ongoing project.

Though not articulating their work in these terms, and though different in many respects, these movements in Spain, the UK, and the US all intuited that popular protagonism needs institutional expression. Yet this was restricted to how we might exercise democratic agency through 'political' power, without consideration of the other types of institutions that might enable us to construct 'social' forms of popular power. Contested reproduction, by extension, remained a far-off prospect — at best a series of important policy proposals like we saw in the Labour *Alternative Models of Ownership* report[18]

— subordinated to the challenge of retaining power and influence in a hostile electoral system.

Much ink has been spilt theorising the origins and shared qualities of this electoral wave. In the imperial core (and its near peripheries) this electoral wave is variously considered to additionally include the Pirate Parties across Scandinavia, La France Insoumise, Syriza, and more ambiguous initiatives like the Five Star Movement in Italy. Theorists such as Chantal Mouffe reflected on this as a moment of left populism,[19] arguing they mark a shift towards the construction of electoral projects triangulated across quite different social identities and class positions. In contrast to right-wing initiatives such as National Rally in France and the Party for Freedom in the Netherlands that base their populism on nation or race, Mouffe suggests that left populisms are those in which 'the people' become articulated through democratic processes. Although this would nominally be grounded in 'a diversity of democratic struggles around issues concerning exploitation, domination, and discrimination', the struggles themselves are effectively relegated to fulfilling a single objective, 'the articulation of a transversal "collective will", a "people", apt to come to power and establish a new hegemonic formation'.[20] Though in practice the proposition of left populism often amounts to little more than advanced electoral arithmetic, a calculation of how and where electoral representatives can be won, Nancy Fraser has gone as far to argue that 'progressive populism could end up being transitional — a way station en route to some new postcapitalist form of society'.[21] If it is a way station, it is one with little sense of where to go next, and in particular little sense of how a fragile and narrowly political electoral project could contribute to a *social* transformation through what Marx calls the 'reabsorption of the state power by society as its own living forces.'

Despite this, there were actors and authors who reflected deeply on the question of how to build popular power within bourgeois political parties that are by their nature, and by dint of the interests they serve, hostile to popular will. Paolo Gerbaudo, for example, has provided a forensic account of how several of these electoral initiatives sought to harness digital technologies to enhance the scope for participatory decision-making within the parties themselves. These have typically led to a 'very different picture of party organisation: a flexible and cybernetic system, to the point where using the very word *structure* becomes questionable' and where 'the adoption of the platform as an organisational mechanism... allegedly allows the expression of the authentic will of the people' in a way that fits well with Mouffe's understanding of left populism.[22] Digital technologies also filled an important function for those who wagered it was possible to reimagine the party-form such that it could both maintain and extend the organisational practices — and some of the wider political philosophies — of horizontalism, while overcoming the perceived limits of attempting to change the world without taking power. The question of how to organise people in the here and now, which was such a central focus of horizontalist movements, in many cases continued to be taken seriously, and yet this line of questioning was generally restricted to the internal machinations of the party and parliamentary elections.

The rise of left populism, though limited in scope and ambition, rightly intuited that the generation of bullshit abundance and artificial scarcity could only be stopped with the help of popular institutions. Yet even in the case of the digital parties which were trying to find technical solutions to how 'the people' could be genuine democratic subjects (rather than an electoral calculus), it was a very specific type of institution — the bourgeois political party — that was the focus of these efforts. By extension, it was also a very restricted understanding of the democratic political subject (one that deliberated on policy frameworks) and form of political agency (the power to decide on those frameworks) that these digital parties were aspiring to create. Ultimately, this electoral turn rested on the premise that parliamentary representation would be the critical first step, or perhaps even that it would be sufficient in itself, to address the world's many compounding social and ecological crises.

INSTITUTING POPULAR PROTAGONISM

In 1984, the French philosophers Gilles Deleuze and Felix Guattari published a short essay entitled 'May '68 Did Not Take Place'.[23]

Written a full 16 years after the rebellions that inspired it, Deleuze and Guattari's point, paradoxically presented in the essay's title, was that the social ills that created 1968's uprisings in France had not yet been resolved. More than this, the energies, collective capacities, and repertoires of struggle learned in the rebellion echoed into the present, informing political practice and challenging the idea that 1968 was a flash in the pan, a passing phase. For both these reasons May 1968 could be said to have not taken place. Or at least not yet. In many ways, the horizontalist and populist turns we've described are similar. The social ills amplified by the 2008 financial crisis have not been resolved. Worse, they are only picking up speed, gaining momentum as they collide and combine with other global crises, not least ecological ones. Similarly, the kinds of collective consciousness and new political understandings produced by the horizontalist and electoral wagers have long-lasting and ongoing effects. This book, and its authors, are products of these struggles. It is as products of them that we note that they have — generally speaking — so far failed to implement the invariant features of transition we described in Chapter Two.

Yet an alternative set of lesser commented-upon practices emerged, or persisted, during the same period, that were guided by a shared intuition that different institutional forms of popular protagonism and contested reproduction must be at the core of how we organise. Some of these emerged from the same melting pot of struggles we've discussed above, while others were born from entirely different conjunctural circumstances.

Here we very briefly present five examples from across the world. None of them use the same conceptual language to organise their struggles. Nor are they illustrative of an already formed and cohesive global movement that takes ecosocialist transition as its aim. Yet from Hernani Burujabe's experiments with radical planning in the Spanish Basque Country through to Venezuela's communes, all are driven by the goal of precipitating a shift 'from a culture in which citizens beg the state to solve their problems to a culture where citizens make decisions, and through struggle get results; where citizens implement, control, and manage things themselves, where citizens govern themselves'.[24] This, as Marta Harnecker argues, ought to be the objective and method of twenty-first century socialism. It is within this tendency that we then locate our proposal for public-common partnerships as an institutional form that is appropriate to our conjuncture.

Hernani, Hegoalde (Spanish Basque Country)

Hernani is a city with a population of around 20,000, located 10 kilometres to the south of Donostia-San Sebastián in the Spanish Basque Country. Beginning in 2020, a coalition of diverse social movements, organisations in the 'transformative economy'[25], and the municipalist government led by the left-wing EH Bildu, initiated a project called Hernani Burujabe. Meaning 'Sovereign Hernani' in Basque, the simplest way to describe Hernani Burujabe is as an attempt to generate popular protagonism through popular-democratic economic planning, and thus to expand the territorially grounded effort to advance circumstances of contested reproduction. But to fully understand its significance, and what the initiative is attempting to achieve, it's critical to understand more about the context of Basque liberation and the disputed understandings of what is meant by the idea of Basque 'sovereignty'.

The Basque region is split in half by the Pyrenees, marking the border between the two nation-states of Spain and France. Composed of seven provinces in total, three form the French part known as Iparralde, and the remaining four make up the Spanish part known as Hegoalde. Since 1979, three Hegoalde provinces have formed the Basque Autonomous Community, or Euskadi, while the Upper Navarre province withdrew from the formation of Euskadi and established its own autonomous area. Though there are sub-national governmental institutions in different parts of the Basque territory, these don't (and haven't in modern history) cohered into a Basque state. Because of this complex territorial situation, left-wing Basque organisers cannot view the sovereign state as the primary agent of social transformation. Instead, popular power must be generated through a new conception of sovereignty that helps to 'transform reality from the bottom up':[26]

> We have to escape from the current power to start building the Basque Republic. But we must do this work of construction through 'creative struggle', and not only through the 'counter struggle'. Along with the destruction of the existing, we must create a free space, today, by making the change and making it a life experience.[27]

It is in this context that we can make sense of counter-hegemonic propositions such as 'transformational sovereignties'[28] or 'territorial sovereignties'[29] as used by many of those organising in Hernani and elsewhere in the Basque territory. Sovereignty is framed as a constitutive process in which 'the goal is to advance towards the recovery of independence in the strategic areas of reproduction of life in society'.[30] Sovereignty isn't something to be channelled through a state, as the singular focus of political expression. Rather sovereignty is articulated and performed through processes committed to 'building popular control over the areas that are essential for the sustenance of our individual collective lives. It is a comprehensive process of feeding, warming, caring, connecting with collective projects... and governing them democratically'.[31] It is spoken of in the plural as sovereign*ties*, rather than as a singular concept of sovereignty, to acknowledge the many aspects of life (food, energy, care, and so on) and the many processes through which collective autonomy and interdependence are articulated. As one organiser put it to us, 'it is a process of constituting a new territoriality, from below. A territoriality planned in a popular-public-cooperative way, which challenges capital in the logic of reproduction of our bodies and territories'.[32]

Hernani Burujabe is one attempt to put these ideas into practice. In coordination between the city government, transformative economy actors, and social movements/active citizens, it functions as an approach to economic planning of the territory, organised into sectoral tables such as biodiversity, food, energy, housing, local payment system, telecommunications, and care. Via citizen assemblies, social movements and local populations collaborate with the transformative economy sector to identify needs, wants, and concerns. In parallel, the transformative economic sector collaborates with the local government, and an action plan is then developed for that sector. For example, the food table might agree to increase local supply of food from agroecological sources, requiring additional land, the creation of a new delivery infrastructure, research into new growing methods, or recruitment of additional workers. This forms an action plan, parcelling out delivery responsibilities between actors and negotiating a budget to support the work. Each of these sectoral plans gets synthesised into a single plan at the Sovereignties Council, which meets five times a year. The final plan is voted upon, with the agreed plan sent for formal budgetary approval by the council. Between April 2021 and the end of 2023, the total investment from the municipality amounted to just over 2.5 million euros.

Although Hernani Burujabe is a nascent process, there are already clear outcomes. The 'local coin' table has supported the development of a local payment system in which 40 percent of companies in Hernani have enrolled, enabling monetary exchange to be 'locked in' to the local economic circuit. Through 2024 there was around 3 million euros circulating within this payment system. The food table has led to the creation of a new consumer association and supermarket in the centre of town, a distribution hub for the cooperative food producers in the area, a farming and cooking school are in development, and land has begun to be acquired to implement an agroecological belt around the entire town. The care table has created a care cooperative which is helping to regularise the work of a notoriously precarious sector, including supporting workers through formal processes of obtaining work and residency permits. The energy table has created a form of public-communitarian energy cooperative, is resisting the development of private energy infrastructure, and is instead promoting the development of socially controlled rooftop energy production.

The relative successes in Hernani have already led to the adoption of the Burujabe approach in the neighbouring town of Oiartzun, while collaborations with the Udalbiltza local government network and the Olatukoop transformative economy umbrella organisation are exploring how to 'scale out' the initiative elsewhere. Through all of this, what is being built isn't just a process for economic development, but the constitution of an approach to collaborative processes of territorial sovereignty. Elements of a new social metabolism are being built through the contested reproduction of vital aspects of the territory's reproduction, coupled with the popular protagonism necessary to defend and expand the process.

Berlin, Germany

In the wake of the 2008 financial crisis, capital flooded into Germany's rental housing market looking for a reliable source of profits.[33] As rental prices began to rise, German social movements started to organise for affordable and accessible housing. These movements emerged primarily in response to the rise of institutional landlords such as the huge German asset firm Vovonia or pension funds like the Dutch ABP, which together have (as of 2022) reportedly captured over 40 billion euros of Berlin's homes and turned them into financial assets. As Daniela Gabor notes, 'this is roughly double the combined value of London's and Amsterdam's institutionally owned houses',[34] putting Germany and especially Berlin in a somewhat unique situation. In the Kottbusser Tor area of Berlin — a mixed working-class, precarious middle-class, and migrant neighbourhood — a group of social housing tenants formed an organisation in 2011 called Kotti & Co. Described as 'a platform for protest that emphasizes migrants' rights', in May 2012 the group occupied the square in front of their social housing complex 'to protest rising rents, falling wages, displacement and racism', establishing a permanent presence through the construction of a 'protest house' which was named Gecekondu, reflecting the Turkish heritage of many of the migrant families in the area. Over the following years, Kotti & Co. was one of a number of tenant organisations that played an important role in launching a referendum movement that ultimately contributed to the Berlin Senate introducing legislation 'guaranteeing social housing tenants that they do not have to pay more than 30 percent of their income for rent'.[35]

In 2019, as tenant organisations across Berlin began mobilising behind a campaign to 'socialise' the housing portfolios of companies that owned more than 3,000 apartments, the Gecekondu served as a campaign hub and meeting point for what became known as the Deutsche Wohnen & Co. Enteignen campaign. Following a successful referendum which put this central demand to a vote in 2021, and following a legal review that confirmed the constitutional viability of the demand, the campaign is, at the time of writing, drafting legislation and preparing an ownership and governance model that it will take to referendum in either 2026 or 2027. If successful, and unless it is blocked by the constitutional court, this referendum will result in the transfer of more than 250,000 apartments into a new model of democratic governance and ownership. How much the corporate owners will be recompensed is still to be determined, but there is a significant legal basis for arguing this ought to be substantially less than market value — indeed, that market value shouldn't be used as a guideline at all. Not only would this demonstrate the viability of using Article 15 of the German constitution to 'socialise' hitherto privately held assets across Germany, but it would establish that the meaning of socialisation — in contrast to nationalisation or expropriation — is to create institutions of popular protagonism and contested reproduction through which resources are owned and governed in common.[36]

The Deutsche Wohnen & Co. Enteignen campaign is a calculated wager that it might be possible to make unprecedented use of Germany's constitution to undermine the sanctity of private property and create a new institution of popular protagonism. Much like the case of Hernani Burujabe, it demonstrates a certain ambivalence towards the institutions of the capitalist state, not viewing them as the privileged site of social transformation but recognising the need to engage critically with these institutions, looking for pathways through which to 'hack' existing legal and political procedures with the aim of building popular protagonism and opportunities for contested reproduction to take root. If this wager proves successful, it's not too much of a leap to imagine it emboldening the already growing German socialisation movement, leading to an explosion of initiatives in other cities and in sectors other than housing. Reportedly, there are already groups exploring how to socialise disused shopping centres and convert them into democratic care centres. If we're being very optimistic, this may in turn prompt a constitutional crisis. Under the pressure of international asset management firms, European courts, financial markets, and a conservative press that would frame this as an assault on one of the fundamental pillars of 'Western democracy', German legislators would likely scramble to try and close the constitutional 'loophole' that had enabled people and movements to undermine the artificial distinction between economy, society, and politics. And if Germany's constitution were to be brought into question, there would be seismic political implications. As with all transitions, none of this is guaranteed, but we entertain the idea to show how even seemingly 'small' assaults on capital's metabolic control can precipitate larger social transformations.

Jackson, Mississippi, USA

In October 2008, the Malcolm X Grassroots Movement (MXGM), a national organisation of 'Afrikans in America/New Afrikans whose mission is to defend the human rights of our people and promote self-determination in our community',[37] successfully listed one of its founders as a candidate for Ward 2 on the council of the majority-Black city of Jackson, Mississippi. Chokwe Lumumba later went on to win the mayorship in May 2013, before his untimely death in February 2014. The decision to run electoral candidates was taken by the MXGM to find ways that the city authorities might 'support the creation of institutions and control of institutions through the community. Candidates steeped in the tradition of self-determination come from an established base that can hold them accountable to their politics'.[38] While electoral politics had never been excluded as a means to foster popular protagonism (or, in the language of the MXGM, collective self-determination), the case for engaging with any 'elected office within the US constitutional framework [is] assessed and conducted on a case-by-case basis according to the potential for that office to either create more democratic space or advance policies that test the limit of structural change'.[39]

With the electoral wager coming up against such structural limits, not least regarding the relative competencies of a Black-majority municipal authority operating within the constraints of the white-majority state legislature, the movement redoubled its focus on developing Cooperation Jackson. A coordinated effort to develop a broad democratic economic base, Cooperation Jackson is one of the central planks in a strategy known as the Jackson-Kush Plan.[40] Developed by the MXGM from the early 2000s and made public in 2012, the lead author Kali Akuno summarises the plan as:

> Designed to build a mass base with the political clarity, organizational capacity, and material self-sufficiency to advance the objective of building an autonomous power... [capable of achieving] four fundamental ends:
>
> 1. To place the ownership and control over the primary means of production directly in the hands of the Black working class of Jackson;
> 2. To build and advance the development of the ecologically regenerative forces of production in Jackson, Mississippi;
> 3. To democratically transform the political economy of the city of Jackson, the state of Mississippi, and the southeastern region; and
> 4. To advance the aims and objectives of the Jackson-Kush Plan, which are to attain self-determination for people of African descent and the radical, democratic transformation of the state of Mississippi (which we see as a prelude to the radical decolonization and transformation of the United States itself).[41]

Here, the invariant features of transition that we described in the previous chapter are on full display. On 1 May 2014, Cooperation

Jackson was launched as the organisational vehicle through which to put into practice the development of a strong, autonomously oriented social and solidarity economy, which through to 2019 had included a federation of emerging local cooperatives, a cooperative incubator, a cooperative school and training centre, and the beginnings of a cooperative financial institution. Ongoing efforts are focused on the development of a light manufacturing digital fabrication factory and education centre, the People's Grocery and Food Security Complex, and the Ewing Street Eco-Village. The latter is constituted as part of a community land trust which owns over 90 percent of the lots on Ewing Street, which is partly conceptualised as a sort of 'firebreak' to the anticipated creeping gentrification in West Jackson. All of this is guided by the understanding that 'economic democracy and the transition to ecosocialism have to come from below, not from above, that workers and communities have to drive the social transformation process through their self-organization and self-management, not be subjected to it'.[42]

The building of this social-solidarity economic sphere was twinned with the development of a People's Assembly, defined in the Jackson-Kush Plan as 'vehicles of Black self-determination and the autonomous political authority of the oppressed peoples and exploited classes contained within the state'.[43] People's Assemblies already had a long tradition in Mississippi, in particular as a form for communities of the Republic of New Afrika — a Black separatist movement formed in 1968 — to develop their own autonomous programmes of action with a view to determine their relationship to the United States. In Jackson, the People's Assembly had been in operation since 2005 and was explicitly understood not as an ephemeral institution focused on a particular issue, but an 'ongoing process and an enduring base of power'.[44] As part of the Jackson-Kush Plan, the People's Assembly is positioned as a vehicle for the self-organisation and promotion of its own social projects, and as a way of mediating between the expanding Black-led solidarity economy and the local state, acting 'as a "dual power" or counterweight to the policies and actions of the government and local and regional business interests'.[45] Or in terms of the concepts we've been developing, it is a means of fostering popular protagonism and contested reproduction.

Kerala, India

Kerala is home to one of the world's largest and most successful experiments in decentralised democratic planning and development, the significance of which becomes clearer if one has at least a loose understanding of the state's history of resistance to neo-classical and conventional theories of social and economic development. Formed in 1956 through the unification of four regions, a socialist thread ran through Kerala from its inception,[46] with the Malabar region in particular having a strong anti-colonial tradition of fierce resistance to British colonial rule.[47] Worker and peasant struggles were initially led by broadly progressive organisations, and later by explicitly communist groups including the Communist Party of India (CPI). The communist movement's influence in Kerala, including early electoral successes, produced a development strategy that prioritised popular protagonism and three lines of social and economic development: the redistribution of income through strengthening collective bargaining and higher wages, a redistribution of assets via land reforms, and guaranteed basic services through public provisioning of education, healthcare, and other critical services.[48]

Up until the mid-1970s this approach achieved remarkable social success, with Kerala leading advancements in the global periphery in relative and absolute terms in literacy rates, education, infant mortality reduction, healthcare, women's rights, land reform, and domestic access to water and electricity. In fact, Kerala's development strategy produced a quality of life for 'its ordinary citizens more akin to the developed countries than their counterparts in other states of India or other underdeveloped countries'.[49] Astonishingly, Kerala achieved these outcomes despite low, and at times stagnant, economic growth. In the words of Marxist economist Prabhat Patnaik, Kerala demonstrated that:

> the elimination, or at any rate the alleviation, of the miserable conditions of life which the bulk of the population in the third world faces, does not have to await that distant day when growth has taken place to a sufficient extent for its 'trickle down' to make an impact upon the people.[50]

Kerala's successes gave rise to the notion of a 'Kerala Model' — the idea that improvements in social indicators could be achieved in the Global South without economic growth, and therefore without further integration into a global capitalist order. Within Kerala, though, it was understood that while incredible progress had been made, an overemphasis on the performance of social indicators obscured a brewing crisis caused by low productivity and high rates of unemployment.[51] In the mid 1970s these concerns were realised. A fiscal crisis hit the state, and Kerala's government was faced with a choice: either reduce government spending through the privatisation of public services or spiral into debt. After decades of limited success battling the economic headwinds, a left-wing government led by the Left Democratic Front (LDF) found a way to refuse this forced choice. Using pre-existing national legislation that promoted the devolution of power within states, but pushing this in a new radical direction, the LDF developed a proposal to pass economic planning and development down to workers and communities. The result was the 1996 People's Planning Campaign (PPC).[52]

The PPC was a 'scientific, participatory and time bound' initiative undertaken by 'local government, elected local government representatives, experts, volunteers, and the mass of people to design and implement regional development plans'.[53] The details of how these plans developed and evolved are too complex to elaborate here,[54] but in broad terms around 35–40 percent of government expenditure was passed to local democratic assemblies ('Gram Sabha') to fund whatever projects were determined to be most pressing. These development plans were developed by the community in consultation with experts and local government. Mid-level bodies called district panchayats or blocks were then given the task of reconciling development needs across regions while the state level ensured overall coherence and allocated appropriate resources. What is crucial from our perspective is that by making a wager on popular protagonism, the state of Kerala avoided the forced choice of privatisation.

Through the PPC and subsequent people's plans, the quality of urban and rural life in Kerala has dramatically improved; access to housing, water, and electricity has increased, critical new infrastructure projects have been built, and public healthcare and education are of a high quality. The participatory planning process has been so popular, in fact, that it has proven politically inexpedient for the right-wing electoral group, the United Democratic Front, to dismantle it in the interests of private capital when it has been in power.[55] Decentralised planning, in other words, has had a disciplinary effect on private capitalist development in Kerala, creating the operating space for further popular protagonism and potentially for a scenario of contested reproduction.

Kerala's participatory planning process has some similarities with participatory budgeting campaigns undertaken in countries including Brazil, Peru, and El Salvador, but there are important differences. Unlike participatory budgeting, Kerala's participatory planning involves large-scale training programmes that give communities the power to self-govern, fostering greater popular protagonism. Popular planning is also sustained by, and sustains, a network of community-owned services and welfare programmes.[56] Kerala has, for example, the largest community-owned palliative care system in the world,[57] while Café Kudumbashree is a community-owned, women-led, food enterprise empowering women across the food sector. By bringing together economic planning, governance training, and common ownership, Kerala is pursuing a development path that eschews capitalist development models and that creates the conditions to curtail capital's metabolic control.

Venezuela

In a substantially different context, the Hugo Chavez-led government of Venezuela passed a series of laws in 2010 known as the Popular Power Laws, which included the Organic Law of the Communes and the Organic Law of the Communal Economic System. Representing a significant evolution in understanding about what practices might actually drive a wider socialist transformation in Venezuela, they also formed the juridical background to Chavez's *El Golpe de Timón* ('Strike at the Helm') speech. Given just two months before his death, the speech is considered important in understanding his vision for the future of Venezuela's socialist project. Heavily influenced by the ideas of Mészáros that we engaged with in Chapter Two, Chavez laid out in this address that the role of the commune was to develop a new basis of social metabolic production through the expansion of social property, promoting participative grassroots democracy, and decommodifying processes of social reproduction. The core of the new revolutionary transition was to be based in the creation and proliferation of communes that would 'form part of a systematic plan, of something new, like a network...a network that works like a gigantic spider's web covering the new territory'.[58]

Writing in 2015, John Bellamy Foster provides a schematic account of the communes' formation:

> In the communes, residents in geographical areas smaller than a city unite in a number of community councils with the object of self-governance through a communal parliament, constructed on participatory principles. The communes are political-economic-cultural structures engaged in such areas as food production, food security, housing, communications, culture, communal exchange, community banking, and justice systems.[59]

Yet, as Chavez himself understood, the communes could not be organs that were created and passed down from above, but institutions of popular protagonism that are constituted by the people themselves. As Chris Gilbert writes in his recent account, the Popular Power Laws were 'aimed at empowering those from below, who would therefore have to assume responsibility for the laws and bring them to realization'.[60] By 2013, the number of registered communes had surpassed 1,000.

Alongside the communes, a number of other democratic economic forms have blossomed across the country. These include several thousand Enterprises of Communal Social Property (EPSC), which the sociologist Dario Azzellini describes as enterprises of 'collective property of the communities, which decide on the organizational structure of enterprises, the workers incorporated and the eventual use of profits.'[61] These are often in sectors that respond to social needs such as public transport, telecommunications, food production, textile manufacturing, production of construction materials, bakeries, and shoemakers. As forms of social property, it is 'not only the workers but the commune itself [which] decides how it will function and how it will produce and what to do with the surplus'.[62] For both the communes and the EPSCs, the place of work retains its central importance as a way of mediating the relationship between people and their environment. Yet it is not workers *as workers* who are valorised as the revolutionary subject and who ought to be exercising control over work processes, but rather a broader community, which aims to align the purposes and processes of production with social needs.

What ultimately ties these different institutions of popular protagonism together, at least conceptually, is their central role in building a new 'communal state'. Underpinning Chavez's perspective of the revolutionary process was that it was possible to harness different administrative, juridical, and financial aspects of the existing state form and bend them towards the creation of a new communal socio-economic system. This is not about building a new 'economy' as a sphere of activity standing apart from the rest of society. The goal is rather to extend new forms of social control over how society as a whole reproduces itself, with the ultimate aim of bringing an entirely different form of communal metabolic control into being. The existing state is thus seen as capable of acting as a midwife for a new form of collective governance, or communal metabolic control, in which the people have been transformed, in Chavez's words, 'into the object *and the subject* of power'.[63]

A decade after Chavez proselytised with the slogan "commune or nothing!", representatives from 60 communes participated in the founding congress of Union Comunera, which since March 2022 has formalised the effort of developing the gigantic spider's web of popular protagonism 'capable of configuring a new society based in daily life'.[64] It is organisations such as Union Comunera which, if they can successfully navigate the contradictions of working alongside the existing state form, not to mention the pressures of US imperialist coups and sanctions,[65] might come to play an integral role in the development of the communal state.

CELL-FORMS OF TRANSITION

The purpose of travelling through these anecdotes isn't to search for a single replicable strategy, nor is it to suggest that any of these offer instances of unmitigated success. Rather, it's to demonstrate that the theory of transition we introduced in Chapter Two already takes many concrete forms. Operating in contexts characterised by different threats and opportunities, people have found ways to advance a popular protagonism in which 'citizens implement, control, and manage things themselves, where citizens govern themselves'[66] in common. Typically focusing on those aspects of life that are necessary to living well — such as housing, food, water, energy, healthcare, and so on — the focus is on extricating these sectors and associated institutions from capital's metabolic control while embedding them in systems of communal control. It's through these institutional practices that people are *contesting the means of their own reproduction* and in doing so are building the foundations for a world of radical abundance. There are many more cases we might have relayed — from the creation of water commons in Naples to popular aquifers in Bolivia, and from the Zhoujiazhuang People's Commune in China to popular banks in California[67] — but those included here are enough to demonstrate that the invariant features of transition can already be located in concrete practices.

We are under no illusion that multiplying these ongoing, precarious, and necessarily contradictory struggles will be enough to extinguish capital's mediation of our lives. As George Ciccariello-Maher reflects in his popular history of the Venezuelan revolution, 'we must first strategically accumulate, consolidate, and develop our own power if we are ever going to be in a position to "disperse" the power of our enemies later'.[68] The nature of the power we must accumulate is rooted in our already existing collective power to reproduce our own lives. This power has been alienated from us by capital's metabolic control and must be regained through the development of institutions of collective democratic planning, at whatever scales we find possible. The problem of transition is the problem of how the communal mediation of our lives can be brought into being.

In different times and places, this struggle may take any number of forms and come about in any number of ways. In Venezuela, the communal system was instigated only after the Chavismo movement took state power and, in all likelihood, will last only as long as imperialist aggression against the socialist governing coalition can be resisted. In Jackson, the racial-political composition of the Mississippi state legislature has played a significant role in foreclosing the prospect of using municipal institutions to further popular protagonism and contested reproduction, with the emphasis consequently placed on the development of an ecosystem of a transformative economy. In the Basque region, the very idea of the state as the seat of sovereign power must be called into question because the movement for Basque autonomy spans across two sovereign states. However, the financial flexibility and relative autonomy of municipalities has opened an opportunity to experiment with a new approach to public-communitarian planning. Whereas in Kerala an alliance of progressive and communist parties was essential to drive forward the People's Planning Campaign, in Berlin the push for the socialisation of housing has been driven by experienced tenants' movements.

Each of these examples has been made possible by contextually appropriate cross-class coalitions, whether that be between propertyless renters or an alliance of urban and rural working classes, Indigenous peoples, and the petite bourgeoisie. None of them reject the prospect of engaging with state institutions, yet this has taken strikingly different forms, ranging from contesting the application of constitutional law, to developing public-communal collaboration at a municipal level, or using national legislative bodies to create new popular democratic forms of local control. All of them are building a 'condensation of popular power from below into a radical pole that stands in antagonistic opposition to the state',[69] while recognising that some form of engagement *with* the institutions and processes of existing states will play a part in bringing an alternative social reality into being.

For all their differences, each of these struggles prioritises creating institutions of popular protagonism that tip the balance in favour of a process of contested reproduction and, ultimately, radical abundance. It is in this general tendency that we find the most hope for a broader strategy of transition. The greatest challenge faced by these approaches, however, is how to reach beyond themselves, to spill over from their particular political contexts to create what must be a truly global process of revolutionary transition. These cell-forms of transition need to multiply and self-replicate. How this might be done is a frustratingly complex question, to which the answers can only be found through shared political practice, but what we know for certain is that part of that political practice necessarily entails what we call, following Antonio Gramsci, conducting a 'conjunctural analysis' of the world around us. It is through conjunctural analyses — political assessments of the intersecting social, economic and cultural factors that more-or-less-precariously balance capital's contradictions in any given time and place — that we find areas of opportunity, sites of potential weakness in capital's metabolic control, and a sense of the class forces who might exploit them to bring about a world of radical abundance. It is to this task that we now turn.

4
Denial and Derisking

The 2021 satirical film *Don't Look Up* begins with an astronomy doctoral student, played by Jennifer Lawrence, discovering a comet headed towards Earth that, when it strikes in six months' time will cause an extinction level event akin to the one that wiped out the dinosaurs. To this extent, the film is similar to two films that came out in 1998, but whereas in *Armageddon* and *Deep Impact,* knowledge of the threat makes governments leap into preventive action, in *Don't Look Up* the scientists are shocked to see the opposite result. The US government — swayed by oligarchs who wish to mine it for resources — refuses to divert the comet, while the media and public struggle to take such an existential threat seriously. As the comet becomes a politically partisan issue, some start to deny its very existence even though the comet is visible to the naked eye. A campaign is launched by comet-sceptics adopting the slogan 'Don't Look Up'.

Criticism of the film's none-too-subtle satire focused on the limits of a comet heading towards Earth as a metaphor for climate change. Rather than an all or nothing, one-off cataclysm, climate change entails a rolling, pulsing, accelerating, and unevenly experienced, series of cataclysms. Despite this failing, the film does manage to capture the sense of unreality that pervades contemporary life and politics. Even when they're briefly acknowledged, the pressing facts of ecological catastrophe are often just as quickly ignored or moved out of view. Like in the film, we can attribute at least some of the tendency to look away to the results of cynical manipulation by those whose interests are against the changes required, but such strategies are only possible because they lean into the psychological discomfort many people experience when the full reality of our situation is brought to their attention. This isn't, we should emphasise, the result of some psychological failing on the part of the individuals concerned; it is better understood as the result of a political failure. We feel discomfort and anxiety in the face of these huge problems because we appear powerless to address them. We are haunted by the chasm between what it is necessary for us to do and what seems politically and socially possible.[1] It is the lack of a viable strategy of transition, and a social base to realise it, that produces the anxiety we all feel.

What's 'necessary' is conditioned by the reliance of human civilisation on what Johan Rockström and his colleagues at the Stockholm Resilience Centre call earth-system processes. In a series of studies since 2009, they have taken the best scientific estimates of the tipping points at which these processes will exit their stable states. They've then added to this schema by extrapolating from the UN's Universal Declaration of Human Rights to define 'social boundaries'. Bringing these together, they've mapped a 'safe and just operating space for humanity'. It is necessary, they argue, for humanity to alter its social, economic, and technical systems so their outcomes fit somewhere within this space.[2] But while the natural boundaries that condition the necessary must be taken as somewhat of a given — only so much CO_2 can be spewed into the atmosphere before the planet becomes uninhabitable to humans — political possibility is much more amenable to human action. The point of producing a map of what's necessary, such as 'a safe and just operating space for humanity', is so we can backcast from where we need to arrive in order to determine the preconditions for getting there. This is, in effect, what we attempted to do in Chapter Two. The invariant features of transition we outlined are necessary components of any strategy of transition to a world beyond capital's metabolic control. Crucially, though, they can't tell us how to organise in the here and now. As we suggested at the end of the previous chapter, there is no general strategy that can be pursued across all geographical or temporal contexts. Because of this, we need to study the shape and form that capital's metabolic control takes in our own context not just so we understand it, but so we can *intervene in it* to bring about a world of radical abundance. This kind of map of what is currently possible is known as a 'conjunctural analysis'.

Conjunctural analysis is rooted in the work of Antonio Gramsci, but is most closely associated with the work of Stuart Hall. His co-written seminal 1978 book *Policing the Crisis* starts by analysing a moral panic fomented by the British press around a confected series of 'muggings', which were taken as 'a sign that the "British way of life" is coming apart at the seams.'[3] The analysis expands from there to discern the coordinates of the emerging project to dismantle the post-war settlement in favour of what soon became known, following Hall's coinage, as Thatcherism. In this way it maps a conjunctural shift beginning from an analysis of an emerging new 'common sense' in which law and order, together with race, are 'the prism through which the crisis is perceived. It is the justifying scheme by means of which the crisis is analysed and explained.'[4] In our case, we're particularly interested in how the contradictions in recent shifts in macroeconomic policy reveal the way our current crises are being conceived and addressed. No conjunctural analysis, particularly one as brief as this chapter, can claim to be comprehensive. Nor does it need to be. Instead, 'the aim of conjunctural analysis is... to map a social territory, in order to identify possible sites of political intervention.'[5]

As we've already made clear, the need for transition, whether seen as just an energy transition or something more fundamental, is the problem that structures our era, even when it is disavowed. This necessity produces huge uncertainty and risk. The only thing we can be sure of is that our future will not look like our present. Capital deals with uncertainty by trying to reduce its own exposure to risk. Sometimes it uses probabilistic assessments of investment risk to hedge against itself, turning risk itself into a profitable phenomenon (the insurance industry being the classic example). Sometimes, capital simply offloads risk onto others.

In recent decades, however, systemic risks have emerged that go beyond what existing modes of insurance or offloading can deal with. It's in this context that we should understand the emergence of new regimes of regulation in which the state is coordinating economic activity with the aim of subsidising specific fractions of capital. The liberal iteration of 'derisking' uses public resources to encourage private investment in line with government-assigned priorities by taking on some of the financial risks involved. The right-wing iteration, which Richard Seymour terms 'disaster nationalism', denies and disavows the climate crisis, diverting the anxieties and energies produced into other primarily imaginary problems and fantasies such as the great replacement conspiracy theory, while seeking to offload the risks involved onto others through repression, tariffs, and clientelist forms of state support for capital.[6]

In this chapter, we will examine these emerging regimes and the conditions that produced them. They are both, we propose, desperate attempts to hold back the tides caused by two of capital's most intractable contradictions: its tendency towards economic stagnation and its ecologically destructive dynamics. The election of Donald Trump to his second presidency has curtailed the liberal derisking regime in the US, yet, as the reception of the recent book *Abundance* by Ezra Klein and Derek Thompson reveals, it still forms the basis of centrist thinking about the conjuncture and will likely form the basis of centrist policy in Democrat-controlled states and municipalities.[7] Meanwhile, derisking remains dominant in Europe and the UK. Rather than derisking capital accumulation through a so-called 'green transition', we propose that it might be possible to pressure public authorities, at the municipal, regional, and ultimately national levels, into derisking a transition towards a new communal metabolic system. Trump's clientelism, meanwhile, opens the possibility of an anti-oligarchical politics based on extending and deepening democracy into the economy. These arguments set the scene for the book's second half, which offers public-common partnerships as a specific political intervention and strategic wager that we believe embodies the invariant features of transition and exploits today's conjunctural opportunities.

TWO SOURCES OF SYSTEMIC RISK

Underlying the prevailing sense of impotent unease are two huge, interrelated crises that threaten to destroy the systems that currently structure our societies. The first, which is generally referred to as secular stagnation, is the long-term trend of slowing economic growth which predates the great financial crisis of 2008, but was made more apparent by it. While this is a global problem, it's become particularly evident in 'developed' or imperial core countries such as the UK, where the growth model is so broken that from 2005 the UK experienced 17 years of zero real wage growth — a period of wage stagnation not seen since the Napoleonic wars.[8] This chronic inability to maintain living standards for large sections of the population has provoked a sustained period of social and political instability. So far, the far right has capitalised on this instability far more effectively than the radical left. The other all-encompassing crisis of the current conjuncture is global heating and capital's undermining of the ecological conditions of life on earth as we know it.

Historically, economic growth has required an increase in material and energy use.[9] Decarbonising the economy by replacing fossil fuels with renewable energy sources would, it is hypothesised, allow the decoupling of economic growth from rising carbon emissions and permit the fundamental coordinates of our social and economic system to be maintained. For 30 years, intergovernmental responses have attempted to realise this hypothesis of 'green growth' through the promotion of market-based mechanisms, primarily carbon trading and offsetting. The catastrophic failure of this approach to reduce carbon emissions has increasingly led to the recognition that market coordination is unsuited to the huge infrastructural transformation required in a green transition. For example, in February 2022 Brian Deese, the former director of Biden's National Economic Council, admitted in reference to failures around decarbonisation that 'the private market on its own, private actors operating to maximise their own utility, will end up underinvesting in areas of the economy that have strategic and economic significance.'[10]

The switch since the late 2010s to a more interventionist state enacting a form of economic planning through an active industrial policy was an attempt by imperial core countries, such as the US and in Europe, to address the problem of economic stagnation, partly through the increased economic activity required to build a 'net-zero' economy — whether through the decarbonisation of hitherto fossil fuel-intensive sectors of the economy, the building of public transit systems, or the retrofitting of housing stock. Yet any project of transition, even if it is predicated on maintaining capitalist social relations, is still subject to many of the problems laid out in the previous chapters. There are, for example, large, entrenched interests that benefit immensely from the current, financialised, and carbon-intensive structure of the economy. States derisking private investment, as opposed to taking direct public action, is predicated on a refusal to tackle the forces that are acting to slow or prevent change. In this sense, it's a strategy in which the pace and extent of decarbonisation is subordinated to the maintenance of the current economic order. But its contradictory nature doesn't end there. As a consequence of its refusal to take the problems of transition seriously, it ends up recruiting the financial forces who benefit most from the fossil fuelled-economy to bring about a green transition that must, by necessity, bring fossil fuel use to an end. In doing so, it also reinforces and exacerbates the very forces and dynamics that have caused and compounded economic stagnation in the first place. The failure to address such problems opens the door to disaster nationalism in its plutocratic and pro-fossil capital form. These contradictions are worth exploring in more detail as they also present new political opportunities to those of us who seek more fundamental change.

Symptoms of Secular Stagnation

The phrase 'secular stagnation', with secular here meaning long-term as opposed to short-term or caused by cyclical fluctuations, was coined during the Great Depression of the 1930s but returned to prominence following a 2013 speech by economist and former Obama-era treasury secretary, Larry Summers. While the debate Summers was addressing was sparked by the failure of developed economies to recover to pre-2008 levels of growth, he suggested the problems were deeper than mere post-crisis aftereffects, concluding, 'the underlying problem may be there forever'.[11] This moment provoked recognition of a long-term decline in rates of growth. In 1966, for example, the trend rate of global GDP growth was 5.5 percent; it has declined steadily, despite oscillations, to around 2.5 percent today. In OECD countries, the trend is even more alarming with per capita growth falling from its mid-1960s peak of around 4 percent per annum to something closer to 1 percent.[12] Yet, this doesn't tell the whole story. For many, even this limited growth has increasingly felt like a bullshit statistic because the benefits have been so unequally shared. Between 1995 and 2021, the top 1 percent captured 38 percent of the increase in global wealth, while the bottom 50 percent captured just 2 percent.[13]

Through the 2010s, a variety of symptoms of economic stagnation came to prominence. The first was income and wealth inequality, which accelerated dramatically through the decade. The richest 53 families in the UK, for instance, now have more wealth than the bottom half of the population,[14] while the wealth of the richest five men in the world has doubled since 2020.[15] Such high levels of inequality have lasting deleterious social impacts. Richard Wilkinson and Kate Pickett's seminal 2010 book *The Spirit Level* shows how inequality correlates with worse health outcomes, more obesity, lower life expectancy, higher infant mortality, poorer educational achievement, and lower social mobility. Large gaps between rich and poor increase the stakes of interpersonal competition and the social shame that comes with losing out. This provokes a cascade of social problems, from exploding levels of stress and anxiety, to collapsing social trust and an increase in violent crime.[16] More recent research has shown how inequality undermines efforts to tackle climate change by reducing recycling levels, increasing status-driven or compensatory consumption, and undermining 'political cohesion and the willingness to support environmental initiatives.'[17] And as oligarchs use their wealth to reinforce their positions by setting up TV stations, buying newspapers and social media platforms, and securing influence through funding political parties and think tanks, it's unclear whether these levels of inequality are compatible with democracy at all. The chaotic and destructive rampage of the oligarch Elon Musk, given unelected oversight of US government functions in the early days of the second Trump presidency, is a frightening illustration of this point.

The unexpected success of Thomas Piketty's 2014 blockbuster book *Capital in the Twenty-First Century* brought the link between inequality and stagnation into focus. While increasing inequality isn't the principal cause of economic stagnation, it certainly compounds the problem. When the already wealthy gain additional money they tend to save it or invest in assets — either way it's removed from the circuits of consumer demand. Conversely when money goes to the less well-off it's much more likely to be spent on immediate consumption, thereby increasing demand. Piketty's work was particularly important because its statistical analysis of large data sets revealed an innate tendency in capitalism for the rate of return (R) on asset ownership to be greater than the rate of economic growth (G), figured in his famous R > G equation.[18] In the absence of counter-tendencies, primarily strong worker organisation and egalitarian political action, inequality increases inexorably as asset ownership and the rentier-based business models that accompany them become a larger and more dominant part of the economy, funnelling money upwards. 'The entrepreneur,' Piketty writes, 'inevitably tends to become a rentier, more and more dominant over those who own nothing but their labour.' This leads to stagnation, 'as the past tends to devour the future: wealth originating in the past automatically grows more rapidly, even without labour, than wealth stemming from work.'[19]

This tendency for capital to become more rentier in character has led Brett Christophers to argue that we've entered the era of rentier capitalism, 'a mode of economic organization in which success is based principally on what you control not what you do.'[20] Across a series of books, Christophers lays out how the privatisation of publicly owned assets, and the financial liberalisation that came with it, far from injecting into the UK economy the competition and efficiency that was promised, has led instead to domination by rentiers deriving their income from the 'ownership... or control of scarce assets under conditions of limited or no competition.'[21] Monopolistic positions allow prices to be raised, costs offloaded, and wages squeezed. The results are most evident in the UK's privatised services in which price gouging accompanies collapsing standards of service across the board. The image that perhaps best sums up this situation derives from the failure of privatised water services. A lack of investment in infrastructure, accompanied by the looting of those companies for huge shareholder dividend payouts, has led to the near constant release of untreated sewage into the UK's river system. It flows from there onto the country's beaches. The British are quite literally swimming in shit! As Christophers concludes, 'if rent is capital's logical destination, social and economic devastation may in turn be rent's logical destination.'[22]

Both Piketty and Christophers date the long-term trends of rising inequality and the rentierisation of the economy back to the 1980s, but both trends were supercharged by the response of many states to the great financial crisis of 2008. Dealing with that explosion of systemic risk took a huge mobilisation of public resources. States underwrote the financial sector by taking on their bad debts, providing favourable loans, and through quantitative easing programmes, gifting them huge sums of essentially free money. In return for this incredible state largesse, many imagined that finance would be reformed to address systemic risk and better serve the public, but any prospect of fundamental reform vanished as the causes of the financial crisis soon disappeared behind a smokescreen of concern about deficits in government budgets. As the risks incurred by the financial sector and the wealthy were underwritten by the state, the severe curtailing of public provision was, in effect, the offloading of the 'risks' of social reproduction from the state onto individuals and families.

From the late 2000s right through the 2010s, interest rates were kept at historically low levels. Indeed, for large periods they were below inflation and so negative in real terms. But while this disincentivised saving, pushing more money into financial markets, public investment was cut and business investment remained stagnant. As a result, money flooded into the purchase of assets. The 2010s saw the economies of the imperial core trapped in a matrix of low interest rates, low wages, and low investments where inflating asset prices was the principal mechanism for boosting consumer demand. This situation was held in place politically by what Will Davies calls a 'rentier alliance' between genuine rentier interests and those who weren't necessarily wealthy but were 'at a point in life where they have paid off their mortgages, and are living off the assets held by pension funds' and so, along with the big rentiers sweating their assets, have little 'immediate interest in labour markets or [the problems of] productive capitalism' such as stagnant productivity.[23] Instead, the interests of older homeowners became increasingly aligned with the performance of the related financial and real estate sectors. When the stock market booms, the value of their pensions increases; when property prices are high, they feel wealthier and can borrow more from their banks. This isn't true for the young who, increasingly cut off from home ownership, are dependent on wages and welfare, both of which diminished through the 2010s.

This divergence of material interests has introduced a dramatic generational divide into the politics of many developed countries, based on the collapse of a post-war story of a coherent life path in which secure employment was the route to increased consumer spending, a stable environment to raise children, secure housing (perhaps through home ownership), and security in retirement with a state-backed pension.[24] In their book *The Asset Economy*, Lisa Adkins, Melinda Cooper, and Martijn Konings argue that the increasing centrality of asset ownership is reshaping our lives as we shift from the state-backed welfare systems of the post-war period to asset-based welfare provision underwritten by home ownership.[25] This combined but uneven entanglement of social reproduction in financial and asset logics is a serious impediment to change. Any disruption that affects stock markets or house prices will impact many ordinary people, not just the rich. Disembedding our lives from dependence on the vagaries of capital is a vital component of transition.

The impact of asset-based welfare provision is most visible in the withdrawal of housing equity to pay for elder care. This familiar story of inheritances whittled away by lengthy parental stays in expensive private care homes also contains another dynamic: the centralisation of wealth. The care industry in the UK is highly privatised and assetised, with 83 percent of care provision in private hands and just 26 companies owning a third of care home beds.[26] Equity withdrawn from housing flows through these rentierised businesses into the pockets of the ultra rich. This pattern seen across different sectors has accelerated in recent years as huge asset management firms have become interested in the care sector, housing, and vital infrastructure. Just as the ladder is being pulled up to prevent younger generations from accessing asset wealth, those with asset wealth are finding themselves subject to the whims of predatory capital. The 'young vs old' binary thus fails to capture the more dominant story of the period in which wealth centralised by flowing upwards to the uber rich and their asset managers.

In his more recent book, *Our Lives in Their Portfolios*, the prolific Brett Christophers reveals the social impact of asset management firms buying up six main infrastructure categories: energy, water, transport, telecommunications, farmland, and social infrastructure, such as schools, hospitals, and care services. These are attractive to institutional investors because they're 'vital physical systems of social reproduction' and so tend to enjoy both monopolistic and essential status.[27] In other words, investing in infrastructure is appealing to asset managers precisely because it's so vital, so bound up with our everyday reproduction. Demand for it is therefore inelastic. Consumers have no choice of suppliers for water services for instance, and have little control over levels of consumption, which makes steady demand all but guaranteed. It is insulated from the volatility of our crisis-ridden present. As such, investing in essential infrastructure is a 'low-volatility, low-risk investment which is very attractive to pension funds that have to make payments out on an annual basis'.[28]

As they gain control over infrastructure, asset managers 'increasingly take on the role of quasi-governments' while escaping the scrutiny democratic governments at least nominally receive. 'It is the asset manager', Christophers writes, 'that decides how the asset is commercially exploited: who electricity is sold to, whether road tolls should be increased, how farmland should be tenanted.'[29] Asset management firms have, however, very different incentive structures to public providers. Christophers identifies three golden rules of what he calls asset-manager society: maximise revenue, squeeze operating costs, and avoid capital expenditure. This acceleration of the dynamics of rentierism and oligopolisation reveals a truth about contemporary capitalism: in an age of stagnation, capital's own need to grow comes at the cost of ever more bullshit provision for the needs of workers and consumers.

Cultural theorists, such as Mark Fisher, argue that this century has been marked by cultural stagnation, as well as economic stagnation.[30] Here, too, the past is devouring the future. The main exception to this rule was prestige TV. Through the 2000s and 2010s, TV drama experienced a new golden age as changing viewing habits, first via DVD box sets and then subscription streaming channels, opened up both new possibilities for long-form storytelling and new revenue streams for creatives. Yet, in recent years that space of cultural flourishing has also been closed down. The culprits, as journalist Daniel Bessner explains, are quite familiar. 'The new effective bosses of the industry — colossal conglomerates, asset-management companies, and private-equity firms... had been stripping value from the production system like copper pipes from a house — threatening the sustainability of the studios themselves.' As a result, by 'early 2023, among those lucky enough to be employed, the median TV writer-producer was making 23% less a week, in real dollars, than their peers a decade before.' Even worse, following the pattern of asset managers offloading risk onto others, independent creatives are now often forced to develop their scripts without studio support. As one writer put it, 'I was expected to take on that risk, when the entities that stood to profit the most from the success of my creative labor, the platform and studio, would not risk a dime.'[31]

Wages and conditions for writers in the US have been kept high by a strong union, the Writers Guild of America (WGA), which in 2023, following an unprecedented 97.9 percent vote in favour, launched a successful five-month strike to beat back the worsening conditions. But union struggles that don't tackle the problem of ownership can only go so far. With the underlying dynamics of the situation unaltered, the wider fight over the direction of the industry continues. Depending on how that turns out, it's unclear if the equivalent of the film with which we opened this chapter would be commissioned in the future. *Don't Look Up* could only be made because it was bought and distributed by Netflix, but the three biggest shareholders in Netflix are now Vanguard, BlackRock, and Fidelity, three of the largest and most rapacious asset management firms in the world. The relentless drive of asset management firms to offload risk, while undermining wages, conditions, and the standard of services is visible in every sector of the economy. The prospect of them gaining even more control over the key infrastructure upon which our lives depend is a truly frightening prospect.

In retrospect, the 2010s appear as a huge state-led effort to ward off the systemic risk revealed by the crisis of 2008. The situation that resulted, in which economies characterised by low inflation, low interest rates, low productivity, and low wages were held in place politically by an electoral 'rentiers alliance', was never going to be sustainable. It contained a series of self-undermining dynamics that produced increasing social and political instability. Then, at the turn of the 2020s, a series of events disrupted the global economy, leading to a dramatic increase in inflation, to which central banks responded by raising interest rates. The tap of easy credit began to be turned off. The immediate trigger was Russia's invasion of Ukraine and the spike in oil prices that followed. This shock was accompanied by environmental crises, most notably the COVID-19 pandemic which was in its second year, but also a succession of disruptions to supply chains caused by the increasing frequency and ferocity of extreme weather events. Climate change, that other great, overdetermining crisis of our era, was making itself felt.

Markets Can't Stop Climate Change

In May 2022, Stuart Kirk, then head of responsible investing at HSBC delivered a talk at a *Financial Times* conference titled, 'Why investors need not worry about climate risk.' It included the statement, 'Who cares if Miami is six metres underwater in 100 years? Amsterdam has been six metres underwater for ages and that's a really nice place.' Financial institutions shouldn't need to worry about 'something that's going to happen in 20 or 30 years', he continued, because at 'a big bank like ours, the average loan term is 6 years. What happens to the planet in year 7 is actually irrelevant. *I don't care.*'[32] The subsequent outcry led to Kirk's resignation, but HSBC's investment record shows his comments reflect the bank's practice far more accurately than their stated environmental policy. Despite the bank's apparent commitment to becoming net-zero by 2050, they've invested well over $130 billion in fossil fuels since the signing of the Paris Climate Agreement in 2016. Indeed, in 2016 alone they invested $19.9 billion in fossil fuels, and in 2021 they *again* invested $19.9 billion. There had been no reduction at all.[33]

What makes Kirk's, and by proxy the financial sector's, dismissive attitude even more egregious is that the financial sector is incredibly vulnerable to the systemic risk posed by climate change. On current estimates, if all available and 'proven' fossil fuel reserves are extracted and burned it would add around 4,777 gigatonnes of CO_2 into the atmosphere. This would on its own lead to a catastrophic 4.3C increase in global average temperatures. And yet fossil fuel companies spend billions each year searching for even more reserves. If carbon capital fully exploits their fossil fuel assets then human civilisation, and a coherent economy, will end. If they are prevented from doing so and that carbon stays in the ground, then carbon-intensive industries and assets are currently massively overvalued in stock markets around the world.[34] The prospect of a sudden revaluation provoked by policy change or a climate catastrophe-driven transformation in public attitudes has led to discussion of a possible climate Minsky moment in which the correction of that overvaluation could provoke the wider collapse of the financial and insurance industries.[35]

Among the key imperatives driving private investment decisions, as Kirk unwittingly revealed, are the maximisation of profitability and a preference for liquidity or, in layman's terms, a preference for short-term rather than long-term investments to better manage the risks involved. These imperatives have proven private investment decisions, and the market mechanisms that accompany them, utterly unsuited for driving the urgent decarbonisation we desperately need. While intergovernmental agreements, notably 1997's Kyoto Protocol, use forms of planning and non-market coordination to set overall national emissions targets, the principal mechanisms for achieving those targets aim to 'correct' the price of activity to include the social and environmental costs of the carbon emitted. This is done either through carbon taxes or market-based systems, such as emissions trading and offsetting schemes. These efforts have been colossal failures. Research shows that 'the environmental benefits' of emissions trading schemes 'have been marginal' at best.[36] In a 2023 investigation, '39 of the top 50 emission offset projects, or 78% of them, were categorised as likely junk or worthless'.[37] But even if they could be made to work on their own terms, such schemes would still not result in the pace or kinds of transformation needed.

Capital has a propensity to minimise risk. This incentivises investments that are likely to show a return over the short term. As such, private investment tends to favour incremental efficiencies to existing technology rather than big infrastructural change with longer-term benefits. One seemingly successful example of capitalist efficiencies is the precipitous decline in the cost of renewable energy brought about by a mix of state subsidies and price guarantees, in combination with efficiencies of scale. Renewable energy is now among the cheapest energy sources available. Yet, this reduction in price has not driven investment in renewable provision at anything like the scale required. In fact, as Christophers points out, it might actually be a hindrance: 'The more that the roll-out of renewables drives down wholesale prices overall, the more that companies hoping to build the world's next generation of wind and solar farms are confronted with the prospect of a diminution in the revenues that those future facilities can be expected to produce.'[38] It's not price but profitability in comparison with other investment opportunities, such as fossil fuels, that drives capitalist investment decisions. As even the neoliberal hawk Martin Wolf admits in a *mea culpa* on market-driven green transition, 'while it is possible to prevent businesses from doing profitable things, it is impossible to make them do things they consider insufficiently profitable'.[39] Capital's drive for self-expansion, maximising returns on investment so those returns can also be reinvested, is imposing artificial scarcity on the expansion of renewable energy. Capitalism can produce only bullshit abundance because it follows the bullshit imperative of undifferentiated profitability rather than targeted economic activity that directly addresses our pressing social and ecological needs.

Thus far, led by the policy proposals we're critiquing, we have spoken mostly about global heating. This could create the impression that our multiple ecological crises can be addressed by just decarbonising the economy. This is far from the truth. The eco-Marxist writer James O'Connor identifies two contradictions in capitalism. The first arises from capital's drive towards automation, which by pushing out workers results in reduced 'market demand for commodities, and lower realized profits'. The second contradiction comes from capital's tendency to 'externalize costs on to conditions of production' which includes the environment, 'with the aim of defending or restoring profits'.[40] As a result, there's a general collision between the inherent dynamics of capital and the ecological systems it depends on but undermines. Climate change is just one of nine earth-system processes whose thresholds make up the safe operating space for humanity. Not only is capital propelling us beyond the safe boundary of the atmosphere's carbon-carrying capacity, but it's also threatening or exceeding the boundaries of several others, including chemical pollution, global freshwater use, and, most visibly of all, biodiversity loss.[41] We are living through the sixth mass extinction in the history of planet Earth, with a rate of extinction 1,000 percent higher than the natural background rate. Average wildlife population sizes have collapsed by 73 percent since 1970. That includes a decline of three billion birds in the North American population and an 81 percent decline in British song thrushes. The eerie silence of the English countryside marks a tragic example of artificial scarcity.

THE EMERGENCE OF THE DERISKING STATE

In a June 2024 speech made at the G7 summit in Italy, Larry Fink, the CEO of the world's largest asset management company, BlackRock, declared:

> Today the G7 average debt-to-GDP is 129%. No matter how much we tax, how much we cut or reduce that debt, it will not be enough... This is why building new infrastructure is critical, especially through public-private partnerships... Between now and 2040, the world will need to spend $75 trillion repairing old and building new infrastructure. Asking taxpayers to shoulder $75 trillion of new debt isn't something countries can fiscally — or fairly — do. Instead, we should look at the growing pool of private investment.[42]

It's a deeply cynical argument that repurposes debunked arguments about unsustainable sovereign debt levels used to justify public austerity in the 2010s. Yet, it does reveal something significant. Asset managers no longer feel able to rely on claims about the efficacy of markets and private investment to legitimise their huge influence over the direction of the global economy. Instead, some are now mobilising the problem of transition itself, arguing that the urgency of the challenge means that they're the only actors with the resources to decarbonise the economy. When Fink proposes public-private partnerships as the principal means of addressing the systemic risks of economic stagnation and ecological crises, he is asking us to trust those who got us into this mess to get us out of it by the simple expedient of giving them everything they want.

Fink's argument contains an obvious sleight-of-hand. When he claims it's unfair to ask taxpayers to foot the $75 trillion bill for new infrastructure, he isn't suggesting that private capital makes that investment in the form of a gift. Quite the opposite. He is asking taxpayers to remove the risks of that investment so as to guarantee huge profits, in the form of rents, for decades to come. That's what public-private partnerships consist of. The taxpayer will pay for that derisking, and then pay again as the users and customers of essential services and infrastructures. The most damaging costs, however, will be to society as a whole. Handing over ownership and control of our key infrastructure to the planet's most rapacious corporations will lead to a precipitous increase in inequality while hollowing out democracy even further.

Despite this prospect, derisking emerged as the favoured liberal policy framework for addressing our interrelated crises, and it lies at the heart of the liberal abundance agenda vying for dominance within the US Democratic Party in the wake of Trump's 2024 victory. The economist most associated with documenting and critiquing the concept, Daniela Gabor, provides us with an initial definition. The derisking state, she says, is defined by the practice of enlisting 'private capital into achieving public policy priorities by tinkering with risk/returns on private investments in sovereign bonds, currency, social infrastructure (schools, roads, hospitals and houses, care homes and prisons, water plants and natural parks) and most recently, green industries.'[43] Evidence of a shift in macroeconomic policy towards active, derisking, industrial strategies is usually drawn from the debates and policies of the Biden administration, but it is also the dominant policy framework in the UK and EU. Moreover, Biden's administration had many continuities with the first Trump administration and, as we will see, despite differences in approach and framing, the policy of the second Trump government has many similarities.

Towards the end of the 2010s, a series of large-scale, and often youth-led, climate justice mobilisations increased the political pertinence of the failure of market-based mechanisms to reduce carbon emissions. This, along with the persistence of post-2008 economic stagnation, formed the background to key figures in the Biden administration coming to the conviction of the need for a new approach. There were also, however, some more proximate triggers for the change in elite liberal thinking. The first was Donald Trump's 2016 election as US president. This, along with the strong showing by Bernie Sanders in the 2016 and 2020 Democratic primaries, convinced key Democratic Party elites of the need to address the falling living standards that accompanied economic stagnation. The second trigger was more geopolitical in nature. Huge countercyclical Chinese state investment did much to prop up the global economy in the aftermath of the 2008 crash, with a massive programme of transport and real estate development sucking in raw materials from around the world. Yet, through this period, US foreign policy rested on the assumption that China would get integrated into the globalised neoliberal order in a subordinate position. Towards the end of the 2010s, however, China's strong industrial policy led to its dominance over the production of solar energy plants, and an increasing focus on state-funded research and development steered the Chinese economy towards the high-tech production of computer chips and superconductors. From 2018 onwards, as the Chinese economy under Xi Jinping became more favourable to state-owned enterprises, US foreign policy attitudes towards China hardened with the imposition of trade tariffs under the first Trump presidency, a policy which Biden continued and expanded. At the same time, the perception grew that the US needed its own industrial policy to compete.

What came to be called Bidenomics signalled a break, however tentative, with the neoliberal macroeconomic orthodoxy that preceded Trump. On the rhetorical level, we can point to a much-discussed speech by former president Biden's national security advisor Jake Sullivan in which he declared the need to overcome the 'assumption... that markets always allocate capital productively and efficiently.'[44] Others in the Biden administration critiqued 'trickle down' economics, the notion that increasing wealth at the top would trickle down to benefit everybody. Instead, Bidenomics promised to 'build from the middle out', by increasing wages for ordinary workers. Trade tariffs, and the accompanying focus of industrial policy towards reshoring production into the US to increase the number of 'well-paying' manufacturing jobs, also constitutes a rejection of a core tenet of neoliberal globalisation in which concerns about the location of production were subordinated to the supposed global benefit of production at the cheapest cost.

The analysis of secular stagnation that underlies the turn to derisking identifies declining productivity, caused by a lack of business investment, as the principal culprit. At the same time, the stalled project to replace carbon-intensive infrastructure with renewable energy alternatives is attributed to the latter's lack of competitive profitability. This produces a new 'logic of statecraft [which] centres on derisking, understood as state interventions to steer price signals, correcting market failures that generate "uninvestable" risk/returns profiles.'[45] Such public derisking of private investment can take monetary, regulatory, and fiscal forms, ranging from providing cheap land for private urban development projects, underwriting financing, or guaranteeing returns through long contracts. But in all cases, it involves the socialisation of the risks and the privatisation of the rewards.

The Biden administration passed four key acts of economic policy: the 2021 American Rescue Plan Act, a $1.9 trillion stimulus package in response to the Covid-19 pandemic; the $250 billion Infrastructure Investment and Jobs Act also passed in 2021; the 2022 CHIPS and Science Act, and the Inflation Reduction Act (IRA) passed at the same time. Of these, the IRA — and, to a lesser extent, the Infrastructure Investment and Jobs Act — most clearly follow the derisking model. The IRA started life as the much more ambitious Build Back Better Act, which contained pledges to invest in social infrastructure, increase wages in the care sector, and increase corporation and top-end taxes to pay for it. This got whittled away through a massive lobbying campaign from capital, with the pharmaceutical and insurance sectors taking the leading role, taking advantage of the Democrats' slender Senate majority.[46] What remained were subsidies to capital whose central mechanisms involve derisking investment through a suite of tax incentives, loan guarantees, and grants. By far the most significant of these are a series of tax credits available if a business aligns with the state-mandated priorities of investing in renewable energy infrastructure — including wind, solar, and battery value chains — as well as electric vehicles and charging infrastructure, nuclear energy, sustainable materials, green hydrogen production, and carbon capture and storage. The total amount of tax credits are not capped, which means there is no limit to the amount that can be applied for. In addition, the tax credits can be stacked, so while the baseline tax credit for building renewable generation is 6 percent, the available tax credit rises to 30 percent if the company pays the prevailing industry wage during the construction of that facility. Projects sited in low-income states can also gain another 20 percent tax credit boost. It's a form of coordination in which the state decides on public goods and incentivises their adoption. The uncapped and stackable nature of the tax credits led to estimates in 2023 that the IRA could amount to $900 billion of state spending over ten years and involve $1.7 trillion in public and private climate spending overall.[47]

While the European Union has its own derisking mechanism with the European Sovereign Fund, the clearest and most direct influence of Bidenomics could be found in the pre-election policy platform of the UK Labour Party. The word securonomics, an ugly portmanteau favoured by chancellor of the exchequer Rachel Reeves, made an appearance in the Labour Party manifesto for the 2024 General Election, introducing the idea that public investment should support and derisk private investment in strategically key sectors. The chief vehicle for this policy is the National Wealth Fund, which will receive £7.3 billion of public funding over the course of the parliament and has a target to supplement this by attracting three pounds of private investment for every one pound of public investment, crowding in 'private capital on a deal-by-deal basis'.[48] This is an explicit return to and acceleration of public-private partnerships, which lost legitimacy in the UK during the fallout of the disastrous Public Finance Initiatives of the New Labour years.[49] The meagre sums involved have led economists Matthias Matthijs and Mark Blyth to term Labour's plans 'homeopathic Bidenomics'.[50] Despite this, the derisking approach is likely to form a major battleground for the rest of the 2020s.

A strong clue to both the direction of Labour policy and the current balance of forces can be seen in the National Infrastructure Taskforce, which was launched in October 2024 and tasked with designing new models of collaboration between government and investors. The taskforce is made up of some of the world's most rapacious, rent-extracting firms, including HSBC, Santander, Phoenix, Fidelity, and BlackRock. The battle over whose interests will prevail will also be fought over the extent to which Great British Energy, a proposed publicly-owned clean power company, will be an energy producer or a derisking vehicle for private initiatives. This battle will also encompass the form to be adopted for the 'public ownership' promised for British train companies as their contracts with private entities expire. The Labour government tied its own hands before even taking office by agreeing to fiscal rules in which 'day-to-day costs are met by revenues and debt must be falling as a share of the economy' five years after their election.[51] That has quickly led to welfare cuts, renewed austerity, and falling growth forecasts — a continuation of the doom-loop that the UK economy has been caught in since 2008. With a deeply unpopular government and living standards forecast to fall until 2030, the room for fiscal derisking in the UK seems to be shrinking. As a consequence, Labour's hopes for growth lean heavily on proposed regulatory derisking of development through reform of the planning system in favour of the big developers. As we will see in Chapter Six, this is unlikely to work.

THE DERISKING HALFWAY HOUSE

We can trace the weaknesses of the derisking state to a contradiction that runs straight through it. Derisking sets up a misshapen halfway house, trapped between neoliberalism and state planning. Public-private partnerships (PPPs), familiar from the high neoliberal period, entailed up-front private finance being used for infrastructure and services to be paid off by taxpayers, along with long-term guaranteed profits. On average, these projects cost 40 percent more than they would have if direct public funding was used. These profits were justified through the notion that private finance took on the risk of cost overruns or project failures. Ultimately that risk transfer proved fallacious as states stepped in when contracting companies went bankrupt. In the contemporary version, PPPs are being applied to different, post-neoliberal problems such as industrial policy. As a result, derisking contains two distinct logics that pull in different directions. One of these logics erects price signals and private investment as the mechanisms through which economic activity should be coordinated, but to do so derisking deploys the public coordination of investment priorities. This second mechanism is an iteration of the logic of economic planning, and as such it contradicts the first. Derisking constructs investability as the key to its solutions, though in doing so it 'reifies the functionality of the price mechanism'.[52] In orthodox economics, profits are justified as a reward for the risks that investors take. When the state removes or attenuates that risk it not only destroys that justification, but also undermines the supposed disciplining effects of the market. This makes a mockery of the idea that price signals are coordinating this activity.

As Gabor makes clear, the derisking state's 'concern with the production of investability forges a state-capital relationship where capital dominates.'[53] As such, it lacks the means to discipline capital. Derisking is all carrots and no sticks. The strategy of rolling out renewable energy while simultaneously allowing, and indeed subsidising, the continued growth of the fossil fuel industry has been a resolute failure. The state must discipline fossil capital, which should be forced to forego trillions in potential future profits, otherwise the planet will be made unliveable. The contradictory logics involved in derisking and its focus on investability means it can't break with the dynamics that drive untargeted bullshit abundance and won't push forward ecological transformation in the timescale required.

This tendency towards bullshit investment might seem less of a problem when dealing with secular stagnation, which is after all assessed through the bullshit measure of GDP growth, itself simply a totalling of all economic activities that have a price. But even here, the contradictory logics of the derisking state import tendencies that reinforce rather than ameliorate the symptoms of stagnation. If we allow derisking and public-private partnerships to be the motor that drives growth, then a tiny number of asset management firms will gain control over the key infrastructure of our era and extract huge rents for decades. Rentier business models relentlessly funnel money upwards, exacerbating inequality, while services deteriorate and wages decline. As oligarchs and asset management companies take over state functions and infrastructure, not only do these rentier dynamics get supercharged but democratic control over key elements of our lives are further eroded, making it harder to actually address the crises engulfing us.

In an age of secular stagnation and wealth concentration, perhaps derisking's biggest weakness is its inability to directly address people's feelings of insecurity and their lived experience of falling living standards. Biden's defeat, for instance, was part of an anti-incumbent electoral wave that swept the world in response to rising inflation and the removal of the Covid-19 era uplifts in welfare provision. Derisking private investment is a circuitous route to addressing urgently felt social needs. It's a policy which supports capital first, workers and citizens second, if at all. Any successful strategy of transition must prioritise immediate, qualitative improvements to people's lives. We have to cut out the bullshit and aim for a more radical form of abundance. The failure to do so opens the door to disaster nationalists such as Donald Trump.

TRANSITION BLOCKED

Trump's victory in the 2024 US presidential election represents the partial blocking of green capitalist efforts to mitigate climate change. Trump has attacked Biden's key derisking policies rhetorically, although the IRA's key tax credit mechanisms remain in place, and as the main beneficiaries have been Republican-controlled states, those subsidies might be hard to remove. Writing at the outset of Trump's second term in office, it seems likely that this term will involve a mix of derisking, direct contracting, and other government support for specific fractions of capital, following a clientelist and transactional logic, focused in particular on what's immediately politically beneficial to Trump. Those fractions receiving government backing will include fossil capital and tech platform monopolists whose interests appear to be aligning since Silicon Valley's version of Large Language Model development (popularly misnamed AI) requires huge quantities of cheap electricity. This alignment of interests partly explains why the tech oligarchs now appear to be more sympathetic to far-right politics. In ideological terms the climate crisis is being both denied and disavowed, with the era's pervading sense of crisis redirected into moral panics around diversity, equity, and inclusion (DEI) policies and racist conspiracy fantasies about declining 'white' birth rates. This misdirection creates room for more material interventions offloading the costs of the crisis onto others, domestically through the withdrawal of social provision, and internationally through radical hikes to trade tariffs. These tariffs were deployed chaotically and transactionally, but in the long term they appear to be aimed at devaluing the dollar and reshoring manufacturing to US soil. On this latter point, there is some continuity with Biden's policy of derisking. Both approaches see the reindustrialisation of the US, and the wave of well-paid jobs they think this will create, as the route to overcoming secular stagnation.

The Marxist social theorist Aaron Benanav argues that secular stagnation coincides with and has a relationship to the wider process of deindustrialisation, which we can define as a decline in industrial activity's share of GDP and employment. Deindustrialisation isn't merely the result of policy choices; it's deeply embedded in capitalism's drive to increase productivity to pursue profitability. Increases in productivity through fixed capital investment and automation are far easier to achieve in the industrial and manufacturing sector than in the service sector. As Benanav explains, one way to understand this is 'that services generally require direct interactions between workers and customers. The more people a worker interacts with, generally speaking, the lower the quality of a service.'[54] As increased productivity through automation pushes workers out of the industrial sector, the service sector picks up the slack and grows in size. It's this process that registers as deindustrialisation and causes a decline of productivity growth, measured in output per labour-hour worked, across the economy as a whole. This innate tendency creates a strong headwind against large-scale attempts to reshore manufacturing jobs through industrial policy and tariffs. Any reshored industrial plant will likely be highly automated and simply won't require much labour to function. Such a strategy will not secure large numbers of new jobs, but it will exacerbate tendencies towards stagnation and declining productivity across the global economy as a whole. If, as therefore seems likely, secular stagnation is here to stay then we can no longer afford bullshit abundance. What growth there is must be carefully targeted to support the transition towards radical abundance.

The interplay between liberal derisking and clientelist, disaster nationalism creates a complicated strategic field for those seeking more fundamental, egalitarian change. The recent book *Abundance: How We Build a Better Future* by centrist journalists Ezra Klein and Derek Thompson, which has proved influential amongst the Democratic Party establishment, advocates a continuation of Biden-era fiscal derisking, shorn of its aims to increase social and labour rights, and amplified by strong regulatory derisking, primarily through the removal of planning regulations. 'If we could build cheaper,' they argue, 'the money would go further.'[55] It seems likely then, despite Trump's victory, that on the US state and municipal levels many Democratic administrations will continue following derisking logics, even if only in this attenuated form. The UK and Europe are also likely to pursue weak forms of derisking while genuflecting to disaster nationalist political framings and policy priorities. While there are differences between the two modes of regulation, they exist in a kind of symbiosis and share elements in common, some of which provide openings to the Left.

CAN POPULAR PROTAGONISM BE DERISKED?

From its earliest days, a key feature of neoliberal governance has been its 'encasement' of markets, as it seeks to insulate economic and investment decision-making from democratic pressure.[56] This encasement was pursued through a number of avenues, from domestic policies such as central bank independence to transnational institutions and agreements, like the EU, the World Bank, and WTO, whose writ supersedes national governments. The re-emergence of tariffs and industrial policies, in both their centrist derisking and clientelist modes, has fundamentally broken this notional separation of the political and economic. Indeed, the entire logic of economic coordination through price signals mediated via markets has been undermined. The state is now picking the winners and making them profitable. In this sense, it's a demystifying moment that opens up a new field of contestability. After all, if the state can act politically in the interests of capital, it can, in principle, also act politically in the interests of workers and communities. What's missing is the popular protagonism to push the state to do so, against both its own inertia and predisposition to reproduce the conditions for capital accumulation.

The prospect of such contestation forms the background to the recent authoritarian turn common to both right-wing and centrist governments. The US, the UK, and many other countries are seeing the dramatic constriction of key, long-held democratic rights to free speech, assembly, and protest. There is an underlying logic to the simultaneity of this turn. If key economic and investment decisions can no longer be insulated from politics, then political decision-making will have to be insulated from democratic pressure. This anti-democratic authoritarianism was opened up by centrist regimes, honed in particular through the repression of disruptive climate activism and pro-Palestinian, anti-genocide protest. Disaster nationalist regimes have followed suit, ramping up their vicious suppression of opposition. Yet repressive overreach — Trump's abandonment of due process in immigration cases, for example — is creating the conditions for a popular anti-oligarch, pro-democracy inflected politics. A defence of democratic rights will obviously play a role in this struggle, but if it's to succeed it must avoid defending the deeply unpopular pre-Trump establishment.

The economist Isabella Weber recently issued an urgent call for an anti-fascist economics, in which the struggle for democracy is made less abstract by directly addressing our deeply felt material needs.[57] We'll certainly need the campaigns that Weber suggests to tax the rich and ensure price controls on profit-gouging companies, but as we've seen in this chapter, the trends towards rising inequality, economic stagnation, and ecological collapse are incredibly strong and deeply imbricated in the core dynamics of capital accumulation. They will not be overcome by mere policy changes. Instead, we must demonstrate that democratic activism is a viable route to a future in which the constraints on our lives are lifted. That means extending and deepening democracy to challenge capital's control of the economic sphere. For this we need institutional forms that can limit the power of capital while building our collective capacity to act and take our collective reproduction into our own hands.

The strategy for doing so will look different in polities where the disaster nationalists are in control versus areas where liberal derisking prevails. When struggling in the latter, we should apply pressure to derisking's contradictions with the hope they will explode in a manner favouring the development of popular protagonism and contested reproduction. We can use derisking and its institutions to open space to discuss and build non-market and democratic forms of economic coordination that point to radical rather than bullshit abundance. As Melanie Brusseler argues, once the institutions of public coordination, such as the UK's National Wealth Fund, have been established they 'can be made susceptible to contesting claims and institutionalisation on different terms over time'.[58] Such an effort could involve a range of tactics — including attempts to attach conditionalities to state support of private enterprises or add additional social incentives to the conditions of derisking — but the ultimate goal is to make public derisking of private investment itself politically unacceptable. Why should public money go to derisking private ownership and gain, we should ask, when it could go to derisking publicly or commonly owned assets and production?

In disaster nationalist contexts, slightly different strategies are required. When access to public funds and derisking seem to be foreclosed then the institutions of economic democracy can initially be established independently, with demands for the public derisking of commonly owned assets used as a powerful mobilising tool. Inspiration for this can be taken from 'bargaining for the common good' strategies developed by US public employees, in which 'workers connect their immediate wage demands to the larger distributional issues of state spending and taxation.'[59] Writing about the 2018 struggle of the West Virginia public-school teachers Melinda Cooper explains,

> A crucial element in the campaign was the drafting of an alternative state budget proposal, recommending an end to the state's

> ultra-generous tax preferences for oil and gas firms. Having built a contestation of state budgetary politics into their campaign from the outset, the teachers were able to transform the meaning of industrial action from negotiated crisis to a genuine battle over spending priorities.[60]

Detailed alternative plans for the extension of workers' and citizens' control over economic coordination could be a vital element in anti-oligarchic struggles. They can expose the interests disaster nationalist regimes really work for, while having a compositional effect on the movements themselves — raising our levels of political consciousness and collective capacities to self-govern.

The history of social and workers' movements shows that we can defeat intransigent governments and compel more amenable but nevertheless hostile state authorities into policy changes and reforms if we make the political costs of doing otherwise untenable. We can ask nicely at first but the severity of the situation means that we will have to insist by any means necessary. As the effects of climate change bite ever harder and both state and private provision becomes ever thinner and more bullshit in nature, we're increasingly pushed into a situation where we need to adopt what social theorist Alberto Toscano calls 'dual biopower — which is to say the collective attempt politically to appropriate aspects of social reproduction that state and capital have deliberately deserted or rendered unbearably exclusionary, from housing to medicine.'[61] This will entail an array of tactics and strategies. Whatever approach is taken, though, we must build the infrastructure for democratic planning from below while preparing the conditions for coordinated planning nationally and — eventually — internationally.

As we demonstrate through the following chapters, this need not start in reference to national or supranational political institutions. In many cases, the easiest way to begin is by applying pressure at the subnational level. The sense of anxious unreality that pervades contemporary life, and with which we started this chapter, is an effect of our failure to meaningfully address the biggest threat to continued human civilisation our species has ever faced. What is needed now more than ever are movements and institutional forms that can set in motion the self-expansion of an entirely different set of social and ecological relations. We turn our attention, from this point onwards, to public-common partnerships as one example of how this can be done.

PART II

5

Public-Common Partnerships

Imagine for a moment a workplace where the workers, and not their bosses, determine what is produced and how. Together, workers make decisions about how many hours a week they work, who does what in the division of labour, and how to maintain or improve the technologies they need. This workplace, whether it's a factory, power plant, farm, or bakery, is worker-owned, but it remains under the influence of capital's metabolic control. It must still produce a profit to reproduce itself, which means that it continues to depend on the extraction of surplus labour from those who work there. But there's a major difference. Whereas in an entirely capitalist workplace, these profits are appropriated by a capitalist owner, and whereas in a cooperative, profits are shared equally among the workers themselves, in a public-common partnership (PCP) the profits are handed to a separate democratic organ, a Common Association, which decides what to do with the surpluses generated. Members of this Common Association include anyone and everyone with an interest in the workplace and what it produces. And since it is they who get to decide what is done with the surplus, it isn't *just* the workplaces' workers who benefit from the fruits of their labour. Rather, it is as many of the people as possible that have helped to (re)produce the workers' ability to work at all. This includes those who consume what the workplace produces, those who do the waged or unwaged reproductive work of looking after their children, of doing the laundry, the cooking, the weekly shop, of maintaining the roads workers use to commute, and much else besides.

The Common Association may choose to invest the workplaces' surpluses in developing the immediate local area. Perhaps more green space is needed. Or a new social centre. But they also know that these surpluses could be used to create other workplaces that similarly prioritise the socialisation of social surplus. For this reason, they choose to give a portion of the surplus to another group of workers who need funds to purchase their own workplace and socialise its surpluses. In this way, the process of commoning — creating social property and spaces for democratic planning — expands. Though these workplaces are not yet outside of capital's metabolic control, by granting one another the surpluses they need to socialise production, they reduce the likelihood of taking loans from private banks that inevitably impose high interest rates and strict repayment stipulations. This, albeit in a small way, diminishes capital's metabolic control, partially limiting its capacity to shape what happens in socially owned workplaces.

These workers and their communities are successfully meeting some of their collective needs and developing their local area in ways that the people who live there want to see. But there's a problem. Competing with private capital means they're forced to maximise profits in the workplace, which means working harder for longer. Worse, the surpluses generated are not enough at first to buy the property needed for a new commonly owned workplace. Seeing how capital's metabolic control constrains the collective desire of workers, people begin to organise. They apply pressure to some part of the state apparatus (perhaps the city government) to support the expansion of the commons. After all, as we saw in the previous chapter, if the state is willing to derisk for profit enterprises, why can't it derisk the expansion of the commons? Under significant pressure — or perhaps, if we're being optimistic, because state actors see the obvious benefits of social property — public bodies decide to use their powers to support the establishment of new commonly owned workplaces. Maybe they transfer a land lease ensuring there are no rents, or perhaps they take out private loans on the workers' behalf to reduce capital's disciplinary mechanisms. By supporting these worker-led initiatives, particular state actors would be empowering workers and communities to shape their own future. They would be helping to derisk a self-expanding dynamic of commoning that might contest capital's own self-expansionary dynamics.

Now imagine that with each commonly owned workplace that is created, new opportunities to prioritise radical abundance take hold: better working conditions, a three or four-day workweek, international solidarity campaigns, and the establishment of mutual supply chains. These in themselves are not instances of radical abundance, but they are its preconditions. Meanwhile, surpluses are invested to meet the immediate needs of workers in the workplace and beyond, often without caring whether an initiative creates a profit or not. And this may happen in frivolous ways that bring people together to socialise, bond, relax, or create. In this way, workers (paid and unpaid) become conscious of themselves as a collective subject with shared interests. Since workers can buy what they need from within this emerging circuit of the commons, or have their needs met without any monetary exchange at all, they're put in a stronger position to reproduce themselves, at least partially, outside of capital's circuits of accumulation. As the commons expands, as sites of contested reproduction multiply, workers are in an increasingly strong position to fight not just for a taste of radical abundance, but for a world that makes its pursuit the utmost priority.

The scenario we've sketched here describes, very loosely, the institutional form that we call public-common partnerships (PCPs). To begin to understand this formulation we can turn to Stuart Hall's 1984 essay 'The State: Socialism's Old Caretaker', which defends 'a conception of the public... as an arena constructed against the logic of capital', but also warns against conceiving of 'the public' as 'identical with the state' so that the only alternative to the marketisation of our lives appeared to be the bureaucratic 'state-management of society in the name of socialism'.[1] This doesn't mean rejecting the possibility of state institutions playing an essential role within a wider politics of socialist transition, but rather that these state institutions could never be the primary instrument. The reference point for socialism is not the state, but society. As Hall puts it,

> Once the logic of capital, property and the market are broken, it is the diversity of social forms, the taking of popular initiatives, the recovery of popular control, the passage of power from the state

> *into* society, which marks out the advance towards socialism. We can envisage a 'partnership' between state and society, so long as the initiative is always passing to society, so long as the monopoly over the management of social life does not come to a dead halt with the state elite, so long as the state itself is rooted in, constantly draws energy from, and is pushed actively, by popular forces.[2]

PCPs offer a concrete approach to embodying Hall's articulation of this 'advance towards socialism'. They embody the proposition that we must focus on 'finding the forms in which [we] can take on the control over an increasingly complex society' and that this will 'not happen all at once, through *one* centre — by simply "smashing the state", as the sort of socialist thinking which is fixated on the state would have it'. Instead, the development of a strategy for transition must 'happen across a multiplicity of sites in social life, on many different fronts, including, of course, the state itself, whose tendency to concentrate power is precisely what constitutes it as a barrier to socialism'. It must, in other words, be focused on the processes that build an entirely different social metabolism, one that embraces a 'struggle to democratise power across all the centres of social activity... from which we can all begin the reconstruction of society'.[3]

Hall was writing in a very different conjuncture to our own. In 1984, the huge post-war expansion of the state-managed public sector was just starting to be undone, but Hall recognised the prevailing currents of 'dissatisfactions with the state' that early neoliberalism took advantage of were 'real and authentic enough — even if Thatcherism mis-describes and mis-explains them. Thatcherism did not invent them — even if its remedies for the problem are fictitious.'[4] In our own time, with everyday life entangled in the unending, predatory, and dysfunctional bureaucracy of private provision, the fictitious nature of neoliberalism's escape from state bureaucracy is apparent, but both the state and society have been transformed in the meantime. The state is well accustomed to using 'partnerships' for development, but almost invariably its partner is capital to which it adopts a subordinate relation. Although there are residual elements of the state acting 'as an arena constructed against the logic of capital', decades of privatisation, outsourcing, and public-private partnerships have hollowed out the public and installed the logic of capital within it.

Neoliberalism has always been defined by the rolling back and constraining of democracy, aiming, in particular, to insulate economic decision-making from democratic pressure. Public-private partnerships have been a key institutional mechanism through which this has been achieved. One way to understand public-*common* partnerships is as a reverse engineering of the effects of public-private partnerships, aiming to reassert democratic control over economic decision-making, while insulating direct democratic deliberation around investment decisions from the distorting discipline of finance capital. As we saw in the previous chapter, the return of public economic coordination, in both its derisking and clientist modes, breaches the separation of political and economic reason that neoliberalism sought to erect. This creates openings to push the state to change the focus of its derisking from capital to the commons. However, the political projects of public-private partnerships and public-common partnerships are not symmetrical. To address the world-historic crises facing us, we must do more than simply undo neoliberalism. We must also fulfil the invariant features of transition outlined in Chapter Two: creating situations of contested reproduction and generating popular protagonism.

For some years now, the authors of this book have been designing PCPs alongside communities across the UK and in France, to think about how to socialise production and to kickstart what we call the self-expansion of the commons. PCPs aren't the only institutional form that might do this. As we saw in Chapter Three, there are many institutional forms that can build popular protagonism and expand the situations of contested reproduction. Yet they're *a* form that might have success within our current constraints by applying pressure to state actors that have begun to renege on the neoliberal commitment to keeping the 'economy' and 'politics' separate. In this sense, they're a wager, a gamble, on a possible course of action.

In this chapter, we present how PCPs function in abstract terms. Some of what we say here, as an institutional description, may appear a little dry. Building popular protagonism involves exciting moments of political mobilisation, but it also includes the more patient work of building institutions, which involves technical processes of institutional design to ensure they best fit the features of transition needed to escape our crisis-ridden present. At a time when we have very few institutions fit for purpose, our aim is to outline the sort of institutions that might lead to a proliferation of popular protagonism and a dramatic expansion in the spaces of contested reproduction. In the three chapters that follow, the design we outline here will be applied in different contexts, for different purposes, starting with urban development in London, then pharmaceutical production in France, and concluding with agroecological transition in England. Together, these chapters help deepen our understanding of what such institutions might look like in our own contexts, exploring the challenges of organising for them and how they might differ across sectors.

HOW A PUBLIC-COMMON PARTNERSHIP WORKS

PCPs are an institutional approach to the co-ownership and co-governance of a productive enterprise that in this chapter's opening vignette we called a 'workplace' but from now on we will call a Joint Enterprise. This Joint Enterprise (JE) is a legal entity that can, in principle, be formed around a broad range of surplus-producing assets or types of work: agricultural land, energy generation infrastructure, market buildings, last-mile logistics, housing, grocery chains, construction firms, forestry reserves, hotels, pharmaceutical manufacturers, restaurants, and so on. In terms of day-to-day operations, a JE would look similar to a worker cooperative. It is those who are doing the work who should make collective decisions about how this work gets done, embedding a principle of worker-management throughout. We won't elaborate upon worker-management structures here as they are contextually specific, but they would include a series of accountability mechanisms that enable transparency amongst workers, as well as for the governance board to ensure the JE is operating in accordance with its organisational goals.

So far there is nothing remarkable about what is being proposed, aside from emphasising the importance of worker-management.

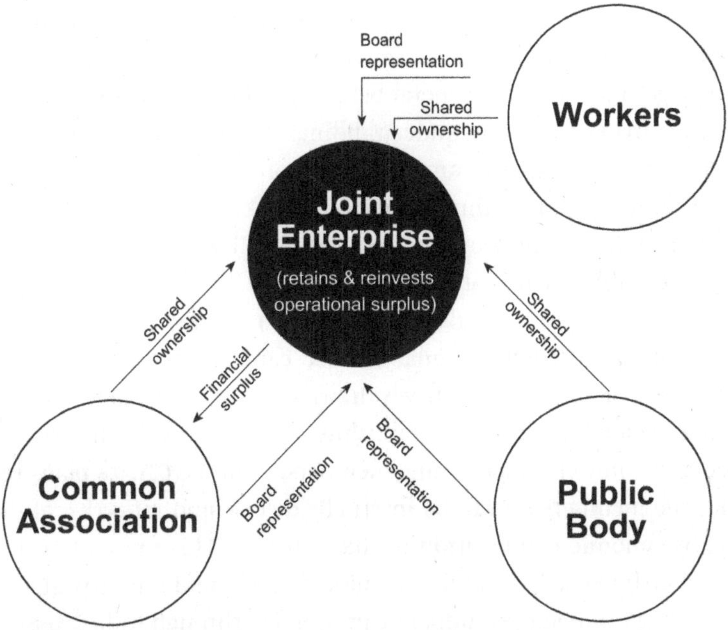

Figure 1 Abstract Model of a Public-Common Partnership

These worker-management structures are ultimately accountable to the board of the JE, which is responsible for the overall governance of the organisation (e.g. setting its goals, direction, broad allocation of resources, limitations, and accountability frameworks). The board includes at least three classes of stakeholder: the employees themselves as worker-owners; a public body, which might be a local or regional authority or statutory organisation; and a Common Association, which is a legally constituted body in its own right. Each class of stakeholder is responsible for electing their own representatives to the board, with the proportional composition of the board being determined on a case-by-case basis. As we'll expand upon in the following section, the composition and subsequent behaviour of this board is a critical site for the contested reproduction of the JE. For now it is sufficient to say that these stakeholders are expected to represent qualitatively different types of interest, which at times might be in direct conflict with one another. The overall governance of the JE should thus be understood as an agonistic space — a permanent site for the negotiation of different and at times competing interests — in which the negotiation comes to determine (or to use our language, 'mediate') the general behaviour of the JE's activity.

It's starting from this understanding of 'different interests' that we can introduce the Common Association (CA). A CA is a separate legal entity governed through decision-making processes that are entirely independent from the rest of the PCP structure, and which is accountable solely to its own membership. The membership itself is composed of individuals that live within a defined territory (e.g. an existing electoral boundary, water catchment area, postcode, bioregion, or an altogether newly drawn territory), with that territory being decided during the establishment of the CA. With territory being the only criteria defining membership in the CA, it's plausible that the membership will be internally diverse and reflective of the socio-economic composition of that territory. This means that the membership of a CA established following an inner-London postcode *really might* range from unpaid care workers through to hedge-fund managers, while the membership of a CA established following a semi-rural electoral boundary *really might* range from seasonal migrant farmworkers to landowners. The Common Association is an intrinsically agonistic organisation that will include people with different class positions and world views which at times might clash significantly with one another.

There are two important factors that serve to mediate this diverse membership of a Common Association. First, as a legally independent organisation it will be bound by its articles of association and subsequently agreed rules (and membership is contingent on supporting them), which commits it to activities that support the development of a wider communal social metabolism. Second, the decision-making processes of the CA must be intrinsically participatory and based on the principle of one member, one vote — with no formal prospect of one's private wealth leading to them having a greater say. There is a great deal of research exploring the possibilities and challenges of developing genuinely participatory democratic processes, which includes Elinor Ostrom's neo-institutional work on commons and the wider work it has informed,[5] as well as historical and current experiences such as those of the Zhoujiazhuang People's Commune.[6] There are a wealth of different mechanisms ranging from deliberative mini-publics, such as citizen assemblies, through to participatory budgeting schemes,[7] and digital participation platforms like Decidem.[8] Whichever participatory processes are developed by a Common Association, they play a fundamental role in fulfilling its broader functions: first, as a communal mediating force contesting the governance and thus the overarching behaviour of the Joint Enterprise; and second, as a vehicle of popular protagonism that works to expand communal metabolic control. Both of these functions will be explored further in the following sections.

PCPs are also distinguished by having a public body as part of the JE's governance arrangement. In practice this might be local or regional government such as a city council or a combined authority or a statutory agency like Transport for London, depending on the specifics of the PCP. The principal basis for the inclusion of a public body is to support what is known as a co-productive approach to policy formation and administration. The relative autonomy of public actors within existing state forms varies with both context and conjuncture, and given that the state's overall function within the capitalist system is to maintain the conditions for capital accumulation,[9] we should have modest expectations about what might be enabled through such co-productive approaches. Nonetheless, the forms of deep and tacit knowledge that may be generated through such close collaboration can enable significantly more supportive environments for the development and operation of PCPs. Just as embedding public actors within public-private partnerships, from private finance initiatives (PFIs) to special purpose vehicles (SPVs), shapes and moulds the 'common sense' of public actors and their day-to-day experience of what 'good government' looks like, so the embedding of public actors in PCPs can affect the everyday mental parameters of public technicians, civil servants, and representatives. As we explore later, this is part of expanding the scope for popular protagonism, contributing to a shift in the prospects for different forms of public support.

The final factor in outlining the abstract form of a PCP is concerned with the ownership and control of assets. First, all of the operating infrastructure and intellectual property, whether in the form of freeholds or leaseholds, is owned by the Joint Enterprise. These assets are all held within what is known as an 'asset lock', which means that any assets or financial surplus cannot be sold, distributed to members, or transferred to another organisation. Such asset locks are a critical part of ensuring these organisations cannot be approached with the goal of extracting private income, immunising them against privatisation and enclosure. Second, while all Joint Enterprises are 'not for profit', they're all designed in anticipation of producing an operating surplus, although, like in any enterprise, this is variable and sometimes minimal or even non-existent. This surplus is used in two distinct ways. On the one hand, it might be expended by the Joint Enterprise as part of its operating costs, such as purchasing new manufacturing equipment, maintaining premises, retrofitting housing stock, and so on. In Figure 1 we term this the 'operational surplus', where the amount of surplus made available for such expenditure is decided by the board of the JE. On the other hand, all remaining surplus (which in Figure 1 is termed the 'financial surplus') will be transferred to the Common Association, which uses it in accordance with its articles of association and as decided through its participatory decision-making processes.

These are some of the fundamental parameters of a public-common partnership, which taken together can help identify what a PCP *is not*. For whatever virtues they might each have, a PCP isn't a participatory mechanism for including civilians in the management of a public enterprise. Nor is it an argument for including employees or 'civil society' on the board of a private corporation, or indeed for the conversion of corporations into worker cooperatives. It's also not a charity aimed at providing resources to those in need (although it most certainly *is* about finding ways to meet people's long-term needs). And it's not a participatory budgeting mechanism for distributing publicly provided resources. And while there are similarities, a PCP is also not just a tripartite arrangement for the governance of assets, as we might find in a Community Land Trust (CLT). Many of these approaches have their own virtues, and some of them (such as CLTs) merit a more thorough analysis in terms of how they might contribute to a process of transition. But we are specific in defining the parameters of a PCP because we are interested *not only* in isolated principles like democratisation, de-privatisation, or commoning, but because we are fundamentally concerned with how they contribute to producing the invariant features of transition: creating situations of contested reproduction and generating popular protagonism.

PUBLIC-COMMON PARTNERSHIPS AND CONTESTED REPRODUCTION

At the core of a PCP is the principle of establishing different types of social property or social ownership. These terms are frequently misused, most often to refer simply to the state ownership of assets or resources and sometimes more expansively to democratic economic forms such as cooperatives. A more accurate understanding of social ownership focuses on the various forces that mediate our relationships between one another and the non-human world around us. As we explored in Chapter Two, there is nothing about state ownership of assets that qualifies these assets as a form of social property, as even under the Soviet model the political extraction of surplus value upheld capital's metabolic control. Despite their internal democratic processes, nor do cooperatives insulate us from capital's imperative to accumulate. Cooperatives are more properly thought of as a kind of collective private property. Even Mondragon — one of the most paradigmatic cases of a worker cooperative that has made impressive strides in terms of internal democracy and worker wellbeing — has found itself outsourcing to non-cooperative production sites in 32 countries. As Noam Chomsky notes, they can't escape operating 'in a market system and they still exploit workers in South America, and they do things that are harmful to the society as a whole and they have no choice. If you're in a system where you must make profit in order to survive, you're compelled to ignore negative externalities, effects on others'.[10] In both capitalist state and cooperative ownership, it's not democratic will that determines our behaviour but the compulsion towards capital accumulation. Social property is thus not simply about who (or what) owns assets, but the extent to which a *communal logic* can become the dominant mediating force shaping decision-making.

Within our current circumstances, it's not possible to create social property in an unadulterated form. This would require us to exist in a world after capital. Instead we must approach the task of creating property as a problem of *contested reproduction*, where tendencies towards the socialisation of property coexist with, and are constrained by, capital's metabolic control even within our institutions. To reiterate Evgenii Preobrazhensky, the challenge is to find ways of establishing a new form of social control while working towards 'the ousting of other economic forms, the subordination of these forms to the new form, and their gradual elimination'.[11] Within a PCP, the primary space in which this contestation occurs is within the overall governance of the Joint Enterprise. On the one hand, with economic surplus ultimately transferred into the control of the Common Association, there is very little left of a 'profit motive' to guide the operations of the Joint Enterprise. While it is possible for a JE to work more efficiently and increase productivity, this would enable those workers to work less, or alternatively to generate additional surplus that would be transferred to the CA. To the extent that a JE is competing within a market (which is relative, and can be militated against through natural, legally granted, or limited/quasi monopolies), it would *still* feel the discipline of profitability as it competed with capitalist firms to 'realise the value' of its products. This discipline, however, would be contested by a different, communal, mediating force.

The principal source of this communal mediating force is the Common Association. Putting aside momentarily the different tensions that might exist within its membership, the CA is able to directly shape critical governance decisions about the JE, from the setting of wages, to establishing limitations on the providence of raw materials and services, to fundamental shifts in what is being produced or delivered. Of course, the CA isn't making these decisions on its own but is governing through a tripartite governance arrangement, along with the workers and a public body. The CA thus exerts a democratic communal 'will' on the overall operation of the Joint Enterprise, which must be articulated through dialogue, and sometimes disagreement, with representatives of the workers and the public body. There will be times when this relationship of mediating forces isn't conflictual whatsoever, and times where there may be quite bitter disputes, but whichever way these unfold they represent the *contested reproduction* of the Joint Enterprise. As such, the JE cannot be thought of as a discrete or pure form of social property that belongs to an 'entirely different' social metabolism. It rather has embedded within it a *tendency towards* social property. The critical point is that the communal mediating force driving this tendency comes from the Common Association.

As a territorially rooted, democratic membership organisation that doesn't produce goods or offer services, the CA is somewhat insulated from capital's mediation. As an organised community rather than an economic unit, there are no productive activities for capital to mediate. This means that, within the shifting constraints of ideology which we'll address later, it's free to make collective socially informed decisions about how the JE ought to act without needing to directly consider the implications. To give a simple caricature of this, the democratic processes within the CA might decide they don't want gambling to be advertised within any of the operating premises associated with the Joint Enterprise. If that JE happened to operate a football club, that decision might not make much economic sense — after all, selling advertising space on club shirts, billboards and stadium naming rights might bring tens of millions into the club. Yet the CA can affirm decisions that run contrary to such strict 'economic' logic, and through accountability to its membership, serve to negotiate or block such decisions at the board level of the JE.

PUBLIC-COMMON PARTNERSHIPS AND POPULAR PROTAGONISM

As we noted above, the CA doesn't only serve as a communal mediating force, but also as a vehicle of popular protagonism that seeks to expand communal metabolic control through contested reproduction. We can think of at least four ways that popular protagonism can be expressed through PCPs. The first is what we've elsewhere referred to as the 'self-expansive dynamic'[12] of a PCP, in which the funds passed into the control of the Common Association can be used to support the development of further PCPs or other elements of a communal social metabolism. This self-expansive dynamic means that PCPs should not be thought of in isolation, but rather as cells within a self-replicating and expanding system tending towards social property and communal metabolic control. For every new PCP supported through such a process, the net capacity of the circuit increases, which in turn accelerates the funding of further, and potentially more financially-intensive, PCPs. This funding is complemented with the free flow of knowledge and skills in a web of mutual support that is so essential to the commons, but that under capitalism is carefully protected as part of a business's so-called 'competitive advantage'. The net effect of this is to create a consciously directed and expansive movement of decommodification, bringing an increasing proportion of our reproductive activity *within* a communal social metabolism. While it's not possible to 'beat capitalism at its own game', this expansive dynamic is designed to compete with the self-expansive dynamic of capital in a way akin to a form of primitive communal accumulation.

In practice, the funds utilised in this expansive circuit may well fall short of what is required to establish additional links in the circuit, which results in the need for a second expression of popular protagonism. Rather than direct forms of market transaction such as the outright purchase of a piece of land, the second form of popular protagonism is premised on people organising to *change the conditions* through which they might gain access to resources. This might look like a campaign to ensure a legislative 'right to communal com-

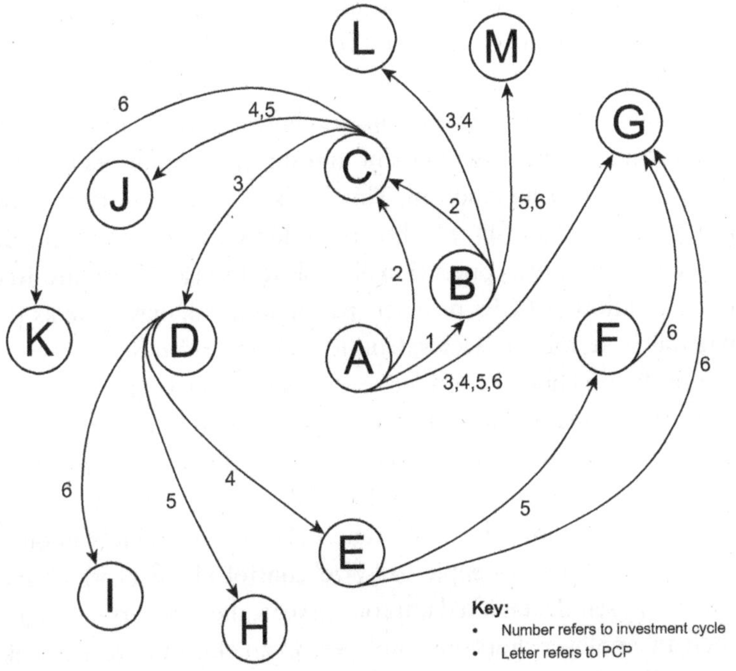

Figure 2 Self-Expansive Dynamic of the Commons

pulsory purchase', which would enshrine the right of communal economy actors to purchase public or privately held assets at a subsidised price — a principle close to that enshrined in Article 15 of Germany's constitution, and which puts the possibility of *socialisation* of private assets on the table, as we saw in Chapter Three. Or it might take a more limited form such as a struggle to take over a particular asset, such as when the metropolitan authority of Marseille responded to pressure and made a 5.3 million euro purchase and asset transfer of a former Unilever factory, supporting the development of a new worker cooperative.[13]

Central to all these examples is that they recognise that there are contextually and *conjuncturally* specific opportunities to episodically 'make use' of parts of the existing state apparatus to support the development of a communal social metabolism. There is no single strategy that either demands or rejects engaging with existing state forms in a particular way. There are certainly times, as we saw in Hernani, Hegoalde in Chapter Three, when it makes sense to form alliances with left-wing parties already in municipal public office. And there are other times, as we saw with Venezuela's communal project, where popular control of the state is critical for creating a policy environment and directing resources towards communal social metabolism. This leads us to a third expression of popular protagonism, which is the role that PCPs might play in a broader and more conventionally political sense. Those involved in the creation of PCPs, or participating in them, may serve as the material base for an electoral project at any given scale. Yet our caution here is not to consider this as having finally arrived at the 'real' site of transformation, but to consider how it might support (to recall Stuart Hall) the continuous passing of the initiative to organised society. In practice, this can look like a series of Popular Power Laws, like those introduced in Venezuela in 2010, which amongst other things allowed people to 'seize' control of assets which had been purposefully rendered unproductive by their owners — such as when an employer shuts out employees in an effort to break a strike — and bring them into a form of communal control.

A final, fourth expression of popular protagonism comes in an altogether more defensive form, and it responds to the problem of what sociologist Erik Olin Wright has termed 'transition troughs'.[14] A transition trough can be summarised as a particular phase of transition in which capital (or the personifications of capital) look to undermine or destroy the social forces that threaten it. A good example of this is capital flight. When threatened with the prospect of significant restrictions to realising profit, capital has the potential to 'flee' a specific jurisdiction, leaving shuttered factories, empty supermarkets, locked farm gates, and dysfunctional basic services. The threat of capital flight and the ensuing chaos and collapse in living standards is often mobilised, whether explicitly or implicitly, as the reason why certain things 'simply cannot be done'. Indeed if such capital flight actually comes to pass, it threatens to rapidly evaporate popular support for anything other than a 'stabilising government' that can work to 'attract capital' back to its shores. But what if a significant part of our social reproductive infrastructure — our farms, housing, energy infrastructure, water utilities, supermarkets — had been integrated into an altogether different communal social metabolism? What if the reproduction of this new kind of communal metabolism was beginning to be viewed by the associated producers as what Marx called a 'self-evident natural law'? What if capital flight didn't pose as much of a threat to our ability to eat and clothe ourselves, to keep our houses warm? Though under very different circumstances, this 'transition trough' problem is precisely what happened in Venezuela in the 2010s. As Chris Gilbert explains, it was after Chavez' death and when oil prices fell to record lows, imperialist attacks on Venezuela heightened, and an economic downturn took hold, that Venezuela's workers adopted the commune as a means for their collective reproduction in earnest. Institutions of popular protagonism and contested reproduction enabled them to weather the storm.[15]

THE ACTIVIST IS DEAD, LONG LIVE THE ACTIVIST!

A question that's been lurking throughout this chapter, and indeed throughout the first half of this book, concerns who it is that is expected to do all this. Who can be a popular protagonist? Who exactly are we claiming is the subject of transformation? And if these Common Associations can prospectively be filled with both migrant farmworkers and hedge fund managers, if they can encompass low-paid care workers and landowners, mothers, coders, land defenders, college students, squatters, accountants, and small shop owners, then why should we place any hope whatsoever in them combining into something we call a communal mediating force? There are two separate responses to these questions. The first regards the enduring importance of worker (and workplace) organising, and the second the subjectifying process of participating in a Common Association.

The establishment of a PCP might often follow from workplace organising. We should caution that this observation might be the result of some of the cases we focus on rather than some general rule, but it should nonetheless be acknowledged. From factory occupations and workplace slow-downs, through to financial and political solidarity and training provided by trade unions, workers will often play a critical role in developing the sort of political leverage that might result in the transfer of existing assets to a PCP. A leading example comes from Brazil, where in 1997 the metalworkers union (SMABC) established the organisation UNISOL to work towards the cooperative takeover of private companies facing bankruptcy, through providing credit, legal support, training, market access, supply chain support, technological support, assistance in developing and lobbying for advantageous public policy, and international cooperation.[16] Within institutions themselves, the democratic organisation of work processes has been, and must remain, a central goal of any socialist politics. It is those who work that must decide *how fast* and *how hard* they labour, whether that means *working less* so there is more time for play and care, or *working more* to support wider goals that the workers themselves have agreed on. Yet waged workers are not the only social agents who matter, and nor are they the only actors who desperately want to end this world of bullshit abundance and artificial scarcity.

This point can be made most forcefully by considering a possible criticism of the idea that any economic surplus produced by those working in a Joint Enterprise should be transferred to a Common Association. Why shouldn't the workers be the recipients of all the wealth that they have produced? This line of questioning, however, ignores fundamental advances made by Marxist-feminist and eco-Marxist thinkers who have, in straightforward terms, explained why the wealth produced within the factory has *never* been produced solely by those who enter through its gates.[17] Taken through to its more expansive conclusion, this means, as Marta Harnecker puts it, that 'wealth is a social heritage that must be used in the interests of society as a whole rather than serving private interests. These assets, incorporating the labor of generations, do not belong to specific people or specific countries, but to humanity.'[18] Beyond the wages that the workers in a Joint Enterprise would receive in compensation for their work, the wealth that is produced is our common social heritage. But how exactly does 'humanity' meaningfully come to control this wealth? The challenge is finding concrete forms that put this concept of social wealth into practice without falling back on the idea that it ought to be accumulated by the state. In the case of a PCP, the transfer of this wealth into the auspices of the Common Association signifies the first step in *socialising* this wealth.

This leads us to the final concern of the composition and processes of the Common Association itself. While we've entertained the *possibility* that a landowner might sit next to a migrant farmworker — subjects who would likely have structurally contradictory interests — in practice the *legally inscribed* function of the Common Association is to act as an institution of popular protagonism to defend and extend a communal social metabolism. Any subject looking to actively work against the interests of the Common Association would thus need to successfully navigate or disrupt the participatory processes of the CA and convince it to act against its collective interests and social heritage. They would also need to meet the requirements that a proposed course of action contributes to the legally inscribed goals of the CA. Those shown to be consistently advocating against the perceived interests of the CA will likely have a tough ride justifying their ongoing participation. Yet we shouldn't be naive and consider that this entirely forecloses attempts to harness the CA against the common interest. In fact we can be absolutely certain that, like any serious political or social force throughout history, Common Associations will share the general challenge of defending themselves against efforts to undermine and disrupt their operation.

A more mundane reality is that, through virtue of the many different walks of life and relative socio-economic positions that are embodied within a CA, a series of non-antagonistic contradictory positions will present themselves. Consider the tension between those who may advocate for building a dam to produce the energy required to expand an electrified public transit network and the fisherfolk and farmworkers using that river to provide fish or irrigation for their fields. While these different participants (in their particular subject positions, each of which is shaped by their relative material interests) might hold contradictory positions on the best course of action, they are *not* fundamentally antagonistic to one another. Indeed, it is plausible to envision a democratic resolution to these contradictions, an agreement that the dam gets built but with modifications to limit its impact on fish stocks, along with replacement land acquired for the farmworkers, and additional aquaculture farms developed with the fisherfolk. The outcome isn't done *to* any of these agents, it's collectively done *by* them. This is a critical step for finding ways in which people might agree to biophysically necessary measures (like ending car dependency, shutting-off hydrocarbons, changing food habits, and so on) which would otherwise be resisted as an imposition on their lives.

Moreover, it is through such dialogue and deliberation that differences between subjects — which although starting from different relative positions (e.g. the wage worker, the unpaid carer), are nonetheless constructed, stratified, and mediated by capital in differing ways — can be reconciled. Instead of seeing one another in opposition, a *new* type of political subject is constituted, one which is shaped by and increasingly embodies this experience of acting in a common interest. To recall Louis Althusser's assertion that 'ideology exists in institutions and the practices specific to them', it is through these institutionally embedded processes of collective democratic deliberation that an altogether different ideology takes root, a new set of parameters about how we ought to act together in the world which have been *forged and negotiated through material relations of (re)production.*[19] As the Italian eco-feminist Stefania Barca reflects on the strategic challenges for degrowth advocates, 'what is missing to move forward with this common plan' of building a world of radical abundance 'is a clearer vision of what political subjects and which processes of political subjectivation can make it happen'.[20] Rather than appealing to an indeterminate 'general public' or searching for a structurally preordained subject such as 'the worker' who only needs to be mobilised, the challenge is to find processes through which we can build the political subject that we need. The answer to the question of 'who is the subject of change' is that it does not exist, but we are everywhere. The political subject of transition isn't out there waiting to be found; it is a subject that we must learn how to make by bringing together waged workers, unwaged workers, the oppressed, the exploited, and everyone else who is fed up with this miserable world of bullshit abundance.

FROM THE ABSTRACT TO THE CONCRETE

In this chapter we have presented the abstract form of a public-common partnership, emphasising how and why such an institution can make a critical contribution to the dynamics of transition. Yet this abstract form leaves many questions unanswered. In moving from abstract form to concrete reality, there are a whole series of practical and strategic challenges that must be addressed: Where do the resources come from to actually establish a productive Joint Enterprise? What sort of public authority is appropriate to involve? And why would they participate? Who is it that would actually initiate the creation of a PCP? Where does a Common Association come from, and who decides how it should make decisions? Why would someone join a Common Association? Must a Joint Enterprise get established *before* a Common Association? Or is it the other way round? What is the appropriate territory for a Common Association? How much surplus could realistically be produced? What legal forms can the Joint Enterprise take? And what about the legal form of a Common Association? What sort of 'popular protagonism' would a Common Association need to act on first? And so on.

The following chapters begin to answer some of these questions by exploring three very different PCP projects; a mixed-use market in North London, the pharmaceutical sector in France, and food production systems in England. As well as exploring how the dynamics of bullshit abundance operate in these three economic sectors, these chapters show how establishing PCPs might open the door to radical abundance. These cases are included in the book because of their differences, helping to demonstrate some of the diverse challenges and opportunities we've faced in our attempts to support the development of PCPs. They don't give conclusive answers, as the questions themselves will differ depending on the case, context, and conjuncture within which they're being developed. But the intention is to share some of the challenges and perspectives that we've worked through, helping you to think about what is involved in trying to establish a PCP where you live. Importantly they also highlight that while we have so far talked about transition as a global phenomenon of shifting from one social metabolism to another — from a world of bullshit abundance to one of radical abundance — the *shape* of this transition will not be the same across different sectors, geographies, and conjunctures.

6
Urban Development

In the summer of 2009, 15 people met in the Barcelona neighbourhood of La Bordeta and launched the Tic-Tac Can Batlló campaign. A former industrial complex, Can Batlló had been earmarked since 1976 for the provision of public facilities and a 4.7-hectare park but little progress had been made. And so, the campaign took the initiative and set their own arbitrary two-year timeline. The Tic-Tac in the campaign name refers to the ticking of a clock, a countdown to the 11 June 2011 deadline. If the transformation of the site remained blocked on that date, then the campaigners pledged to squat the site and socialise it directly. This countdown and pledging campaign allowed the movement to snowball, applying increasing pressure on the city council and the site's owners as the time ticked away. Large, colourful marches paraded through the city, while the words 'Tic-Tac Can Batlló', accompanied by the image of a clock, spread through the area on posters and paintings. The campaign proved both pedagogical and radicalising, with its demands shifting from simple public provision to self-managed community control. As the deadline approached, the initial 15 had grown to 2,500 local people pledging to occupy the site.

On 15 May 2011, just a month before the campaign's deadline, a huge social movement exploded into existence with massive demonstrations, occupations, and assemblies in city squares across Spain. Shaken by this display of widespread political unrest, the conservative Barcelona city council agreed that 'Block 11' of Can Batlló — a large warehouse complex — was to be handed over for community use. Beginning with the installation of a self-managed library, the Can Batlló collective gradually expanded to include a bar, social centre, auditorium, restaurant, brewery, community garden, food bank, sports facilities, a climbing wall, artistic spaces, a publishing house, and a print shop. It also houses the cooperative incubator Coòpolis and work spaces for carpentry, construction, and vehicle repair. In 2019, while the city was under the leadership of the new municipalist party Barcelona en Comu, the city council formalised the project through a 50-year right of use contract. The city council also committed to covering the annual utility bills for the site, whilst providing further financial resources for the community-led renovation of the buildings. In early 2024, the site expanded to include a renovated former warehouse known as 'Block 4', which is now an impressive cooperative development hub.

Close by and emerging out of Can Batlló is the now famous housing cooperative La Borda, which developed a new model of housing and inspired a series of other housing developments. The construction of La Borda started in 2016, with residents moving into their apartments in 2020. Before 2016, there were fewer than 45 cooperative housing apartments in Catalonia. By 2022 that number had jumped to 259, with a further 571 in construction. These are linked together in a network of mutual support, along with other solidarity economy projects called Xarxa d'Economia Solidaria (XES). La Borda follows a public-common model of collective ownership in which the land remains in public hands but guaranteed rights of use are granted to the cooperative and its members. Applicants must qualify for social housing before they can apply for cooperative membership. Once membership is granted, they must participate in the governance and management of the building while also feeding into the expansion of the commons through the XES and similar networks. This cooperative ethos is built into the very architecture of the building. Individual or family living spaces have been made smaller to facilitate large amounts of shared space, such as laundry rooms, dining space, collective offices, multi-use meeting rooms, and play areas.

Can Batlló and La Borda show how the commons can expand not just geographically but also to cover ever greater areas of social reproduction, removing them from the direct control of capital. The achievements may be humble, and the barriers to expanding social property in housing are manifold, but it is a working example of the contested reproduction of urban space, illustrating a strategic approach to contesting the dominant model of urban development in a city plagued by skyrocketing housing costs. In this chapter, we contrast this model of urban development with the extractive bullshit urban development we are so used to seeing, before looking at detailed plans for turning a 20-year struggle over the redevelopment of a mixed-use market in North London into a PCP with ambitions that match Barcelona's experiments.

URBAN BULLSHIT

The dialectical pairing of bullshit abundance and artificial scarcity in urban development should be easy to grasp as most of us experience it viscerally on a daily basis. For centuries, wealth has poured into core cities while being extracted from the rural and peri-urban periphery. In both the US and the UK, for example, the process of deindustrialisation has structurally underdeveloped large swathes of the country with poor-quality jobs, shuttered high streets, and a deteriorating housing stock since the mid-1970s. The same process has underdeveloped non-urban spaces to such an extent that, in the United States, non-urban residents are at a greater risk of death from a host of factors including heart disease, unintentional injuries, COPD, lung cancer, stroke, suicide, and diabetes. Even after adjusting for relative poverty levels, residents in urban areas experienced larger mortality reductions during the past four decades than non-urban residents, contributing to a widening gap.[1]

At the same time, especially in the centres of major cities such as London, Manchester, Chicago, or New York, we see glass towers proliferate — the very image of urban bullshit. Yet, this combined but uneven spatial development also takes place within cities, between richer and poorer areas, and also, most importantly, between richer and poorer segments of the population, as developments aimed at bullshit abundance displace poorer communities through processes of gentrification.[2] As economies of the core countries deindustrialised, urban development and housing took on an entirely new importance for capital. Whereas buildings had historically been developed to facilitate the extraction of surplus value from the work done *within* construction yards, workshops, and department stores, the process of urban development *itself* became the dominant process for realising profit. It was the buildings themselves, and the built landscape they created, that became the primary source of wealth extraction, not whatever work might be done inside them. Both a major driver and symptom of the wider dynamic of financialisation, urban development — now talked of as a sector — displays all the symptoms of deindustrialised secular stagnation: domination by oligopolies, rentier business models, massive inequality, and the assetisation of key aspects of social reproduction. We have a scarcity of libraries, public space, and the other infrastructure needed for a vibrant urban culture. Instead, cities are inundated with 'luxury' apartments that promise the biggest asset price appreciation, or purpose-built student accommodation (PBSA) which, with less stringent building regulations, can be built smaller and to lower standards. Contemporary urban development produces bullshit results because consideration of local, existing needs rarely takes priority. It's driven instead by the imperative to maximise profits through asset appreciation and rental income.

At one end of the bullshit continuum, we see luxury developments bought or constructed purely for asset appreciation and consequently left unoccupied. These so-called 'buy to leave' developments are exemplified by One Kensington Gardens, a nine-storey, 500,000-square foot, luxury apartment building on Kensington High Street, London. It has a gym, swimming pool, sauna, and valet parking. Flats there cost from £6 million to £30 million. Yet, in the evenings there's rarely a light to be seen in the whole building. Most flats are either unoccupied or used just a few weeks of the year. They function primarily not as housing but as a safe store for the wealth of the global elite. The practice pushes up local house prices, further incentivising similar developments, with the local population getting little in return. The Abu Dhabi consortium who developed the building in the early 2010s were required by the local council to provide 48 units of off-site affordable housing. That number is deeply inadequate when the borough has 2,300 residents living in temporary accommodation and 3,500 households on the social housing waiting list.[3] Such ultra high-end, luxury developments are comparatively rare, but they illustrate *in extremis* the wider problems of treating housing as an asset rather than a place to live.

The assetisation of housing has, as we saw in Chapter Four, delinked house prices from wage levels. In the United States, the average price-to-income ratio on buying a home has increased by 57 percent since 1990, with many cities far outstripping the average, including Boulder, Colorado (150 percent), Tucson, Arizona (94 percent), and Seattle (93 percent). In nearly half of all US metropolitan areas, you now need an annual salary of over $100,000 to afford a median-priced home.[4] The average annual salary is $59,428. The same is found in the UK: 20 years ago, a British household on an average income could afford an averagely priced house; now it can afford only the cheapest 10 percent of houses.[5]

What average figures hide is an underlying geographical inequality, which further exacerbates the problem. Cheap homes tend to be in areas with the fewest well-paying jobs, leaving young people in a catch-22 situation. They are trapped into either the private rental sector, or, in cases where this is possible, into living with their parents. The rising costs of housing in Spain has further exacerbated a European-leading trend, with 64 percent of 25 to 29-year olds still living with their parents, though it should be noted that this is traditionally more culturally accepted in Spain than the UK.[6] In the UK the figure is around 30 percent, with 700,000 joining their ranks over the last decade.[7] At the same time, the cost of private renting is unprecedentedly high, rising 60 percent faster than wages between just 2011 and 2017. In the 1950s and 1960s, UK renters spent just 10 percent of their income on housing, by 2016 this had risen to 36 percent.[8] The individual and social consequences have been severe. Many key workers such as teachers, nurses, and social care assistants find it impossible to live anywhere near their places of work. High rents make it difficult to save for a deposit, locking out an ever-growing segment of the population from home ownership. Increasingly, some form of inheritance is needed to secure a foot on the housing ladder. The dynastic dynamics that follow from this, in which access to familial wealth can be more important in determining life outcome than income from the work you do, undermine ideas of merit which for several decades have been the key mode of legitimation for the inequalities we see around us.[9]

Conventional economic wisdom blames a simple lack of housing units for high rents and house prices, arguing simplistically that the problem is one of supply and demand. Ezra Klein and Derek Thompson's liberal version of the 'abundance agenda', for example, mirrors the YIMBY (Yes In My Backyard) lobby in the US and UK by arguing that it is planning 'red tape' that's holding back development.[10] Yet, keeping with the UK example, Brett Christophers has detailed how, in 2015, Britain's four biggest housebuilders had already hoarded enough land to build 450,000 units, while more than 475,000 successful residential planning permissions had been left unimplemented.[11] By 2022, the number of plots banked by the big developers had soared to 918,823. With that number, they could keep building houses at their current rate until 2040, even if no new plots were acquired or planning permissions gained.[12] The real constriction on house building is the drive to maximise profitability. Private developers intentionally produce an artificial scarcity of new housing by strangling the pace of development to what's called the 'optimum absorption rate' — the rate at which newly constructed homes can be sold into the housing market without bringing down prices.

At the same time, what gets built is often, to be blunt, shit and getting shitter. UK homes have been decreasing in size since the 1970s as developers maximise the number of properties on each piece of land.[13] As a result, the average amount of living space has reduced by a quarter over 50 years, and those houses are built 'using inferior materials'.[14] More than 50 percent of purchasers complain that their new builds suffer from 'major problems'.[15] They then face significant difficulties getting them fixed.[16] Standards in the private rental sector are even worse. A quarter of privately rented homes are rated 'non-decent', while 14 percent are classed as 'below minimum standards', which means they contain 'a hazard that can cause death, or that otherwise poses a serious and immediate risk to human health and safety.'[17] Like many other contemporary markets, construction in the UK is dominated by a handful of large firms. Until recently, just ten companies built more than half of the new homes. Now that number has consolidated down to six.[18] This oligopoly, assisted by permissive and poorly enforced regulation, creates little incentive to produce good-quality homes, yet the companies' owners and executives are handsomely rewarded.

Before 2008, an average UK home netted big housing developers around £30,000 in pre-tax profits. Just ten years later, this had risen to £62,000, and profitability has only boomed since.[19] Between 2010 and 2022, the profits of the UK house building firm Persimmon, for example, quadrupled. In 2018, their CEO Jeff Fairburn was awarded a bonus of £82 million, among the largest in British corporate history. Yet, those increased profits weren't the result of rising productivity, which has been essentially flat in the construction sector since 1994. Fairburn was simply the beneficiary of government derisking in the form of the disastrous 'help to buy' subsidy scheme introduced in 2013. Given this level of oligopolistic rent extraction, it's unsurprising that the large asset management firms are moving in, leading to an increasing concentration of ownership. Already just three big investment managers (Legal and General, Vanguard Group, and Norges) have the largest shareholdings in eight out of the nine biggest housebuilders. At the same time, the aforementioned problems of housing affordability and quality have been compounded by the development of housing as an asset for large institutional lenders and asset managers. Indeed, the world's largest institutional landlord is the asset management firm Blackstone, which was once part of BlackRock, the world's largest asset management company.

This development is accelerating the worst trends of the financialisation of housing. As the work of Daniela Gabor and Sebastian Kohl makes clear: 'the presence of transnational investors such as Blackstone have been associated with evictions, rental overburdens and housing shortages.'[20] As the primary clients of institutional landlords are its shareholders rather than the tenants, the housing itself becomes entirely incidental to its operation. Indeed, the German investor Deutsche Wohnen, which is one of the targets of the Berlin socialisation campaign discussed in Chapter Three, emphasised in their 2018 annual report a commitment to 'measures with rent increasing potential', a euphemism for terminating rental contracts, displacing tenants, and cutting maintenance expenses.[21] It's a dynamic that's likely to grow for a number of reasons. Institutional investors can use their scale to buy up large volumes of property during the collapse of housing bubbles. They can afford to finance new 'buy to let' projects, often borrowing against already acquired housing assets in a self-reinforcing cycle. Most importantly they can lobby on a city, regional, national, or even continental level for governments to derisk their investments both directly, through public-private partnerships, and indirectly, through regulatory change. As in so many other areas of the economy, the dysfunction of urban development is accelerating into a crisis.

HOW TO THINK LIKE AN ASSET

The transformation of housing and urban development over the last 40 years has, in part, been the result of a deliberate political project not just to remake the sector, but to create new political subjects by changing how people see their place in wider society. The project predates the 1980s. Already in the 1920s, conservatives were responding to universal suffrage with proposals for a 'property-owning democracy' to counter the forms of collective property advocated by socialists. Conservative writers, such as Noel Skelton, argued democracy could be 'stabilised' if enough people bought their homes and took on the perspective of individual property owners rather than collective workers.[22] That project was constrained during the years of the post-war settlement and then redoubled as neoliberalism was imposed. Let's take the UK as a detailed example, in 1971 while half of homes were owner-occupied, around one-third were social housing, owned by the local authority. By 2023, the social rented sector had been cut almost in half to just 16 percent of the total, while owner-occupation had risen to 65 percent. This transformation took a concerted programme of regulatory and institutional reform to bring about.

Although what would come to be called neoliberal policies were first introduced into the UK as a stipulation of an IMF government bailout in 1976, the key moment in the transformation of UK housing came shortly after the 1979 election of the Conservative prime minister Margaret Thatcher. The 1980 Housing Act established the right of council tenants to buy their homes from the local authority, provided they had lived there for a minimum of three years. Under the 'right to buy' scheme, residents were incentivised to buy through considerable discounts, 33 percent below market value if they had lived there for three years, rising by 1 percent for each additional year of tenancy up to a maximum of 50 percent. As 1.5 million publicly owned homes, worth £40 billion, were sold off in the first 25 years, this represented a huge privatisation of the social wealth built up through the post-war years.[23] While the policy benefited one generation of council tenants, it was designed to impose an artificial scarcity of social housing over all. Local authorities were effectively forced to hand over the income from 'right to buy' sales to central government rather than use it to build new stock. This policy heavily disincentivised building council houses, and yet councils retained a statutory duty to house eligible households with priority needs. As the social housing stock declined, councils were forced to house people in the private rental sector. With 41 percent of council homes sold under the right to buy scheme and now often being let on the private market, this means councils are paying vastly inflated 'market' rents to private landlords for housing that the council previously owned.[24] The cost of housing benefit, which is a direct public subsidy to private landlords, currently sits at around £22 billion a year, double what it was in the early 2000s.

The other side of the embedding of asset logics was addressed through the 1988 Housing Act, which massively reduced the rights of renters and set the legal framework for the rise of the private rental sector, which increased from just 9.3 percent of households in 1991 to 19 percent today.[25] Not only did the act abolish rent controls, it also introduced assured shorthold tenancies, which guarantee the right of landlords to evict tenants without cause at the end of, often yearly, tenancy agreements. With the increased opportunities for rent rises, and the weakened ability of renters to assert their legal rights, renting in the UK became expensive, insecure, and transitory. This made owning rental properties more financially attractive, increasing demand for housing.

Beginning in the late 1990s, the huge increase in asset prices primarily benefited the generations who owned property before that period. Indeed, during the early 2000s, 17 percent of working-age adults earned more from the increase in their house prices than they made from their income from work.[26] As that generation retired, or came close to it, their material interests became more closely linked to the performance of the financial and real estate sectors than to the level of wages. As many bought properties to rent as a means of securing retirement income, the adoption of what we might call rentier subjectivities became even more pronounced. Now 59 percent of private landlords are 55 or older, while one in three are retired.[27] These material interests are clearly reflected in political behaviour, with older homeowners far more likely to vote for right-wing parties than younger cohorts, or indeed non-home owning pensioners.[28]

It's not just voters who have been inculcated into adopting the logic of assets. The huge extra costs imposed on local authorities by the 'right to buy' programme is part of a series of measures forcing council budgets into artificial scarcity. Council income has been restricted for 30 years by the continued use of 1991 property values as the basis for local property taxes. The 2003 Local Government Act hamstrung councils by making it illegal for them to run a deficit. Then from 2010 a regime of severe austerity has been imposed on local government with cuts of almost 50 percent in central government funding.[29] These huge constraints on council budgets have provoked a massive sell-off of public land and assets. A report from the IPPR think tank estimated that '75,000 council assets, including buildings and land, at an approximate asset value of £15 billion' had been sold off since 2010.[30] Most of this newly enclosed land has been captured by developers, often through public-private partnerships in which the local authority facilitates and derisks the plans of the big developers through huge discounts on assets, sometimes amounting to virtual or actual giveaways.

THE HALFWAY HOUSE FOR HOUSING

While the shift towards a derisking state is primarily focused on industrial policy, there's also a significant role assigned to urban development, as the agglomerative effects of bringing people together can improve productivity by, for instance, building housing closer to sources of work and reducing commuting times. The incumbent UK Labour government, for example, has pledged to build 1.5 million new houses during its five-year parliament. These plans include the creation of four new towns, the first in the UK since the 1970s, and a promise of the 'biggest boost to social and affordable housing in a generation'.[31] True to the formulae of 'homoeopathic Bidenomics' discussed in Chapter Four, the amount of public money promised to this end isn't substantial. The focus is instead on regulatory derisking, reforming the planning system to make life easier for the big developers. In this, it's similar to the liberal 'abundance agenda' in the US.

Building will be encouraged on previously used land known as 'brownfield' sites, but restrictions will also be relaxed on building on previously protected low-quality green land (now reclassified as the 'grey belt'). The stated aim is for half the homes built on such sites to be 'affordable', classified by the government as 80 percent or less of the market price. This will likely be much higher than the house price ratio of five times average annual earnings, the indicator of housing affordability used in government statistics. There will, however, be no new money for the Affordable Homes Programme and rather than abolishing the disastrous 'right to buy' law, Labour are merely allowing councils to keep the receipts. The Labour government is relying on the big developers to build the new homes and towns, and on the asset management firms to build the infrastructure that will service them.

The difficulties faced by such a strategy are manifold. Most obviously, there is little incentive for private developers to increase the rate of house-building. Even the UK's Competition and Market Authority accept that the optimum absorption rate (mentioned above) dictates the pace of private development, not the lack of available building plots with planning permission.[32] And the chances of them building 50 percent affordable housing are even slimmer. In 2018, for example, the large house-building group Berkeley was found to have secured reductions in their required affordable housing quotas in 93 percent of their London developments.[33] So, the UK government's plans to address the housing crisis through derisking the big developers is unlikely to work on its own terms, but it's worse than that: their diagnosis of the problem is so wrong, they might end up exacerbating the real causes rather than addressing them.

The economist Josh Ryan-Collins, among many others, convincingly argues that the financialisation of housing, specifically the increase in available mortgage credit, has contributed most significantly to the explosion of house prices. As he explains, 'in the last 20 years... real house prices have increased by 50%. During that same period, real average incomes have flatlined — but mortgage credit has risen exponentially. There is a clear correlation between the two variables since the 1990s.'[34] The financial deregulation of the 1980s triggered this dynamic, with mortgage credit rising from just 20 percent of GDP in the late 1970s to 55 percent a decade later. The OECD estimates that between 1980 and 2005, mortgage credit expansion increased house prices by 30 percent. Meanwhile, a later IMF study found that 'a 10% increase in household credit leads to a 6% increase in nominal average house prices.'[35]

Failing to address the financialisation of housing and relying on asset managers to deliver infrastructure and housing is almost certain to accelerate the dysfunctional form of urban development with which we are now familiar. Deregulating planning laws will lead to the further expansion of low-quality, cookie-cutter developments which fit the needs of developers rather than local communities. Instead of producing a diverse urban life that guarantees the space for many different social and cultural needs — from day-care centres, greenspace, and markets to music venues and hardware stores — the assetisation of housing is driving processes of cultural and social sterilisation. But these developments will also lead to an explosion of anti-gentrification campaigns and similar struggles as communities seek to assert their interests. For such campaigns to be successful, it is typically never enough to just oppose this process of urban development. At a certain point, there is a need to produce alternative plans, contesting a form of urban development mediated by capital and furthering a strategy that emphasises communal forms of urban development. In the next section, we will trace one such approach in the community struggle around a mixed-use market at Wards Corner in Tottenham, North London, which led to the proposition of a public-common partnership model to first develop the site and then democratically plan the development of the local area.

THE ROAD TO RADICAL URBAN ABUNDANCE

Opened as an Edwardian department store and row of residential terraces in 1901, the Wards Corner buildings sit at the busy intersection and railway station at Seven Sisters Junction in Tottenham, Haringey. The department store closed just three years after the opening of the Victoria underground line in 1969, while the freehold of the land was acquired by Transport for London (TfL) via a Compulsory Purchase Order in 1973. TfL's long-term interest in the site reflects its concern with the structural integrity of the surrounding transport infrastructure, including the Victoria line, which runs directly underneath Wards Corner. The building sat disused for more than a decade, until 1985, when TfL began leasing the ground floor to independent operators, leading to its development into an indoor market. Initially serving the local Afro-Caribbean community, the market became increasingly important for Latin American traders and customers, becoming established as a significant cultural site for the wider diaspora. The market grew organically, based around people's needs for services, goods, and social contact. Filled with cafes, grocers, butchers, beauty salons, money exchange services and clothes shops, it also played a critical role in supporting newly arrived people with legal and immigration support and translation services. The market, with its constant hubbub of conversation, became a vibrant community hub known locally as the Latin Village.

The Wards Corner site (along with an adjacent council office building and the Seven Sisters underground station) was earmarked by Haringey council for redevelopment in 2003 with a stated vision of creating 'a landmark development that acts as a high quality gateway to Seven Sisters'.[36] In 2007, a development agreement was signed between Haringey council and the UK-based developer Grainger PLC, followed in 2012 by the granting of planning permission for Grainger's proposed redevelopment. In 2015, the local authority approved the use of a Compulsory Purchase Order (CPO) to acquire the property interests for the development, which includes the Wards Corner buildings, along with the residential and commercial properties linked to it.

Grainger's plans — which included 196 build-to-rent flats and commercial restaurant and retail units, alongside a smaller replacement market — were opposed from the outset by many of the market traders, local businesses, and community groups. The threat that Grainger's development plans posed to this community was underlined by a 2017 review by the UNHRC (United Nations Human Rights Council), which condemned the plans on the basis that 'the destruction of the market and scattering of the small businesses to other premises would not only seriously affect the economic situation of the people working there, but it would also make this cultural life simply disappear'.[37] Grainger's development plans typified the bullshit model of urban development, riding roughshod over the needs and desires of existing residents, fuelling wider gentrification, and ensuring that profits get extracted out of the area.

Just as the council understood the site as a 'gateway to Seven Sisters', a coalition of community actors, primarily the market's traders, along with community groups and anti-gentrification campaigners, saw the potential for Wards Corner to act as the nucleus of a broader community-led and community-owned revitalisation of the area. Starting in 2008, this coalition of actors formed a constellation of campaign groups, including the Wards Corner Community Coalition and the West Green Road / Seven Sisters Development

Trust, which led the iterative development of four alternative community plans, each building on the previous one. The fourth plan sets out to restore the three-storey steel-frame building, revitalising and expanding the market across the ground floor and vacant upper storeys, adding around 400 square metres of office space and introducing two new community spaces totalling 235 square meters. The application also incorporated a detailed business plan that forecast an £880,000 annual turnover for the market alone and included a housing study that demonstrated the potential for between 52 and 120 socially-owned housing units that could feature as part of a longer-term development of the wider site. While the plan did not set out details of its ownership model, it explicitly framed this development as part of 'new approaches to community wealth building and bottom-up local economic development'.[38] The plan received planning permission in November 2019, demonstrating the feasibility of the community-led alternative, although it can't be put into practice without control of the site.

Despite a crowdfunded legal challenge led by the Seven Sisters Market Traders Association, the local authority compulsory purchase order (CPO) was approved by the Secretary of State in October 2019, marking what looked like the end of more than 15 years of campaigning. The campaign though refused to give in. They redoubled their efforts, meeting with and lobbying the mayor of London. Then, on 7 April 2021, over 12 months after the UK entered its first Covid-19 lockdown, Grainger PLC wrote to all the market traders informing them that 'an in-depth review of the wider Seven Sisters regeneration project... has identified significant challenges to the project's viability'.[39] In August 2021, Grainger formally withdrew from the development, handing a significant victory to local people and leaving the Community Plan as the only credible proposal on the table for the redevelopment of Wards Corner.

In 2019, we were invited by the campaign to fill out the general commitment to a PCP and bottom-up local economic development that the Community Plan already contained, into a more detailed, place-specific model for the governance of the site in its relation to the wider development of the area. Following a process of interviews

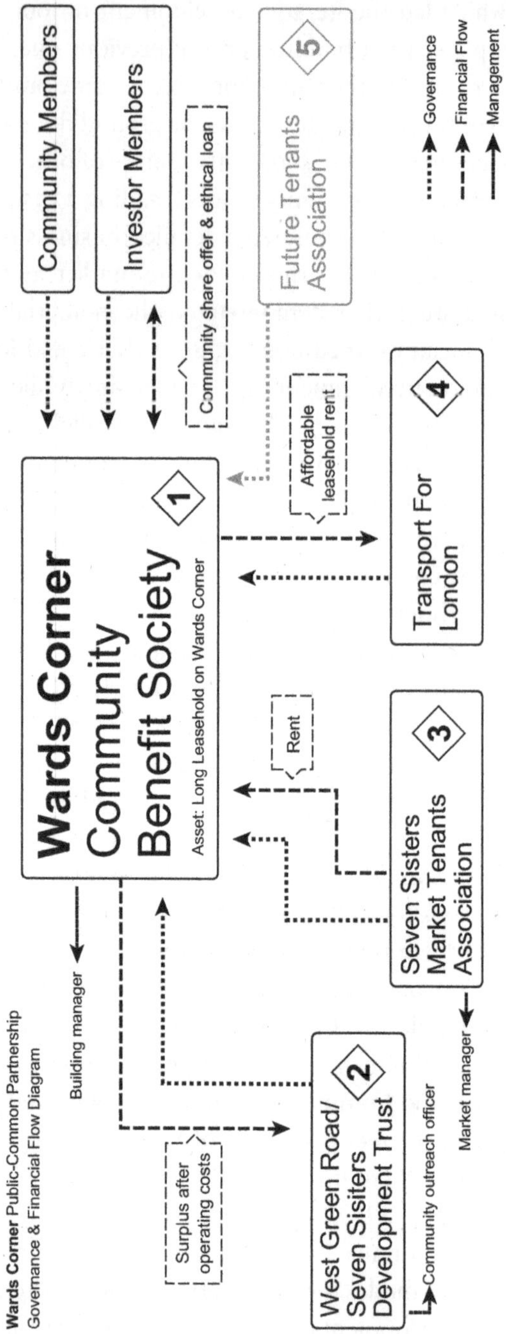
Wards Corner Public-Common Partnership
Governance & Financial Flow Diagram
Community Members
Investor Members
Community share offer & ethical loan
Future Tenants Association
5
Governance
Financial Flow
Management
Wards Corner Community Benefit Society
1
Asset: Long Leasehold on Wards Corner
Affordable leasehold rent
Transport For London
4
Rent
Seven Sisters Market Tenants Association
3
Market manager
Building manager
Surplus after operating costs
West Green Road/ Seven Sisiters Development Trust
2
Community outreach officer

Figure 3 Wards Corner Public-Common Partnership Model

1. The Community Benefit Society (CBS) will be established by the West Green/Seven Sisters Development Trust. The CBS will be responsible for the overall governance of the Wards Corner site and will act as the leaseholder. A CBS is governed by a board that can have different membership types, each of which have different voting rights and obligations. We anticipate this board may represent:

A. local residents and users of Wards Corner and the town centre (community members);
B. investors (i.e. ethical loans and the community share offer);
C. market-traders, other tenants and businesses in the wider town centre;
D. West Green Road/Seven Sisters development trust;
E. TFL.

2. The West Green Road/Seven Sisters Development Trust is a registered charity. The Trust receives any surplus after operating costs from the CBS. The Trust's aim is to enable the CBS to fulfil its commitment to a wider community benefit. We anticipate that this includes the participatory allocation of resources in supporting the wider community redevelopment of the West Green Road/Seven Sisters neighbourhood.

3. The Seven Sisters Market Tenants Association is the representative body for the Wards Corner market traders. The association will lease the market space within the restored building, and be responsible for the affairs of the market, including the appointment of the market manager.

4. TFL retains the freehold on the Wards Corner site. The membership type will ensure that TFL can attend to their interests and concerns around the infrastructure of the site.

5. The Future Tenants Association allows for the participation of future tenants that may arise in the further development of the Wards Corner site, e.g. community nursery, office users, residents.

and discussions with key actors, including the board members of the West Green Road / Seven Sisters Development Trust, and attendance at meetings between the Trust and TfL, we drew up an initial diagram of the governance and financial flows for the proposed Wards Corner PCP. This went through a series of iterations in consultation with the Trust. The report and proposal we produced through our research included a version of the diagram reproduced as Figure 3.[40]

At the core of the Wards Corner public-common partnership is the Wards Corner Community Benefit Society (BenCom). Introduced in the 2014 Co-operative and Community Benefit Societies Act, BenComs provide a model of ownership in which the use of assets or 'a business, industry or trade' must be 'conducted for the benefit of the community'. By carefully defining that community benefit, we can ensure that the BenCom maintains its key purpose of establishing the Wards Corner building as a community-controlled asset that functions as the motor of a wider democratic revitalisation of the local area.

A BenCom has a democratic membership-based structure, and Wards Corner BenCom is composed of five different membership share types: Community Members, Investor Members, Transport for London, the Seven Sisters Market Tenants Association (SSMTA), and West Green Road/Seven Sisters Development Trust (the Trust). Eligibility for each kind of share is defined by the rules of the BenCom, and each shareholder member has a single vote regardless of how many shares they own, a rule known as 'one member, one vote'. For example, Community Member shares (typically available for £1) may be made available to anyone that lives within a defined geography, such as a postcode or combination of electoral wards. Likewise, the SSMTA would access shares exclusively for market traders, and so on. On an annual basis, shareholders elect a specified number of representatives for their share type to the board. This approach ensures that specified types of interest, from community members to market traders, are always represented on the board. The membership types in a BenCom can be assigned different rights and obligations. For instance, TfL's primary interests could be guaranteed via decision-making powers over the infrastructure of the site, ensuring it fulfils its statutory responsibility to maintain transport-adjacent infrastructure. In return, it is proposed that otherwise hard to access ethical loans to support the redevelopment be facilitated through TfL acting as loan guarantor. TfL as a quasi-public body would in effect be derisking the common ownership of the asset.

In this model, the Trust pre-exists and creates the BenCom but then aims, through a process of community organising, to build its membership. It evolves to become the participatory democratic body that enables local community members to have a direct say in how the surplus produced by a redeveloped Wards Corner should be used in the regeneration of their local area. As the Trust is the recipient of the BenCom's surplus after operating costs and debt servicing, the decisions the Trust takes receive a certain level of insulation from the mediating effects of finance capital, allowing a different logic of development to take place. In addition, the Trust is free to follow the community's own mode and temporality of decision-making because the interface with other interests and institutional logics is conducted in a separate body, the BenCom.

The Trust's ambitions don't stop at the Wards Corner site. It is anticipated that the surplus will be used to finance new PCPs in the wider local area. The surpluses after operating costs of those PCPs would also feed back into the Trust, producing a self-expansive dynamic for the extension of economic democracy. In this way, the Wards Corner PCP forms a potential nucleus of an alternative model of development of the whole area which would attend to the needs of residents rather than financial interests. The Trust would develop a common plan for the local area using the tools of participative, democratic planning. As Haringey council have their own neighbourhood plan, the Trust's common plan would have to be drawn up in negotiation with it, but for once the community would have the unity of vision and material force that developers enjoy in their negotiations with public bodies. The Trust would not only enjoy the legitimacy produced by its democratic practice, but also the legal rights gained from its control of assets.

The project of building public-common partnerships is primarily political in nature. It involves campaigning, community organising, and lobbying, but it also entails a more technical element of institutional design. The act defining BenComs was passed by the Conservative and Liberal Democrat coalition government as part of their Big Society programme, which was rhetorically paired with the 'small state' they sought to bring into being through severe cuts to public spending. Our use of BenComs puts them to new purposes beyond, and even against, the intentions of their originators. In this we can see similarities with other examples of 'hacking' and repurposing existing legislation to create space for the composition of new political forces, such as the Deutsche Wohnen & Co. Enteignen campaign's use of Article 15 of the German constitution to socialise Berlin's housing. Such legal activism requires a reflexive understanding of the law, aiming to hack existing legal and political procedures with the aim of building popular protagonism and opportunities for contested reproduction.

The public-commons partnership model outlined here has been largely adopted by the Wards Corner Community Benefit Society, the BenCom which will take the development forwards. In 2024, TfL invited community-led bids for the Wards Corner Site and, in a significant step forward for the Community Plan, has begun partnership discussions with the Wards Corner Community Benefit Society. As the only operative plan in place for the site, there is growing optimism amongst campaigners that the Community Plan will be delivered. But new models of ownership are always an outcome of, and shaped by, the struggles that surround their implementation. As the hitherto contested history of the Wards Corner site shows, the realisation of the Community Plan isn't a predetermined outcome, and the continued development and composition of an active and visible community will likely be essential to its viability.

HOW TO THINK LIKE A COMMONER

The neoliberal reform of housing and urban development wasn't only about who gets to own and profit from assets. It was also a project to form new political subjects by extending asset ownership or otherwise inducing people to adopt the logic of private assets, ultimately providing the basis for a political alliance of the highly differentiated asset-owning classes. Similarly, the project of developing popular protagonism isn't only about extending forms of community control and contesting the ownership of resources, it also aims to forge collective democratic subjects through their participation in the governance of commonly owned assets. When people collectively deliberate over how to spend the surpluses produced by PCPs, and when they engage in the democratic planning of how they would like their local area to develop, they're generating their own collective modes of valuing, and so prioritising, activity. Participating in these processes acts as a training in the logic of common ownership, a training in the democratic practices of commoning, a training in democracy itself. This is what Stuart Hall would call 'the deepening of democratic life. Without the deepening of popular participation... ordinary people don't have any experience of actually running anything. We need to re-acquire the notion that politics is about expanding popular capacities, the capacities of ordinary people.'[41] This is, of course, far from straightforward. Communities capable of popular protagonism aren't given, they're built. Our wager is that commonly owned assets can be the infrastructure around which this happens.

Communities are made up of people with different material interests. Most obviously, in terms of urban development the interests of homeowners can be in serious tension with those of renters. But as we've already seen, this division of interest was engineered through political and economic interventions. Material interests aren't just given, they're partly formed. Indeed, we always have multiple potential interests, some of which may even be contradictory. These different sets of interests are, as Jeremy Gilbert and Alex Williams argue, linked to different 'horizons of realisability', they're 'operable, expressible and realisable at different temporal and spatial scales.'[42] Any assessment of what's in your interest necessarily includes, for instance, a conception of probable futures, the future in which those interests will be enacted. The speculative logic of assets is also temporal, acting to pre-empt and shape future possibilities and life courses. They operate as though they are, for all intents and purposes, given, yet the brute facts of climate change means that over the medium term, the future around which those assets are oriented is largely illusory. It's this disjunction between the logics that animate the institutions we interact with and the scientific consensus on global heating that drives climate denialism, but it also offers up the possibility of breaking with those logics and embracing new ones. The practice of commoning, the collective governing of common assets and resources, is precisely the difficult process of constructing common interests.

The struggle over the Latin Village market illustrates how this can work. The campaign around the Wards Corner site was initiated by the market traders whose interests were most directly impacted. They took the leading role in defeating the plans for a gentrifying redevelopment of the site. It was their organisation, the SSMTA, for instance, that organised legal challenges to Grainger's plans. But as the struggle moved to include more of a propositional mode, through development of alternative community plans of the site, the interests of the market traders had to come into conversation with different interests in the local community. Fortunately, many of the traders carried an inheritance of Latin American community organising traditions, which helped promote a participative democratic ethos. The participative process through which the Community Plan was developed included not just traditional door knocking, but also public workshops in which members of the local community discussed how a potential surplus from the market could be deployed in the local area.

We can see the same process from a slightly different register if we shift focus from material interests to the closely related category of class. Class is also often conceived as something given, rather than formed. Indeed, in popular discourse it is often seen as a form of inheritance, of cultural markers developed through your upbringing. For a more coherent and useful conception of class, we can look to theorists who see class formation as a discontinuous process of organisation and disorganisation, a process that happens in fits and starts. Adam Przeworski, for instance, argues that 'concrete analysis is incompatible with the view of classes as economically determined, spontaneously emerging subjects... Classes form as effects of struggles', and, to go further, 'as classes struggle they transform the conditions under which classes are formed.'[43] Class then is something that retains a link to material interests and 'objective conditions', rooted in the way capital shapes and constricts our lives, but it is also shaped by struggle. Class formation is a process into which we can intervene through the building of institutions or 'collectivities-in-struggle', such as 'unions and electoral parties' but also 'cooperatives, clubs, intellectual circles, neighborhood associations, and so on.'[44] That doesn't mean the objective conditions of capitalist development can be ignored but, as Przeworski argues 'objective conditions appear to historical actors as structures of choices, as realms of possibility and impossibility.'[45] Some courses of action seem more possible or less possible based on concrete, everyday experiences of work and life, as well as operative conceptions of what the future might look like.

We can look once again to the case of Wards Corner and the central role played by the market traders. While an assessment of the traders' class position must include the migrant backgrounds many share, their material interests are also structured by their experiences as sole traders or small business people. Classically, this type of work would lead to categorisation as members of the petty bourgeoisie, who historically have been a frequent source of right-wing politics. The material interests of the petty bourgeoisie have traditionally been shaped by the anxious position of dependency on making sufficient profits to survive, if not grow, while being in a powerless position relative to big capital. It's also a form of work that tends to lack moments of collectivity, as people are forced to face economic problems as individuals or family units. Participation in a PCP adds not just the logic of collective rather than private property, but also allows for collective responses to shared problems. The SSMTA, for instance, retains firm control over the affairs of the market by appointing and overseeing the market manager. The wider Wards Corner PCP also acts as the arena through which class alliances are formed, as market traders act in concert with the (predominantly) working-class users of the market and other residents of the local area. Building institutions for collective action to facilitate the constitution of collective subjects could have huge impacts far beyond the ranks of the traditional petty bourgeoisie; it must be applied, for instance, to the growing ranks of the self-employed who are increasingly subject to individualised contact with managerial apps.

We can theorise the best methods for creating new political subjects through common ownership, but ultimately this must be worked out in practice. Using surpluses to build networks of PCPs, addressing ever greater areas of social reproduction in a local area will teach us the necessary techniques and capabilities needed for participative democratic planning. The strategic promise of urban development PCPs, like Wards Corner, is that by acting as the cell-form for building popular protagonism in a locality, they could have both exploratory and exemplary effects. In this we can learn once again from the neoliberal project that we wish to unwind. In the UK, urban development projects played a key role in making neo-liberal ideas hegemonic through the creation of exemplary enclaves called enterprise zones, with London Docklands as the most famous example. These operated under different economic principles to the rest of the economy. Indeed, neoliberal planners also pioneered new anti-democratic institutions to create and coordinate these zones, Urban Development Corporations for example.[46] Urban development PCPs can play a mirror role, pioneering the techniques of democratic economic coordination and planning, building new institutions to coordinate this activity, while providing proof of the concept to inspire others along a similar path.

None of this, of course, will be plain sailing. Even when they are fully functioning, PCPs won't be the only institution that participants engage with, so identification with those common interests will be far from automatic. Participation will, however, create moments of shared lived experience on which particular political narratives, framings, and conceptions of the future, can be anchored and thus become more intelligible and convincing. As we've already made clear, the full transformative potential of PCPs can only be fully realised as part of a much wider transitional and hegemonic project.

There are a number of ways that those wider projects could develop. In the US, for example, we could imagine a strategy of building bases of local power in response to right-wing Republican dominance of the federal level. The self-expansion of commonly owned assets in a locality, building a density of overlapping projects and struggles, could pair well with an electoral wing aiming to build on and facilitate the democratisation of the local economy. The building of popular protagonism would need to be rigorously prioritised in this strategy if the tensions between the two sides are to be navigated, and, as the experience in Jackson discussed in Chapter Three suggests, when and how to engage with electoral institutions must be a question of ongoing strategic assessment. A key problem here is often the lack of capacity in a hollowed-out state sector, but the dynamic of re-democratisation could also affect public bodies, that, through both participation in the governance of PCPs and negotiation over common plans for local areas, would need to engage urban development through the problems and perspective of common ownership. We can glimpse how this works by looking at Barcelona, where the successful example of the La Borda housing cooperative had a large impact on the technical officers of the city council, who during negotiations with the social and solidarity economy network XES developed a new approach to the allocation of municipal land much more favourable to public-common partnerships.[47]

In the UK, we've already suggested the possibility that the Labour government's deregulation of planning could spark a wave of campaigns objecting to the kinds of public derisking that leads to asset manager control over key infrastructure and urban development. The relative success of independent candidates in the 2024 general election, when four left-wing independent candidates gained seats, is an indication of the likelihood of campaigns and alternative propositions around infrastructure and urban development. From there you could see how building networks of PCPs and the campaigns around them could help to force open a broader field of contested reproduction over urban development, with repercussions for how we might approach the institutions of electoral politics. The current model of housing and urban development is so broken that even the glimmer of such an outcome could fundamentally shift the boundaries of what seems socially and politically possible, which in turn could provoke a more widespread re-evaluation in people's perception of their material interests.

7
Pharmaceuticals

In 2016, the St. Regis Mohawk Tribe, whose reservation is located in Franklin County, New York, sent a medical delegation to Cuba to explore the potential of Heberprot-P, a type 2 diabetes drug. Federal data suggests that 17 percent of Native Americans in the United States are living with diabetes, more than double the rate of the white population, with some tribes reporting that over half of those over 65 years of age suffer from type 2 diabetes.[1] Heberprot-P is used specifically to treat diabetic foot ulcers, which are estimated to affect around 1.6 million Americans and is the principal complication associated with diabetes. In the UK, where more than 7,000 diabetes-related amputations are reported each year, diabetic foot ulcers make up more than 80 percent of these.[2] More than 160,000 Americans undergo amputations for a diabetic foot ulcer each year,[3] while around half of those who undergo such amputations don't survive beyond five years.[4] Yet this suffering and loss of life can be radically reduced, with Heberprot-P capable of healing severe Grade 4 and 5 diabetic foot ulcers within 45 days, with research suggesting that 77 percent of patients could be fully healed.[5]

The Mohawk delegation — which aimed to pressure federal government to approve and fund Heberprot-P — continued a long relationship between Native Americans and the Cuban government reaching back to 1959, when an eleven-member pan-Indian coalition led by 'Mad Bear' Anderson, a prominent advocate for Native American rights, was invited to attend the 26 July Cuban independence celebrations in Havana. The invitation had been made in recognition of the common struggles of Native Americans and the Cuban people, in particular the deteriorating relations with the US government which at the time was imposing both a full economic embargo on Cuba and a policy of termination towards Native Americans.[6] In the time since that early delegation, Cuba has become notorious for its successful public healthcare system, and its pharmaceutical sector is no different. Along with developing the world's first synthetic vaccine against the life-threatening Haemophilus influenza type B,[7] it was the smallest country in the world to develop its own Covid-19 vaccines,[8] while its unique CIMAvax immunotherapy treatment has led many Americans suffering from advanced lung cancer to make the illegal journey to Cuba to obtain treatment inaccessible on US soil. In 2006, the Heberprot-P treatment was registered for use in Cuba, and has subsequently been made available in 23 other countries — not including the United States.

The lack of access to Heberprot-P serves as a particularly devastating example of artificial scarcity driven by two related factors. On the one hand, the United States' long-standing embargo of Cuba has for almost 20 years denied millions of Americans access to a drug that may have drastically improved or even saved their life. As the recent initiation of trials on US soil demonstrates,[9] such a loss of life — which disproportionately affected Native American and other oppressed populations — was entirely preventable. On the other hand, despite this politically enforced scarcity, US-based pharmaceutical giants failed to undertake the research that might have brought an alternative product to market. No doubt this reluctance to fund the development of an alternative was, in part, due to the concern that Cuba had already developed a public alternative which would undermine the ability of Big Pharma to price gouge individuals and healthcare systems worldwide. Yet even in the US, where the embargo on Cuba effectively created the opportunity for a legally-granted monopoly on an alternative product, pharmaceutical companies didn't deem it sufficiently profitable to develop a drug that might save hundreds of thousands of lives and prevent millions of unnecessary amputations.

This is no surprise. As Artie Vierkant and Beatrice Adler-Bolton argue in their book *Health Communism*, under capital's metabolic control, pharmaceuticals are *not* about preventing, ameliorating, or curing diseases. First and foremost, they are an instrument for the management of populations.[10] The provision or non-provision of pharmaceuticals shuttles people back and forth from the category of an employable and exploitable 'worker' to the category of 'surplus', the latter referring to those deemed either of no use to capital's circuits of accumulation or a threat to them. Cuba's pharmaceutical sector poses a threat to such an approach. It demonstrates the viability of a different model of pharmaceutical production. It proves that vast corporate profits aren't needed to incentivise research into drugs that might improve our lives and that human need can and should be the basis for pharmaceutical research and production. However, aside from a small number of public pharmaceutical infrastructures, the trillion-dollar pharmaceutical industry — dominated by a handful of major companies colloquially known as Big Pharma — is systematically and structurally oriented towards the dual production of artificial scarcity and bullshit abundance. Like so many other sectors of the economy, something absolutely critical to well-being is intrinsically structured to function *against* our collective interests. Rather than a handful of greedy executives or a few bad apples, this is an industry that is rotten to its core.

Awareness of these structural challenges and calls to prioritise and fund public alternatives to Big Pharma are starting to take root. In early 2024, a series of European-based organisations — including the People's Health Movement, Oxfam, Health Action International, Medico International, Viva Salud, the Pharmaceutical Accountability Foundation, and others — held a conference in Brussels entitled 'Public Pharma in Europe'. Many of these organisations have a long history of campaigning against the for-profit pharmaceutical industry and have lobbied for everything from policy interventions aimed at preventing the evergreening of patents or tackling the use of plastics in packaging through to increased public research funding. With the resulting launch of a Public Pharma for Europe coalition at the end of 2024, there are signs that a concerted and coordinated effort is emerging — one that may go further than lobbying for regulation of the existing industry and advocate for an alternative model of provision.

However, the challenges in advocating for and building a 'public alternative' are steep. Illustrative of the problem is the vast amount of money spent by the industry on lobbying governments, drafting and shaping policies, and trying to influence referenda. In the United States, this amounted to an estimated expenditure of $4.7 billion between the years 1999 to 2018.[11] In the EU, a conservative estimate of Big Pharma spending is 36 million euros annually, although the actual figure is expected to be much higher due to lack of reporting by companies, and no official record of industry funding to think tanks, advocacy groups, or patient groups.[12] Recent research has found that the latter has amounted to an additional 110 million euros annually, threatening the independence of the sector and resulting in industry-backed patient groups functioning as unofficial lobbying groups.[13] To give some indication of the impact, a major lobbying focus during the pandemic was opposition to the waiver of the World Trade Organization's Trade-Related Aspects of Intellectual Property Rights (TRIPS) on vaccine patents, something which would have allowed the production and distribution of vaccines at low cost. A piece of legislation that was only required due to companies such as Pfizer and Moderna refusing to share IP and technology in the first place, the final TRIPS waiver was watered down and delayed by over 18 months in large part due to this lobbying. In the end, it was denounced by the international president of Medecins Sans Frontieres (MSF) as no longer representing 'a true intellectual property waiver' and thus 'will not address pharmaceutical monopolies or ensure affordable access to lifesaving medical tools'.[14]

The pharmaceutical industry has enormous structural power to resist any attempts to develop public alternatives. As Nick Dearden argues in his recent book *Pharmanomics: How Big Pharma Destroys Global Health*, the underpinning issue is a global intellectual property (IP) framework that has induced companies to 'behave more like hedge funds than medical research firms'.[15] For example, instead of conducting pioneering research, the focus is often on high-cost and speculative acquisitions of pharma start-ups with the hope this will lead to control of valuable IP. Common practice is to then misleadingly account for such acquisitions as part of reported R&D budgets, even if no research and development has taken place. Meanwhile, pharmaceutical companies maintain that the high cost of clinical trials justifies the subsequent high price of medicines, simultaneously foreclosing the possibility of public bodies bringing their own products into circulation. While recent research conducted by MSF found that industry claims of high trial costs are dramatically overstated, the relative lack of publicly owned infrastructure means governments often find themselves over a barrel. Lacking the capacity to conduct the necessary trials for a drug to receive approval, governments have minimal bargaining power and are left with little choice but to hand over the research to Big Pharma.[16] As with many of the Covid vaccinations, not only does this result in the public paying twice, but it also takes control of production and distribution out of public hands — often with dire health implications.

A 'pharma commons', one that is free from the imperative to accumulate and instead mediated by collective democratic decisions, is thus critical in securing a 'safe and just operating space for humanity'. Yet the track record of Big Pharma suggests it will do everything in its capacity to undermine such efforts, whether through lobbying national and international government bodies for favourable policy, harnessing IP litigation as a strategy to force up costs and bankrupt alternatives, smear campaigns against generics and competitors so as to raise doubts over safety or efficacy, or undermining key supply chains through acquiring the producers of active ingredients. These are specific examples of a general problem in advancing a strategy for transition, where entrenched interests that benefit from the current situation will actively look to disrupt and prevent change to the point of sabotaging essential parts of our social reproduction.

Hoping that governments will legislate into existence an alternative to the dominant pharmaceutical model when it currently fails to regulate even the worst of its excesses is wishful thinking. We need a strategy that immediately addresses many of the critical artificial scarcities produced by the current system, a situation which in May 2024 was described as 'beyond critical' by Community Pharmacy England when 79 percent of UK pharmacists perceived medical shortages were putting patients at risk.[17] Yet the odds are dramatically stacked against the emergence of an alternative. Any strategy must therefore also function to change the political calculus of tackling Big Pharma, undermining its structural dominance through developing new forms of popular protagonism that change the stakes of political (in)action. While there are many pieces to such a puzzle, public-common partnerships could play a critical role in such a strategy.

THE PHARMACEUTICAL INDUSTRIAL COMPLEX

There has long been discontent with the global pharmaceutical industry, but the Covid pandemic brought it to the fore. Seeking a rapid response to a global crisis, vast sums of public money were directed towards accelerating the development of a vaccine and to rapidly scale up production, not least in the United States where as of August 2020 — only five months after the first lockdown had been introduced — eight companies had already received $11 billion in public funding. By May the following year, the pandemic had created nine *new* Pharma billionaires: individuals with 'a combined net wealth of $19.3 billion (15.8 billion euros), enough to fully vaccinate all people in low-income countries 1.3 times'.[18] At the same time, it was widely reported that much of the research underpinning vaccine development had come from public sources. This included the Pfizer vaccine, where the underpinning technology was financed by a $445 million research grant from the German government to BioNTech, and the Oxford-AstraZeneca vaccine, where an estimated 97 to 99 percent of development funding had come from public or charitable sources. The development of the Moderna vaccine, a company which accounted for four of the nine new billionaires, had reportedly been funded entirely by the United States National Institutes of Health.[19]

In what amounts to public subsidy to Big Pharma, vaccines developed largely or entirely through public and philanthropic funding had effectively been gifted to the pharmaceutical companies. Vaccines were systematically overpriced, with research indicating that the Pfizer/BioNTech and Moderna vaccines 'could be mass produced for as little as $1.18 to $2.85 a dose' but were being sold 'at an average price of $16.25 and between $19.20 and $24 per dose respectively'.[20] When donations were made to lower and middle-income countries, the vaccines were often unusable due to being past their expiry dates, a bullshit abundance of over 100 million doses being refused by recipients in December 2021 alone.[21] The stark global inequality in access to vaccines led to declarations of a 'vaccine apartheid'[22] which not only left billions of people unprotected, but also critically undermined the global effort to further contain the emergence of new variants. India and South Africa's effort to secure a TRIPS waiver on vaccine patents was watered down and delayed under intense lobbying, such that when a text was finally approved in June 2022, the World Health Organization estimated there had already been at least 6.4 million Covid-related deaths worldwide.[23]

Yet while the pandemic created a situation in which the pharmaceutical industry was under unprecedented public scrutiny, it provided only a small glimpse into the systemic tendencies of the entire sector. A wholly financialised industry structured through a global system of intellectual property rights has for decades resulted in an artificial scarcity of necessary pharmaceuticals through the systematic lack of research into 'less profitable' conditions and diseases (which includes vaccine technologies); overpricing enforced through monopolistic behaviour, resulting in an increased strain on both public and individual finances; cartel behaviour of coordinated price-fixing between companies; 'pay to delay' strategics where major pharmaceutical companies, intent on maintaining high prices on a given product, pay generic competitors to delay the release of a cheaper competing product; and increasingly severe shortages as manufactures cease production of products, especially generic off-patent medicines, that are no-longer considered sufficiently profitable. We have also been subjected to a bullshit abundance of drugs that have undergone minor adaptations solely to extend a company's monopoly privileges, a practice known as evergreening. Not only do these adaptations often offer no clinical advancement on the drug they're replacing, and not only are the associated research costs then used to justify higher prices, but some drugs have been found to be of *more harm than benefit.*[24]

Even before the Covid vaccine gold rush, these systemic failures should be understood in the context of corporate profit margins that typically outstrip most other sectors of the economy. One cross-sectional study found that between 2000 and 2018, the profit margin of the 35 largest pharmaceutical companies listed on the S&P 500 Index averaged 13.8 percent, significantly higher than the 7.7 percent margin of 357 other, large non-pharmaceutical companies listed.[25] In the same time period, the total payout to shareholders 'increased from 88% of total investments in research and development in 2000 to 123% in 2018', which at $146 billion was an increase of almost 400 percent.[26] Meanwhile in the UK, NHS spending on hospital-prescribed medicines increased by 35 percent between 2018 to 2022, rising from £6.7 billion to £9.1 billion, a figure which *excludes* expenditure on Covid-related vaccines and treatments.[27] Even the European Commission has recognised that 'access to affordable and innovative essential medicines may be endangered by a combination of (i) very high and unsustainable price levels; (ii) market withdrawals, or other business strategies by pharmaceutical companies; and (iii) the limited bargaining power of national governments against those pharmaceutical companies'.[28]

Efforts to regulate this industry have proved ineffective. In the US alone, a sample of 26 publicly listed pharmaceutical companies — including giants such as GlaxoSmithKline, Pfizer, Sanofi, Merck, and Eli Lilly — found that between 2003 and 2016, 85 percent of companies had received a financial penalty for illegal activities, totalling a value of $33 billion.[29] This eye-watering sum is demonstrative of the failure of government efforts to effectively regulate industry behaviour because, given the profit margins of the industry and the inflation in shareholder and executive payouts over the same period, these fines can be perceived as little more than a 'cost of doing business'.

DEVELOPING AN ALTERNATIVE

In mid-2021, a small group of French health and commons activists began exploring the possibility of organising pharmaceutical production as a commons. This proposition soon cohered an alliance of interested parties, including chemists, unionists, pharmacists, pro-commons activists, members of the French cooperative society (SCOP), and organisations such as the Open Insulin Foundation and Medicines Sans Frontiers, along with two members of our organisation. From the outset, the group's focus was not on developing isolated examples of best practice or creating an all-encompassing future vision, but to focus on specific sites to help us think through which organisational forms might be realisable in the present context, and how they might contribute to a wider transitional politics in the pharmaceutical sector. This meant not only exploring what strategies might result in the contested reproduction of pharmaceutical production, but what expressions of popular protagonism might help drive this forward.

Much like the UK, France is typically considered to have an excellent healthcare system, yet there was a reported shortage of 3,530 pharmaceutical products during the period 2012–18, with a 'fourfold increase between 2012 and 2018 [in shortages] and a sharp rise in 2017 and 2018, along with a rise in the number of active substances on shortage'.[30] The situation became progressively worse. In 2022 alone, the National Agency for the Safety of Medicines and Health Products (ANSM) reported there were more than 3,000 drugs 'of major therapeutic interest' either in shortage or at risk of shortage, including antiseptics, anti-epileptics, antibiotics, and anti-diabetics. In 2019, there had been 1,504.[31] There is a simultaneous challenge of newly marketed drugs failing to offer 'added therapeutic value', meaning they offer no advancement on already available products. An exhaustive analysis conducted by *La Revue Prescrire* in 2014 found that of all new drugs marketed in France, 'less than 25% of drugs represented a therapeutic advance, including very minor advances. Over 50% represented no advance at all, and on average 15 to 20% were judged to be even of more harm than benefit'.[32]

Ostensibly in response to this increasing severity of shortages, in June 2023 president Emmanuel Macron announced plans to initiate production of a number of key medicines to France, drawing up a shortlist of 450 molecules and 50 'core drugs' that ranged from antibiotics to paracetamol. Among the beneficiaries of this 160 million-euro reshoring programme was a factory based in Saint-Genis-Laval in Lyon, owned by the Lebanese company Benta. Formerly owned by the Greek company Famar, the Saint-Genis-Laval site had gone into receivership in 2020, and was transferred to the ownership of Benta by the Parisian commercial court. Despite the promise of creating 268 jobs over the following six years, the takeover itself resulted in 125 of the 240-strong workforce being made redundant. The estimated annual production of 110 million units at the time of the takeover fell to only 4 million in 2022, meaning that the site was running drastically under capacity. By July 2021, as a result of the company being 'in danger of cessation of payments' the site was already at risk of re-entering administration. In November 2022, Benta entered into a 12-month subsidy agreement with the French government worth 2.8 million euros, amounting to a little over 50 percent of total wages, creating deep uncertainty about the future prospects for the site. However, as part of Macron's announcements, Benta was allocated a further 4.8 million euros of state subsidy in exchange for initiating production of six new products.

The short history of Benta's acquisition of the Saint-Genis-Laval site is, in effect, an extension of the logic of public-private partnerships as an operating mode of the derisking state. Despite the view of Gilbert-Luc Devinaz,[33] the senator for the Rhône region of which Lyon is the regional capital, that 'what would have been a good thing is for the government to carry out at least a partial nationalisation' of the site, the Parisian commercial court transferred essential productive capacity to a private company at a peppercorn price. Despite promises this would contribute to both improved employment prospects and help to address pharmaceutical shortages, under Benta's leadership the facility shed jobs and ran drastically under capacity, only to be rewarded with a further 7.6 million euros in subsidies. The 'public' explicitly ameliorated the risk of a private enterprise, repeatedly mobilising public resources to underwrite the accumulation of private profits. The obvious question stands that, if there is the administrative capacity to appropriate and redistribute existing assets from failing companies, and if public financing can (repeatedly) be found to underwrite the risks of for-profit companies, then why are we not facilitating alternative models of production that are more systematically aligned with principles of public health?

PCPs FOR THE PHARMA COMMONS

We cannot think of the 'pharmaceutical commons' only in terms of individual manufacturing facilities, just as we can't approach it only as a question of research, access, or prices. Rather it implies extending processes of democratic self-governance across the entirety of the sector, from what research ought to be prioritised through to how to organise production, what new facilities are required, and how active ingredients should be extracted and produced. There is no place for 'price signals' to stand in as a proxy for human need. Instead, the entire circuit of pharmaceutical research, production, and distribution must be mediated directly through something akin to what Pat Devine calls the political economy of a self-governing society — people making collective, democratic decisions about what pharmaceuticals we need, incorporating all of the processes that lead up to a drug being made available in a hospital or pharmacy.[34]

Given the sheer scale of what is required, what hope is there in focusing initially on a handful of production facilities — as we suggest here — rather than lobbying to change the much wider regime of intellectual property rights, to demand more punitive measures for evergreening, and so on? We are not arguing against any such initiatives; efforts to radically restrict the deleterious effects of the profit motive on research and production are necessary goals. New forms of collective intellectual 'property' to ward against enclosure are essential. But there are three critical issues. First, how will efforts to legislate against the worst excesses of the industry help to address chronic shortages when these are often the result of products simply not being produced due to a comparative lack of profitability? Second, what forms of popular protagonism — what social forces — are required to achieve even the most modest of reforms to Big Pharma? What is the social and material base that would sufficiently empower or force government actors (whether at national, European, or WTO level) to radically discipline Big Pharma? Third, short of taking more fundamental steps such as socialising parts of the industry (which itself rests on the prior existence of necessary social forces), legislative approaches don't challenge the fundamental structure and tendencies of an extractive profit-orientated pharmaceutical industry. To put it another way, it is not only the excesses of Big Pharma that are the problem; it's the fundamental incompatibility of an industry whose decisions about research and production are guided by the extraction of maximum profit instead of collectively defined human needs.

The creation of PCPs in generic medicine manufacturing does not answer the question of what a future pharma commons might look like, nor address all of the steps that would be necessary to get there. Nevertheless, our wager is that they're a key strategic intervention that not only begins to address issues of shortages in the present (and are thus justifiable on their own terms), but that they can play a strategic role in helping to compose the social and political forces necessary to a broader transition. Building from our collaborative work around the site in Saint-Genis-Laval helps us to understand what this might look like in practice.

The structure of a pharmaceutical PCP follows the general approach outlined in Chapter Five, in which there is a model of co-ownership and co-governance of an organisation that includes three stakeholders: a public body (the Saint-Genis-Laval Commune/ Lyon Metropole), the employees (as worker-owners), and here a Common Health Association (a legally constituted body in its own right). In France, such an arrangement is possible in the legal form of a Société Coopérative d'intérêt Collectif (SCIC), an ownership model introduced in 2001 based on the premise of a cooperative explicitly aimed at pursuing social objectives and which must contribute to the development of the territories to which it belongs. In many ways, there are parallels with the structure of a Community

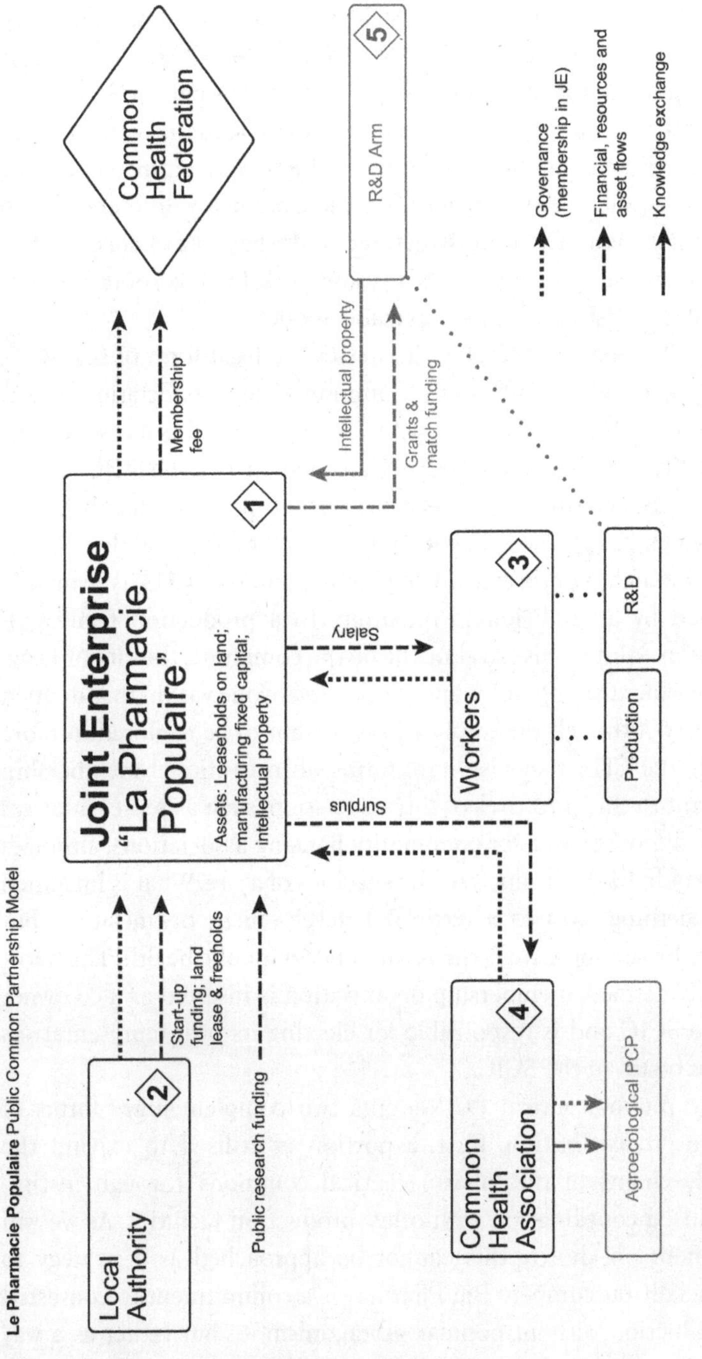

Figure 4 La Pharmacie Populaire Public-Common Partnership Model

Benefit Society in the UK. The SCIC model is now somewhat established; as of 2020 there were 1,060 registered SCICs, with 34 percent of them including at least one local authority as part of their structure. Yet there are no pharmaceutical manufacturers structured as SCICs, with the majority being in food and agriculture, education, electricity, and the arts. In addition, there are many differences as to how individual SCICs are structured and what sort of stakeholders they mobilise; they offer a legal framework for incorporation, but they don't exist as a simple replicable model.

A PCP approach therefore harnesses the legal form of the SCIC, but — crucially — includes a Common Health Association (CHA) as one of its three stakeholders. A CHA is conceived as its own legally constituted body whose objectives are aligned with the SCIC (e.g., to expand the pharma commons while furthering public health needs), but which has its own constitution, board, and internal democratic decision-making processes. The membership of a CHA is primarily defined by an individual's proximity to a production facility — which in Saint-Genis-Laval might be the commune, the city of Lyon, or the wider metropole — and is open to anyone within that defined territory. Although the implications remain to be explored in more depth, the CHA may also have forms of institutional membership relevant to the objectives of the association, such as representatives of local food growers or community housing associations, although this would be determined by the specifics of a site. What is imagined is something akin to a territorial development organisation, but whose broad objective is the furtherance of public health. This territorially defined, membership organisation is inserted as a co-owner of the SCIC and is responsible for electing its own representatives to the board of the SCIC.

The pharmaceutical PCP adopts two complementary forms of surplus redistribution. First, a portion is utilised to expand the supply chains of the 'pharmaceutical commons' through institutionalised coordination with other production facilities. As we will comment on shortly, this cannot be approached as a strategy to financially outcompete Big Pharma — a commitment to contested reproduction without popular protagonism — but rather as a way of financially resourcing the necessary *political work* of developing the pharma commons. Second, a portion of surplus is transferred annually to the Common Health Association. In practice this is much like a company paying dividends to one of its majority shareholders, except in this case the 'shareholder' is a territorially rooted, democratic membership organisation with the defined objective of intervening to further public health objectives. What exactly these interventions look like are the prerogative of an individual CHA, but they will share the fundamental characteristics of being upstream, collectivised, and citizen-led responses that further public health objectives.

LEVERAGING TRANSITION

Although it might feel implausible given the political realities most of us have lived through, there is nothing about a liberal democracy that structurally forecloses the possibility of public authorities providing financial or legislative support to democratic enterprises such as those we describe. Indeed, there is some precedent for how the Saint-Genis-Laval factory could have been transferred into the ownership of a newly formed PCP. In 2010, Unilever decided to close the 'Fralib' tea factory in Gémenos near Marseille, a decision which would have led to the dismissal of 182 workers. Supported by the General Confederation of Labour (Confédération Générale du Travail, CGT), workers at the plant occupied the factory in a struggle that lasted for more than three and a half years. Finally, in September 2013 the Marseille-Provence Metropole (the regional authority) supported the takeover of the factory through a 5.3 million euro purchase of the land, along with a symbolic one euro payment to take control of the site machinery.[35] Although they did not incorporate as a SCIC or form a long-term partnership with the metropole, the combination of worker-led popular protagonism and local authority support resulted in ScopTi operating as a 60-person strong worker-owned tea cooperative.

Yet, just as public bodies might provide critical support to emerging initiatives, what is also true is that without the mobilisation of the former Unilever workers to contest the future of the site, it is highly unlikely that the regional authorities would have stepped in to help secure the assets. A central question that arises, especially when acting without the support of a wider circuit of PCPs, is what alliances can be built and what expressions of popular protagonism might be effective in obtaining the resources necessary in establishing a PCP? It is only through political mobilisation that what was 'derisked' was a worker-led initiative, rather than — as in the case of Saint-Genis-Laval — yet another extractive profit-driven business. While different government bodies will be more or less receptive, it will unquestionably take concerted and focused organising to bring them on board.

But why exactly should those concerned with establishing a pharma commons — which in many instances is a challenge of research or access, rather than production — use their limited organising capacities trying to establish PCPs? What is it about this proposed approach that lends itself towards supporting a wider politics of transition in the pharmaceutical sector? There are three principal arguments that have some specificity beyond those outlined in Chapter Five, which we'll address in turn: the development of a collective action frame; the control of financial surpluses; and material capacity that provides governments with 'leverage'. We are not suggesting that creating such organisations is a 'silver bullet' that can take the place of other forms of organising. But we are wagering that the development of pharmaceutical PCPs can significantly improve the prospects of both radically curtailing the worst excesses of the dominant pharmaceutical industry and laying the foundations upon which to expand the development of a global pharma commons.

First, participation in a Common Health Association can play a critical role in developing the 'collective action frame' necessary to cohering an effective social movement for the pharma commons.[36] As a reader of this book, you may individually already be convinced of the need to radically constrain or even wholly replace the existing pharmaceutical industry. Yet not only have you most likely never taken any form of action to follow through on this belief, you probably expect that someone else is in a better position than you to do so. Pharmaceuticals might appear as a bit of an 'expert field' in which you feel unqualified to act, and it's not particularly clear what action you could even take. If you're a patient you might connect with important advocacy groups such as Just Treatment, but otherwise you're probably limited to signing petitions or joining demonstrations. To put this otherwise, although you might have a belief that things must change, what you don't have is a collectively articulated lens for viewing the problem, a way of relating to others as a collective actor, and an associated framework of understanding regarding what can be done about it.

Contrast this with what might feel possible if you were one of many members in a CHA, perhaps associated with a production facility in your region producing generic diabetes medicine (such as metformin). It is well established that the prevalence of type 2 diabetes is linked to environmental risk factors such as lack of access to affordable good food, high-quality public transport options, and accessible green space. Whereas the dominant pharmaceutical sector views type 2 diabetes as an 'expanding market' for its products, from a public health perspective the goal is to undermine demand through supporting interventions that mitigate these risk factors. While PCPs might form initially within specific sectors, this illustrates how the operation of a Common Association (here CHAs) can cut *across* sectors, such that a single Common Association might find itself acting as force of communal mediation in quite different sectors at the same time. For example, this might mean the CHA using its resources to expand agroecological PCPs in the region (see Chapter Eight). Not only is this a collectivised 'upstream' response that may improve access to affordable and nutritious food, but it also supports the expansion of the communal social metabolism while making interventions into wider issues of food sovereignty.

Participation in the CHA leads to concrete outcomes, but more than that the processes of participating help to articulate an understanding of 'health' as (primarily) the outcome of socio-economic processes (rather than the neoliberal discourse of health as the outcome of individualised decision-making) and as something that you have a collective capacity to intervene in. It isn't through an abstract appeal for 'people' to 'mobilise' that this can be achieved, but through your territorial rootedness in the pharmaceutical PCP and its intrinsic connection with broader prospects for improved health. In this regard, the Common Health Association may function as a 'conduit' between the technical and specialised functions of pharmaceutical production and a broader collective interest that ties individuals together. Indeed, part of what gets produced through the development of a new collective action frame is also a new subject or agent of change; it is neither 'patients' nor 'citizens' that act, but a cadre (something like health commoners, for want of a better term) with a new shared language, way of relating to one another, and understanding of the actions they might take to defend and expand the pharma commons. Although the initial formation of a CHA will invariably bring together people with relatively different (although not hostile) class interests, it's through this participation that a new collective political subject can be forged.

The formation of this cadre is critical to the second proposition, which is that the surpluses generated through a pharmaceutical PCP, governed under forms of participatory democratic control, provide a tangible capacity to expand the pharma commons. In its simplest form, this can be thought of as a coordination between production facilities in order to invest in and establish a new part of a wider supply chain, whether that be for the production of active ingredients or new research laboratories. This necessarily leads to questions concerning democratic economic planning such as how we decide how to prioritise expenditure, who decides, how different firms coordinate with one another, where forms of public and inter-firm finance are utilised, and so on. Yet these questions should *not* be approached (as they often are within democratic planning thought) as a theoretical design problem that can be sketched out on a *tabula rasa*, with the aim of building a model that can then be implemented unilaterally and in its totality. Such approaches typically assume a set of ideal conditions that do not yet exist, whether it's the presence of a benevolent and democratic state or the mediating role of capital having been partially or entirely overcome.

To the contrary, any efforts to expand the pharma commons will take place in circumstances that are overwhelmingly hostile, both in terms of the Big Pharma industry we are trying to undermine (which itself is supported through a state-enforced regime of intellectual property) and the practical lack of resources for an emergent pharma commons. To put this latter point into context, one estimate for the construction of a new manufacturing plant on the outskirts of Paris suggested it might cost around 90 million euros over five years — and that is presuming you already had the land. Even if smaller investments might be realised, we should quickly abandon any idea that it is possible to 'outcompete' the existing pharmaceutical industry. Not only is such an endeavour financially impossible, but it fails to confront the reality in which Big Pharma is systematically supported by the states of the imperial core (through legislation, direct financial support, knowledge transfers, enforcement of IP, and so on). Expanding the pharma commons therefore demands a multifaceted and politicised approach to economic development, one that puts an emphasis on different expressions of popular protagonism that may enable gaining control of new infrastructure, rather than simply financing it outright. Indeed, the relative futility of individual pharmaceutical PCPs attempting to address the challenges they face provide one response to Michael Lebowitz's concern about 'collective atomism', in which the solidarity generated within a PCP fails to be articulated as solidarity across PCPs. It is through necessity that these PCPs must find ways to act in concert, for without this collaboration any broader efforts to expand the pharma commons will likely be futile.

This is where the importance of the cadre becomes clear — if you're going to expand the pharma commons, you need a coherent and well resourced movement that is capable of implementing a diversity of strategies (targeted takeovers of failing companies, impacting negotiation of prices with the national health system, lobbying for compulsory licences to expand generic production of in-patent products, supporting campaigns to ban evergreening, and so on). What different future might have been possible for the Saint-Genis-Laval site, if instead of the Parisian commercial court transferring ownership of the site to Benta in 2020 there had been a competing proposal for a pharmaceutical PCP? What if the pharma commons had been able to resource the development of the business plans and worker-management structure for the factory while also helping to fund on-the-ground organisers? What if investment into the site could be match-funded between the Lyon Metropole and the pharma commons? What if the workers were backed by a strike fund such that a factory occupation could continue indefinitely? What if there was a well organised cadre of 'health commoners' that could rapidly turn the fate of a local factory into a struggle of national interest? These 'what ifs' are what it means to adopt a politicised approach to expanding the pharma commons and point to the intersection between popular protagonism and contested reproduction.

Finally, the development of a pharma commons might have a significant impact on what the European Commission recognises as 'the limited bargaining power of national governments' when engaging with pharmaceutical companies. This goes some way to addressing why a public body would, given the different options available, use financial and/or legislative means to support the development of pharma PCPs and the wider pharma commons. The realities of this are complex, and there are a number of ways in which this might be possible, but one of the most significant is through undermining the lack of transparency in the costs of bringing a drug to market — with the implications this has for saving costs directly in terms of the wider public health system, as well as in relation to socio-economic costs of ill-health.

Big Pharma currently holds something of a monopoly on the ability to conduct clinical trials, which companies have long argued are extortionately expensive (although the costs of this have always been kept hidden) justifying the high costs of final products. In an effort to understand the true costs of medical trials, Médecins Sans Frontières recently undertook its own trial into a four-drug combination treatment for drug-resistant tuberculosis, arriving at a total cost of £29 million — which *included* having to invest in upgraded infrastructure (such as TB clinics) to make the trial possible. This figure was dramatically lower than the £1.7–2.5 billion figure that the International Federation of Pharmaceutical Manufacturers and Associations (IFPMA) suggests is the average cost for bringing a product through trials to market.

A pharma commons with the capacity to run its own clinical trials might significantly change the stakes for national governments negotiating with Big Pharma. Through breaking the monopoly on clinical trials, developing a new (non-private) industry standard of the associated costs, and offering an alternative route for bringing a drug to market, Big Pharma would find it increasingly untenable to demand a high price for drugs without introducing transparency over its costs. In the UK and other countries where the cost of drugs are negotiated centrally before being purchased by the NHS, this could result in dramatic reductions in the overall cost of sourcing pharmaceuticals from private companies. On the other hand, a pharma commons with the capacity both to conduct clinical trials and manufacture a product might be able to circumvent entirely the need to source certain drugs from the for-profit sector. Ultimately, the capacity to do this is a matter of scale, but it is one that can begin through specific interventions to convert production facilities into public-common partnerships.

CHALLENGING EXTRACTIVE ABANDONMENT

Having read our vision for a pharmaceutical commons in France, you may wonder why this chapter belongs in a book about how to win a green and democratic future. Wouldn't it make more sense to discuss the high-emitting industries that must be transformed for a green transition of any kind to occur, such as the energy sector, transportation, or manufacturing? One answer to this objection is to point out that per dollar of revenue, emissions from the pharmaceutical sector are 55 percent higher than the automotive industry.[37] As a ratio compared to their contribution to GDP, then, pharmaceuticals are worse for the environment than the automotive industry. This kind of answer isn't terribly satisfying, though. For one thing, GDP is an appalling metric by which to evaluate social wellbeing. When someone gets sick, the cost of treating them boosts GDP but this doesn't mean society is getting qualitatively better. As we've argued in this chapter, it's just another example of capital's bullshit. For another, in absolute terms, the global healthcare sector contributes around 4.4 percent of global greenhouse gas emissions.[38] While this isn't insignificant, the automotive industry is responsible for more than double that at around 10 percent.

The reason for including pharmaceuticals has less to do with driving down emissions than it does with the task of composing a collective subject that can dismantle capital's grip on human and non-human life. There's no question that highly polluting industries must be sites of struggle, but to privilege them in the fight for a green transition would be a grave error. Invariably on the Left, privileging highly emitting sectors leads to a strategy of building power among those parts of the working class employed by them. This usually leads to promoting a strategy of trade union mobilisation, winning social democratic reforms through electoral struggles, and ensuring that those employed in the fossil fuel industry, for example, are not disadvantaged by the transition to renewables. This is all good and important work.

Yet, as critical health scholars and radical health campaigners argue, one of the ways capital's metabolic control manifests itself is by arbitrating over who is and isn't considered a 'productive' worker. Through the demarcation of people as either eligible or ineligible to work, capital cleaves the working class into two categories: those available to be directly exploited to create surplus value and those it deems 'surplus' to its requirements. As Adler-Bolton and Vierkant argue, even those deemed surplus are viewed as an opportunity to make profits. Through a process they call 'extractive abandonment', surplus populations become important sites of income for insurers, pharmaceutical companies, and other private healthcare systems.[39] This makes both those who are out of work and dependent on pharmaceuticals, and those who are perhaps in work and dependent on them, important agents of transition.

One of the things that makes PCPs an important strategic wager is that they can span across struggles at the sites of production and reproduction, across those deemed 'productive' and those deemed 'surplus'. The strategy of building PCPs in the pharmaceutical sector is well positioned for this. As this chapter shows, it brings together trade unionists in the pharmaceutical sector, and those (by which we mean everyone, in principle) whose health outcomes are socially determined. Democratic control over pharmaceuticals therefore has the potential to strip capital of its ability to shuttle people back and forth between the categories of productive worker and surplus. It can allow more people to lead richer, fuller lives than they ever could without processes of contested reproduction. And importantly, it acknowledges that those deemed surplus by capital not only have an interest in bringing capital to an end, but should be part of the struggle for a green and democratic future for all.

8
Food Systems

Cloudberries are a small orange to peachy-pink fruit produced by the Rubus chamaemorus plant native to northern Europe and northern America. They can be found in boggy areas across Russia, Finland, Sweden, Greenland, Alaska, and Canada. If you're lucky, you might even find them in parts of the Scottish Highlands and northern England. A delicacy across Scandinavia, where they're known as 'arctic gold', Inuit and Sami tribes traditionally collected the precious berries in autumn, freezing them to enjoy in the winter months.[1] The Yup'ik combine the berries with whipped seal oil and reindeer or caribou fat to make a calorie-dense treat called *akataq*. Long before sailors of the British Empire learned to take citrus with them on imperial voyages, Vikings brought preserved cloudberries with them to sea to ward off scurvy. What they didn't know then, but we do know now, is that cloudberries are an excellent source of vitamin C.[2] Cloudberries were once so highly prized in Norway that a law was passed to grant exclusive harvesting rights to people in the north of the country where they are most frequently found. Still today they're the most collected wild fruit in Finland. They even appear on the Finnish version of the two Euro coin.

Cloudberries are part of the *rosaceae* family, which includes some more commonly consumed plants like apples, pears, blackberries, cherries, and almonds, but their tart flavour is perhaps best described as a cross between a raspberry and redcurrant.[3] Given their unusual taste, cultural significance, and nutritional benefits, why don't we see cloudberries in our supermarkets? One reason is that they're notoriously low yielding. While strawberries and other popular commercial fruits are monoecious, meaning each plant is both male and female, cloudberries are dioecious which means each plant is either male or female. To get a harvest, a would-be farmer needs a mix of male and female plants. Of those, only the female bears fruit and it can take up to seven years for them to start producing, far longer than any return-on-investment-focused farmer wants to wait. Cloudberries are also extremely labour-intensive to pick. Since berries on the same plant tend to ripen at different times, it takes a keen eye and a delicate hand to get a decent crop. Finally, cloudberries are only ripe for a short period. A harvest takes vigilance.

For all these reasons, cloudberries have never been commercially farmed. Little wonder that a small jar of cloudberry jam sells for an extortionate price; that the fruits are a favourite among Scandinavian Michelin-starred restaurants; or that settlers in Canada have appropriated the berry, and its rich connection to Indigenous cultures, to market the 'wildness' and 'purity' of tourist destinations.[4] The cloudberry's rarity and labour-intensive harvesting make it a luxury to be enjoyed by the few.

Cloudberries may seem like an improbable place to begin a chapter about worldwide food system transformation, but they put us in precisely the right mindset. One of the things that makes cloudberries special is that their growing habits stubbornly resist capitalist agricultural systems, which aim to maximise yield, drive down costs, and extend the post-harvest longevity of foodstuffs. While these aren't bad goals in themselves, conventional agriculture pursues them almost exclusively through the exploitation of labour, destruction of ecosystems, and reduction in the quality and diversity of foods available.[5] What is produced, who by, and how is under capital's metabolic control.

It's because cloudberries resist inclusion into capitalist food production that they provide a window into a food system organised around radical abundance. Imagine, for a moment, that the world's agricultural and aquacultural territories produced foods, fuels, and fibres to meet the needs of people and planet rather than to generate a bullshit abundance of profits for private monopolies in the agricultural and food sectors. In this future, agricultural landscapes don't feature row upon row of corn, wheat, and other ecologically simplifying monocultures. In their place is an array of biodiverse food systems that look almost nothing like what we think of as an agricultural landscape today. Biodiverse intercropped fields, silvopasture featuring fruit-bearing trees and livestock, and light food-processing centres manufacturing everything from yoghurts to flour are interspersed with conservation areas in a mosaic-like pattern. Such landscapes protect habitats, reduce the risk of diseases spilling over into human populations, and ensure landscape-scale resilience to climatic shocks.[6]

Nearly no pesticides or fertilisers produced off-farm are used in this system, and no inputs are derived from fossil fuels because farmworkers use well-known on-farm pest control and soil fertilisation strategies. Crop rotations including nitrogen-fixing legumes ensure a constant supply of nitrogen in the soil, green manure or animal manure from on-farm livestock fertilises soils, deeper rooted plants ensure soils are aerated to retain water and require less frequent microrhizome-destroying, carbon dioxide-emitting ploughing. Habitats created by intercropping provide homes for predators of common agricultural pests.

In this food system, rather than private farms employing seasonal, super-exploited, and often racialised labour to drive down labour costs, as many farms do today, more of us participate in producing what we eat. We get our hands dirty together at important times of the year to bring in harvests, or we use some of our time to help with local food distribution hubs, or with processing to produce yoghurts, breads, and cheeses. We do this because a world of radical abundance for all is only possible when the divisions of labour established by capital's metabolic control are unravelled, and we do it because it's enjoyable to work together, to socialise, to bond.

In this future, everyone, everywhere, has access to culturally appropriate nutrient-dense foods that they helped produce and that they have collective democratic control over. In this world, it's not difficult to imagine the fussiness of cloudberries and similar foodstuffs makes their arrival a cause of excitement and celebration — a treat valued not in monetary terms, or for the nutritional benefits they bring, but for the love, care, and dedication they take to source, grow, and harvest. Were the associated producers in northern regions of the world to choose to grow cloudberries, perhaps intercropping them with less challenging plants that enjoy similar conditions like lingonberries and cranberries, or perhaps foraging for them as practised by Indigenous communities to this day, they would add taste and diversity, to our diets. Their labour-intensive production would no longer make them a luxury to be enjoyed by a wealthy few. They become an example of the kinds of communal luxury that is possible in a world defined by the communal pursuit of radical abundance, one where we collectively choose to use some of our time to generate splendour.[7] Cloudberries become testament to the success of wresting our food supply from capital's metabolic control.

There are no ecological or technological impediments to this vision. The technologies and agricultural practices described exist and are well known. The barriers are purely political. Today's food system is under capital's metabolic control, which means that the production of food, and hence the reproduction of human and non-human life, is secondary to the reproduction of capital on an ever-expanding scale. For a new, just, food system to become a reality there must be a revolution in how we live our lives, including how food is produced, who produces it, and where. In this chapter we'll join a chorus of voices, led by the international agrarian movement La Via Campesina, in arguing that this is possible through the adoption of agroecological farming methods and the principles of food sovereignty.[8] To this we'll add the public-common partnership as an appropriate institutional form — in England, and perhaps beyond — to facilitate a transition towards the exercise of popular protagonism throughout the food system from production to consumption.

The chapter builds on our previous examples of PCPs in two ways. First, it shows how PCPs can respond to a series of conjunctural opportunities in England's agricultural sector. Like many agricultural sectors in the imperial core, England is undergoing a transition towards a supposedly greener and more sustainable future. The present course of this transition is towards a continuation of the dialectics of bullshit abundance and artificial scarcity, but it's not too late to change direction. This chapter argues that England's dwindling council farm estate is a pre-existing form of agricultural property that offers a unique conjunctural opportunity to kickstart a transition towards agroecological food sovereignty. Second, the chapter shows how agroecological PCPs facilitate integrated food systems and ecological planning across local, national, and international scales. This is essential because a sustainable and globally just food system cannot be secured by 're-localisation' alone.[9] The food system is a global problem in need of a global solution.

CONVENTIONAL AGRICULTURE: LIVING ON BORROWED TIME

Few sectors in the global economy have been hit as hard by the world's converging crises as agriculture. The outbreak of war in Ukraine in February 2022 caused significant pressure to global grain supplies, leading to increased prices for household staples in the UK and beyond. Meanwhile, cutbacks of foreign aid budgets have led to aid agencies working in Yemen, Afghanistan, South Sudan, and Ethiopia being left with 'no choice but to take food from the hungry to feed the starving'.[10] To make matters worse, global heating is having dire effects on localised crop production, the most spectacular of which get mainstream news coverage. Global heating is expected to reduce crop yields by as much as 12 percent by 2050 and 25 percent by 2100, with the worst effects felt by those in the Global South.[11] Already global heating has slowed agricultural productivity growth by around 21 percent since 1961[12] and negatively affected yields globally.[13]

Understandably, facts and figures like these could lead one to assume the world will soon produce too little food to feed its growing population. Indeed, there's no shortage of research suggesting food production must increase in the coming decades. This is only true, though, if we don't call into question capital's metabolic control over the global food system. The truth is that today's food system produces more than enough to provide everyone alive today with a healthy diet, but a full 30 percent of what is produced goes to waste. Meanwhile, hunger and undernourishment have increased since 2019.[14] Nearly one in ten people across the world — 892 million people — go to bed hungry every night, and a shocking 45 percent of all deaths among children under five are associated with undernutrition. Inflationary pressures in the global economy, driven by increased demand after the lifting of Covid-19 lockdowns, the war in Ukraine, and powerful companies driving up prices through 'greedflation' have exacerbated food insecurity worldwide.[15] A UK Food Standards Agency report found that 25 percent of the UK was food insecure in January 2023.[16] Meanwhile, food insecurity in much of the global periphery is aggravated by the effects of climate change and import dependency for staple crops imposed through the developed world's loan stipulations and development programmes.[17]

Tragically, on the reverse side of this artificial scarcity, millions of people suffer from obesity caused in part by unhealthy but cheap diets rich in calories but low in macronutrients and fibre. In 1997, the World Health Organization declared obesity had reached 'epidemic' proportions and was associated with increased risk of type 2 diabetes, heart disease, strokes and some cancers. Obesity is responsible for 30,000 preventable deaths each year in the UK, and 300,000 in the US. In both countries, it is the second largest cause of preventable deaths behind tobacco.[18] This bullshit abundance of health complications — caused by a structurally unjust food system, and not by 'unhealthy lifestyle choices' — costs the National Health Services around £6.5 billion a year.

The global food system's vulnerability to global heating and the paradox of food scarcity and insecurity amidst abundance are hallmarks of a food system organised around producing food for profit rather than social and ecological need. This prioritisation of profits over people and planet shapes how food is grown, by whom, and where, throughout the world. Capital's metabolic control results in an overproduction of food, reducing the price of food for consumers in some parts of the world, which in turn drives down wages across all sectors and maximises the surplus value accumulated by rentier and capitalist classes. The food system's prioritisation of bullshit abundance also means it is responsible for 30 percent of global greenhouse gas emissions, making it the second-largest contributor to global heating behind energy production.[19] Though some of these emissions stem from transportation, packing, retail, and waste disposal, the vast majority originate in land-use changes and on-farm practices of conventional agricultural systems.[20] Conventional agriculture's contributions to global heating are so pronounced that even if the world stopped burning fossil fuels tomorrow, emissions from the global food system alone would still put planetary warming above the Paris Agreement's targets of 1.5C or 2C above pre-industrial levels.[21]

Ample evidence suggests that biodiverse food systems are more resilient to climatic shocks and less likely to spread pathogens and zoonotic diseases including bird flu, swine flu, and Covid-19, yet conventional farming is effectively an all-out assault on biodiversity. Much of the world's food is produced through ecologically simplified and heavily mechanised farming systems reliant on fossil fuel-derived pesticides and fertilisers, enhanced and privatised seed varieties, concentrated animal feeding lots, and animal antibiotics and hormones.[22] Each one of these practices reduces biodiversity. The United Nations Environment Programme (UNEP) has identified agriculture as a threat to 86 percent of all species at risk of extinction,[23] while the UN's Food and Agriculture Organization finds that agriculture is responsible for 90 percent of global deforestation.[24]

Perhaps worst of all, conventional agriculture is also destabilising the very ecological conditions it needs to exist. Biodiversity collapse driven by conventional agriculture has caused dramatic declines in essential pollinating species, as well as species that provide natural forms of pest control. In the UK, one in six species are threatened with extinction, while numbers of pollinating insects have crashed by 18 percent in the same period.[25] A change in farming systems could reverse the damage caused by this artificially imposed scarcity. Instead, start-ups are touting the benefits of mechanised pollination by 'RoboBees' or pollen dusting with fossil fuel-guzzling aircraft. More bullshit abundance.[26]

The notoriously anti-democratic practices and enormous market shares of large agribusinesses make changing the agricultural sector exceedingly difficult. The so-called 'Big Four' agribusinesses — Bayer, BASF, Corteva, and Syngenta Chem-China — together control a staggering 67 percent of proprietary seed sales and 70 percent of the agrochemical industry.[27] Just two companies control 40 percent of the global commercial seed market, while 90 percent of all soya seeds sold in the US are owned by Monsanto, a subsidiary of the German conglomerate Bayer.[28] Since many seed varieties are patented by multinational corporations, it is often illegal for farm-workers to keep seeds from one season to the next or to exchange seeds among growers. As companies reach into the genomes of seeds and livestock to secure profits, life itself is rendered the property of a few, posing major barriers to more democratic models of food production.[29]

These anti-democratic features of the global food system are the effect of ongoing and historic actions taken by imperial powers, including the UK, to secure cheap access to foods, fuels, and fibres.[30] Colonial occupation pressed the periphery's lands and labour into the service of the dietary whims and profit-making impulses of the imperial core. Taking sugar as an example, Chris Otter shows, that the mass production of sugar on slave plantations across the Caribbean and America was not only profitable, but provided a high caloric foodstuff that in turn helped to cheapen the cost of labour in the imperial core, maximising capitalist profits.[31] Liberalising trade deals and loan stipulations have long exacerbated the situation, while invasions, coups, and assassinations of leftist leaders maintain it. The Green Revolution of the 1950s and 1960s, which increased agricultural productivity by introducing proprietary high-yielding crop varieties and synthetic pesticides and fertilisers, meanwhile, suppressed demands for progressive land reform in the periphery and ensured producers were reliant on global markets for off-farm inputs and loan repayments.[32] All of these practices have limited the capacity for countries in the Global South to democratically pursue a green transition and self-directed economic development.

The undemocratic character of conventional agriculture also shapes food systems in the imperial core. Anti-democratic ownership structures, along with control over market access, have severe impacts on agricultural profit margins, promoting the super-exploitation of seasonal labour, inhibiting best ecological practice, and encouraging ecologically destructive corner-cutting such as dumping slurry into waterways. The British food and farming alliance, Sustain, finds that farmworkers receive only a miniscule share of the profits generated by their own labour, if they receive any at all. Across five British staples, the farms themselves receive just 0.03 percent of average profits generated.[33] The majority of profits are captured by supermarkets, food processors, and the producers of off-farm inputs. Yet farmworkers occupy the part of the supply chain that is expected to take the greatest risk. As the climate becomes more extreme and weather more volatile, farmworkers are facing ever-more challenging growing and working conditions. Nevertheless, they are locked into unfavourable contracts with retailers that forcclose the possibility of experimenting with climate-resilient growing systems like agroecology and more democratic forms of land management.

Conventional agriculture as we know it exists on borrowed time. Through its profligate use of fossil fuels and fossil fuel-derived inputs, simplification and pollution of ecosystems, contributions to global heating, and production of low-quality standardised foods, it robs future generations of a climatically stable biodiverse planet and the health they need to enjoy it. Like several of today's sectors, agriculture cannot carry on as it is.

Many states, agribusinesses, and conventional farms are painfully aware of this and have begun to integrate so-called 'climate-smart' technologies and farming practices into for-profit farming systems. Climate-smart agriculture is a broad term covering a suite of technological fixes — from drone imaging systems to 'nature-based solutions' — that vainly seek to minimise or eliminate the destructive consequences of conventional agriculture without tackling the problems at their source: capital's metabolic control. In the imperial core, emissions targets are pursued through policy interventions like Europe's Green Deal or England's Environmental Land Management schemes that aim to reduce emissions or sequester carbon in farming systems. These changes aren't working. Carbon sequestration in agricultural landscapes is notoriously over-hyped and poorly evidenced. More than that, it puts the risks and burden of decarbonisation onto farmers, and beginning in 2019, farmers' protests exploded across Europe in response to green capitalist legislation for that reason.

In the global periphery, meanwhile, the necessity of decarbonising food systems has been seized upon by agribusinesses domiciled in the imperial core and by the periphery's domestic bourgeoisie as an opportunity to accumulate capital through the dispossession and disempowerment of farmworkers and rural communities. Rather than empowering them to adapt farming systems to shifting local climatic conditions, the use of big data, financialisation of agricultural production, and interventions by neo-colonial non-profits have deepened dependency relations that have blocked popular and rural development in the periphery for centuries.[34]

AGROECOLOGICAL FOOD SOVEREIGNTY: A REVOLUTIONARY ALTERNATIVE

Today's monocultural, fossil fuel-intensive farming systems have become the norm in many parts of the world, including in the Global South. Nevertheless, there remain large parts of the Global South's food systems that are still managed by smallholders practising some form of sustainable farming or agroecology, using growing systems, technologies, and knowledge that has been developed over hundreds, if not thousands, of years. Such agroecological farming systems are not outside of capital's metabolic control. Often, farms practising agroecological methods are complexly entangled, in one way or another, in the capitalist world economy.[35] Even so, agroecological farming systems have to some extent avoided being restructured by capitalist imperatives, persisting as spaces of a different kind of viable, modern, and more ecologically regenerative alternative to so-called 'conventional' agriculture. This gives agroecological systems a strange temporality. They're at one and the same time a fractured remnant of pre-capitalist means of provisioning, a part of the capitalist world-system's food system, and a precursor to a new, communal system.

Though definitions of what constitutes agroecology vary, most describe it as at once a science, practice, and social movement.[36] As a science, it draws on historical knowledge of growing foods, fuels, and fibres in biodiverse, socially, and ecologically sensitive ways and combines this with cutting-edge research into how to boost yields and reduce labour time. As a diverse set of practices, it feeds millions across the world through an iterative socio-ecological practice of growing, learning, and adapting food systems. As a movement, it is composed of growers, food justice campaigners, policy makers, and academics who see agroecology as the future of farming and who propagate good agroecological practice through *campesino a campesino* knowledge exchange.[37]

Agroecology's critics like to say that it's incapable of feeding the world's growing population. Yet numerous studies show that agroecology can indeed be scaled up to feed the global population in ways that are socially empowering and ecologically sustainable.[38] A study conducted by the Institute for Sustainable Development and International Relations found that agroecological methods could feed Europe's growing population, reduce the continent's use of lands and labour overseas, reduce emissions in the sector by 40 percent, and help to restore biodiversity.[39] Agroecology's use of biodiverse farming systems has also been shown to deliver numerous benefits for the natural environment and human populations including soil regeneration, improved biodiversity, increased nutrient density in foods, greater equity and connections among rural communities, and reduced risk of zoonotic spillovers.[40] Because agroecological production is more biodiverse than conventional monocultural farming systems, it is also more climate resilient, which is a critical consideration on a warming planet.[41]

The gradual acceptance of these benefits among mainstream (by which we mean capitalist) non-profits, international organisations, and some commercial farms has caused agroecology to go 'from being ignored, ridiculed and/or excluded by large institutions that preside over world agriculture to being recognized as *one* of the possible alternatives to address the crises caused by the Green Revolution.'[42] This uptake and mainstream acceptance has come at a heavy cost, with agroecology being repurposed as something akin to a 'technofix' alongside drone and satellite-supported precision agriculture, vertical farms, patented climate-resilient seed varieties, and robotic harvesters. Such 'climate-smart agriculture' feigns political and technological neutrality while buttressing capital's metabolic control over the global food system. Stripped of its wider system-critical implications and rendered solely as a set of 'techniques', agroecology threatens to be captured and deployed as a counter-revolutionary measure to ensure workers remain dependent on the wage relation for their food and hence their very survival.

In contrast, agroecology, when properly conceived, is intrinsically political. Instead of abstracting technologies and growing practices from the social and ecological relations they reproduce, agroecology's proponents emphasise the kinds of democratic, socially reparative, and ecologically regenerative farming practices that cannot exist under capital's metabolic control: an end to labour exploitation, the decommodification of food, attentiveness to the needs of non-human nature, and an intergenerational approach to land management, among others. One step to resist agroecology's capture is to think of it in proximity to the ideals of food sovereignty. Originally advanced by the international agrarian movement La Via Campesina, today food sovereignty has captured the imagination of growers, academics, and policymakers across the world. Though there are competing ideas about what food sovereignty involves, one of the most common definitions emphasises:

> the right of peoples to healthy and culturally appropriate food produced through ecologically sound and sustainable methods, and their right to define their own food and agriculture systems.[43]

For some, especially those influenced by the alter-globalisation movement of the late 1990s and early 2000s, food sovereignty is about creating a localised, self-sufficient food system that empowers agricultural workers by freeing them in part or in full from international trade and corporate control. While this is important, it does not go far enough.

Food sovereignty is about securing the associated producers' independence from capital's metabolic control. This necessarily means common democratic control and ownership over the production, distribution, and consumption of foods, fuels, and fibres for all workers the world over. From this perspective, it's not enough to give local agricultural producers control over food systems, as agrarian scholar Jan Douwe Van de Ploeg proposes, because this implies collectively owned private property and control over food production rather than the formation of social property and social democratic control.[44] Nor is it enough to make merely localised inroads into capital's control when the capitalist food system is defined by a global division of labour. Acknowledging this is especially important in the imperial core, where the pursuit of food sovereignty has very different resonances to its pursuit in the periphery. Food sovereignty in the UK, for example, must not come at the expense of the periphery, nor must it become an inadvertent instance of 'lifeboat ethics', where the core's food system is made more resilient to social and ecological shocks while the periphery remains in its situation of exploitation and dependency on commodities, inputs, and financing supplied by imperial powers. North-South solidarity must therefore be front and centre to struggles for food sovereignty in the imperial core in concrete, practical, and implemental ways.

ARE COUNCIL FARMS ENGLAND'S ROAD TO AGROECOLOGICAL FOOD SOVEREIGNTY?

In 2023, the New York Times ran an article breathlessly warning that 'If You Don't Use Your Land, These Marxists May Take It'.[45] Unsurprisingly, given the publication, the headline interpellates its readership as the property-owning bourgeois and plays on anti-communist sentiments. More surprisingly for the NYT, the headline isn't too much of an exaggeration. The article was referring to Brazil's Landless Workers' Movement (MST), one of the most famous contemporary examples of an agrarian movement successfully combining agroecological practices with forms of popular protagonism necessary for fully realising and embodying the transformational principles of agroecology.[46]

MST has been so successful, in part, because it has creatively mobilised elements of the Brazilian constitution which empower peasants and social movements to expropriate land that isn't serving a 'social function'. After identifying and occupying such land, the MST initiates legal proceedings to 'expropriate the land and grant title to the landless workers'.[47] As of 2017, having secured land titles for over 350,000 families, this had led to a proliferation of small-scale agrarian production cooperatives, schools, and processing plants. By mobilising its base and encouraging participatory democracy it generates popular protagonism. Through its opposition to private property and establishment of collective farms instead, it facilitates a scenario of contested reproduction. Organised in such a way that encourages the active and participatory democracy of its 1.5 million members, the MST has built itself into the largest social movement in Latin America.

While the MST is a hugely inspiring movement, its story also illustrates that the successful conjunctural wagers of one movement cannot be straightforwardly transferred into new times and places. Unlike Brazil's constitution, Britain's uncodified constitution doesn't require private property to serve any social function whatsoever. And while Britain has a long and glorious history of peasant and worker rebellion, it lacks a large population of landless workers who have been rendered marginal or superfluous to capital and who are steeped in a popular culture and history of anti-colonial and Marxist struggle or communal forms of self-organisation.[48] What Britain *does* have is a much-overlooked pre-existing form of agricultural public property which, if repurposed, could serve as the cell-form for a transition towards agroecological food sovereignty: the council farm estate.

Few outside the agricultural sector may have heard of them, but council farms provide an important and rapidly disappearing opportunity to kick-start a transition towards agroecological food sovereignty in the UK. Council farms are parcels of agricultural land owned by local authorities and leased to tenant farmworkers, usually below market rates. The UK's council farm estate was established in the late 1800s with the goal of easing access to agricultural land for young and first-generation farmworkers, who, by leasing council farms, could gain the experience and capital they needed to run their own private farms in the future. The country's council farm estate would, it was hoped, enable access to farming for new entrants in return for a dependable source of rental income for local authorities. However, for much of the past century, council farms have not been supported by the central government and their potential to facilitate access to farming for those historically excluded from the sector has been undermined.[49] Rather than serving as vital anchor institutions in the English countryside, or as a crucial stepping stone towards private farm ownership, rising land values have made it increasingly difficult for council farm tenants to move on and purchase their own farms or rent elsewhere.

More significantly, in recent years local authorities have taken to selling off their council farm holdings to plug spending deficits and support struggling social services. Since 1977, the acreage of council farms in England has declined by more than 50 percent. In just the eight years between 2010 and 2018, 15,000 hectares of the UK's council farms were privatised, which amounts to 7 percent of the total estate.[50] These sell-offs, which are indicative of a deep, systematic, politically motivated, and anti-democratic wave of land privatisation, amount to a new enclosures movement,[51] producing at least two severe long-term negative consequences. First, the loss of council farms makes farming a less accessible profession at a time when new entrants are urgently needed. Industry commentators have warned that British farming is on the 'verge of a crisis' that can only be averted by bringing younger people into the sector.[52] The average age of UK farmworkers is 58, and around 40 percent of farmworkers are beyond retirement age. Indeed, 120,000 family-owned farms are 'retiring or transferring ownership over the next few years', two thirds of which don't have a succession plan.[53] While there's growing interest in agriculture among young people and traditionally excluded groups, land prices are beyond most people's reach and the regenerative, agroecological systems they tend to favour are not supported by current legislation.

Second, the sale of council farms robs councils of long-term dependable rental incomes or, as suggested in our model below, the social and ecological benefits that accrue from ecologically regenerative and community-focused land management. This stopgap solution to politically enforced scarcity only further impoverishes and erodes the competencies of local government, narrowing the prospects for local government to support a socially and ecologically just green transition. If in the late 1800s council farms could be used to derisk entry into the agricultural sector for new farmworkers, a rejuvenated council farm estate today could be used to derisk a transition towards agroecological food sovereignty in the UK. Council farms, if managed as agroecological food systems, could become 'lighthouses' or beacons of best practice that demonstrate the desirability and viability of a broader agroecological transition of the country's agricultural land.[54]

The plight of council farms and their potential to deliver various social and ecological goods has received considerable attention from left-leaning think tanks and the alternative agricultural community in recent years,[55] but proposals to save them generally require national policy shifts or funding from central government. This regulatory support and funding are unlikely to be forthcoming. Our approach here is different. Much like the clauses in Brazil's constitution that invite land occupation, the plight of the UK's council farm estate is a conjunctural opportunity. If managed as public-common partnerships, they are an already-existing institutional form that could help the struggle for a transition towards agroecological food sovereignty. Here, we provide a speculative vision of what it is possible to do with the UK's council farm estate, in the hope that we can inspire current and aspiring farmworkers to mobilise for a transition towards agroecological food sovereignty.

COUNCIL FARMS AS AGROECOLOGICAL LIGHTHOUSES

In lieu of central government intervention to support council farms, it's essential that farmworkers, communities, and social movements exercise their collective power to defend and expand the UK's council farm estate. The self-expansion of the commons facilitated by PCPs is one way to achieve this. The institutional design described below imagines council farms as part of a local authority-supported reimagining of the UK's agricultural sector. More so than in our previous examples of PCPs, several elements of this design project into the future. One key development is that we introduce a body called the National Federation for Food Sovereignty that coordinates land management and production nationally. This is of critical importance because without some degree of centralised coordination and planning, the UK's food production cannot be made as efficient as possible across distinct biomes and growing conditions, nor can its depleted ecosystems be repaired. We are conscious that resolving the world's ecological crises, and at the same time efficiently coordinating the production of foods, fuels, and fibres, will ultimately require planning systems on a *global* scale that are accountable to, and can be directly recalled by, farmworkers, forest peoples, fisherfolk, and their communities. For now, we focus on the institutional apparatus needed for England to contribute to such a system by showing how council farms can kick-start an agroecological transition. Our design points towards a future of national planning, but this doesn't mean growers and local authorities can't pursue agroecological PCPs today. Rather, these groups would act as trailblazers, or lighthouses, of agroecological food sovereignty, demonstrating its social and ecological benefits and establishing the conditions for a broader transition of the UK's food system.

The logical starting place for explaining agroecological PCPs is the Food Sovereignty Council (FSC). This would be the democratic body responsible for governing the social, ecological, and food production objectives of participating council farms. Several farms would work together to define and implement a collectively developed and place-specific plan within the territory of a single FSC. The plan would reflect farm and landscape-specific needs and realities, regional social and ecological priorities, and (in its fully realised form) nationally agreed objectives. In an advanced stage of development, each council area in the UK would have its own FSC. The FSC also enables farms to exchange best agroecological practice, collab-

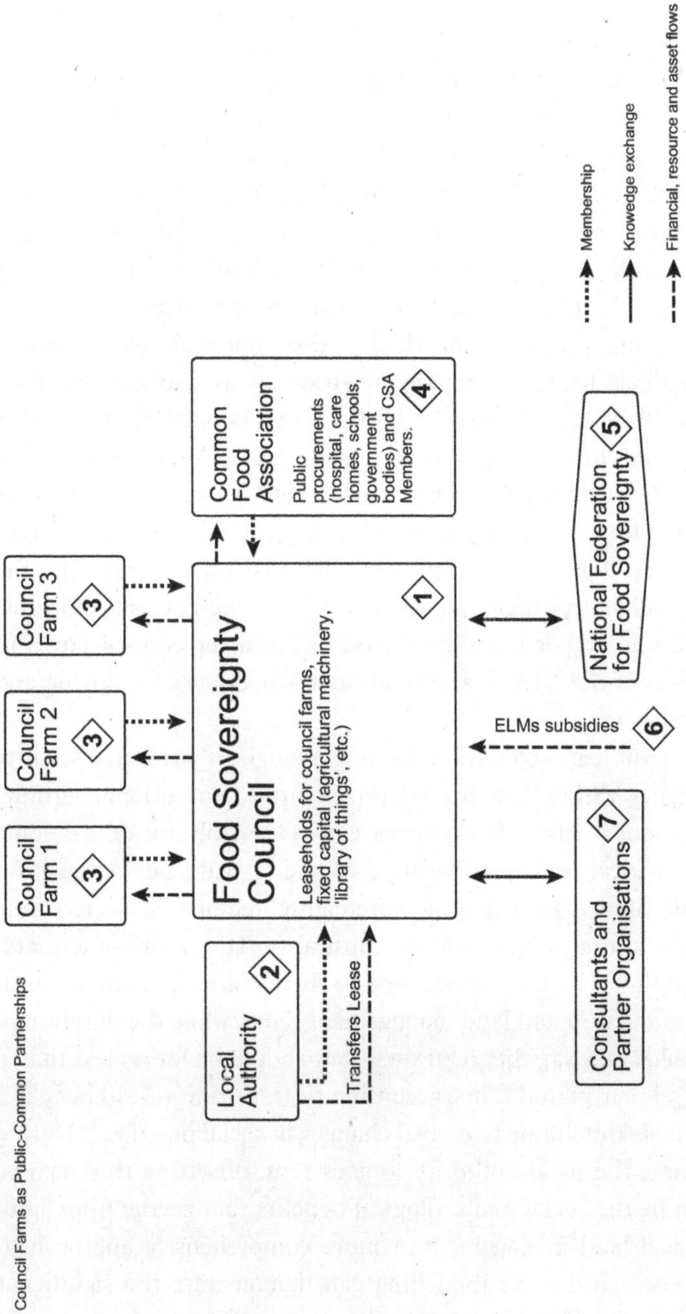

Figure 5 Council Farm Public-Common Partnership Model

orate in divisions of labour, and share fixed capital such as farming equipment and seeds.

As with the Wards Corner PCP, the FSC uses the legal form of a Community Benefit Society. The board is formed from participating farms, the local authority, and representatives from the Common Food Association (to be described below). All participating council farms have worker representation on the board. Besides its governance role, the FSC holds at least three kinds of assets that are critical to the PCP's functioning. First, the land leases for participating council farms, from which it does not seek rental income. The freehold for these remains provisionally with local authorities. Second, fixed capital used by participating council farms, such as farming machinery. This can be imagined as a 'library of things' to which all participating council farms have access.[56] This reduces the need for council farms to independently own farming materials, driving down production costs, material throughputs, and the PCP's overall ecological impact. Third, since the FSC is responsible for the sale and/or transfer of produce from the council farms to members of the CFA, it also holds assets necessary for boxing and distribution.

The farm leaseholds must be long enough to guarantee security of tenancy throughout the transition from conventional farming to agroecology. Individual farms can reasonably introduce some agroecological principles within a couple of years, but a transition towards agroecological food sovereignty requires a society-wide shift in cultural values. Non-agricultural workers, farmworkers, and local authorities alike must learn to democratically participate in food production and land management. Thus, while the duration of leaseholds may vary between sites, they should be for no less than a 25 to 50-year period. This, according to transition researchers, is a reasonable timeframe to embed changes in social practice.[57] During this time, the local authority forgoes rent, offsetting this income stream by the social and ecological benefits that accrue from agroecological land management. A more comprehensive approach to social-ecological value modelling can demonstrate the significant long-term benefits for the council in terms of restored ecosystems, local employment opportunities, increased biodiversity, soil health, wetlands restoration, increased use of greenspace, and high-quality locally produced food for residents and public services. Participating council farms are thus not only focused on their direct nutritional output, but will be required to meet various social, ecological, and production objectives, democratically agreed by the FSC in accordance with a plan ultimately co-developed through the National Federation for Food Sovereignty.

Whereas the PCPs we discussed in previous chapters featured a single site of production, here we are introducing the idea of having multiple production sites — in this case farms — within a single PCP. Each council farm is independently run through structures of worker self-management, with the aim of delivering objectives agreed by the FSC. This reflects the central importance of worker self-management and protagonism in the production process. At the same time, it acknowledges the need to align specific sites of production with wider social and ecological priorities determined by the entirety of the associated producers, and not just those working at one specific site of production. It should not, in other words, be up to the farmworkers alone to decide what they produce. It should, and must be, a decision arrived at by society as a whole in accordance with a democratically determined plan.

Bringing multiple farms together under the FSC also allows for a better use of existing government subsidies paid to England's farms, such as the new post-Brexit environment and land management (ELM) scheme. Under our proposed model, these subsidies would be received by the FSC and would serve as an important revenue stream to support an agroecological transition. Today, ELM payments are received by owner occupiers or tenants farming or managing land, in return for meeting land-use and restoration targets stipulated by Westminster. Each farm therefore chooses, in isolation from neighbouring farms and communities, how it wishes to manage the land to receive government support. This, in effect, reproduces the problem of unplanned production found in the capitalist economy. Without coordinated land-use across farms, and without society-wide input into land-use, how the land is managed is mediated by capital's metabolic control. Soil and waterway management, biodiversity protection, and food production are all subordinated to the landowner or tenant's need to maximise farm income. Rather than delivering social and ecological necessities directly, then, they're mediated through the profit motive.

In contrast, the more collectivised approach we propose has several benefits. Even during the process of transition in which capital's metabolic control dominates, making decisions about how to manage the land at the level of the FSC would allow for joined-up landscape restoration, biodiversity recovery, and food production across several farms at once. Though council farms are not always on contiguous land, those that are could co-manage and co-plan landscape restoration to maximise financial returns and the delivery of what the English government calls 'public money for public goods'. As capital's metabolic control is constrained by the expansion of spaces of contested reproduction, the receipt of government funding by the FSC socialises income streams from individuals and individualised land-use planning, helping to compose a new collective agrarian subject that manages the land not in accordance with the need to make a profit, but to meet social and ecological needs.

As an important part of breaking with the individualised and individualising use of agricultural land, tenants do not pay rent to the council nor to the FSC. Instead, tenants become workers in receipt of a wage and pension benefits — along with other guaranteed rights such as holidays and sick pay — as employees of the FSC. All workers, whether permanent or seasonal, are employed by the FSC. This wage is conditional on managing the land in accordance with agroecological principles and objectives collectively agreed by both the FSC and National Federation for Food Sovereignty.

Common Food Association

Whereas a FSC's primary function is to plan production across participating council farms, thereby kickstarting a transition towards agroecology, the Common Food Association (CFA) is responsible for making democratic social and economic interventions to expand common food production and provisioning. Each local authority would have a single CFA. Membership in the CFA is modelled on a subscription system similar to Community Supported Agriculture schemes (CSAs). There are two kinds of membership to the scheme. First, private individuals can pay an annual subscription to the CFA and in return receive fresh produce from the FSC on a weekly basis. This subscription scheme is tiered so that those with higher incomes can support the needs of lower-income households. Those unable to pay would ideally receive food freely, in accordance with the principle of 'from each according to their ability, to each according to their needs.'[58] A more developed scenario could see individuals receive tokens (rather than a literal basket of goods) that could be used within a national supermarket chain owned and governed by the Federation of Food Sovereignty.

Second, the CFA would be open to a local authority's anchor institutions, such as hospitals, care homes, schools, and government bodies. As with private individuals, in return for an institutional subscription fee to the CFA, these public institutions receive fresh produce to feed workers, patients, and students. As the FSC expands and begins to purchase its own processing equipment, it could distribute value-added products such as yoghurt, ice cream, bread, and pre-prepared meals to regional anchor institutions. In a developed scenario, these institutions would agree to consider procurement through the region's FSC before private providers.

This kind of subscription system addresses several of the challenges faced by existing community-supported agriculture schemes. Research into these schemes has shown the difficulty they have scaling up to contest conventional agriculture, in part because each scheme must compete with others on the open market for subscriptions.[59] Such schemes are also based on receiving a premium from subscribers to offset the challenges farmworkers face producing food in accordance with free market pressures and coercions. These pressures often lead farmworkers to 'self-exploit', by paying themselves below the amount of social value they create with their labour. These conditions of self-exploitation and intra-scheme competition are leading reasons farmworkers may end up leaving the sector. While some community-supported agriculture schemes struggle to make a liveable income, well-established and experienced schemes can thrive and flourish, leading to a significant discrepancy in income and opportunity.[60]

In contrast, subscriptions to the CFA are integrated with a potentially unlimited number of participating council farms, the workers of which receive a living wage and benefits. This removes the element of intra-farm competition for subscriptions and potential for self-exploitation. It also enables more successful farms, which are perhaps working more productive land or with a more advanced agroecological system, to support those still undergoing an agroecological transition. This helps to 'derisk' the agroecological transition across all participating council farms, insulating and fostering spaces of popular protagonism and contested reproduction.

In our previous examples of PCPs, the Common Association was responsible for democratically investing surpluses received from a Joint Enterprise. In the food system, however, these surpluses are likely to be small to non-existent. Even under capitalism, food production is rarely profitable without subsidies or forms of state protection. As Jason Moore and Raj Patel argue in their book, the capitalist world-system is dependent on 'cheap food' to keep the price of labour power to a minimum, thereby maximising profits across all sectors of the economy.[61] Farms that do turn a profit either grow specialised produce or implement practices that have no place in a green and democratic future, such as super-exploiting immigrant labour, hiring unwaged 'volunteers' and 'interns', and externalising costs of production onto non-human nature through ecologically damaging farming practices.

Surpluses on agroecological PCPs could be obtained by incorporating value-added processing such as yoghurt, cheese, or flour production into a CFA and selling these on the capitalist market. In cases where surpluses can be generated, the CFA is responsible for democratically investing surpluses in whatever way it decides. This does not need to be in the agricultural sector, but if it is, surpluses could support local growing initiatives, invest in the agroecological improvement of existing council farm estates, or invest in infrastructure for food processing. Other agricultural uses of surpluses might include agroecological colleges, such as funding scholarships to ensure the next generation of agroecological farmworkers.

In most cases, however, we accept that agroecological PCPs are unlikely to generate a sizeable surplus. While this might seem like a problem, it is in fact a good thing. PCPs are a transitional institution because they foster popular protagonism and contested reproduction. They can do this in part because in the aggregate, across a future network of PCPs spanning multiple sectors, they generate a surplus that contributes to what we've called the self-expansion of the commons. But it doesn't follow from this that each PCP must contribute a monetary surplus, providing it can support the dismantling of capital's metabolic control in other ways.

It is on this front that agroecological PCPs and CFAs have a role to play in the broader contested reproduction of our food systems even if they don't return a surplus. In removing the need to generate a surplus, agroecological PCPs alleviate the pressures that lead to exploitative employment conditions — including self-exploitation — or the degradation of nature in agricultural landscapes. This facilitates a qualitative transformation in labour conditions and metabolic exchanges with non-human nature. More fundamentally, since the production of food is no longer mediated through the profit motive, it can instead be produced to meet the immediate needs of the associated producers. Food production becomes, in other words, a space of contested reproduction. Those subscribing to an agroecological PCP subscribe with wages most likely paid to them from their participation in a capitalist economy, but insofar as farms cease to function as surplus-generating enterprises they cease to function capitalistically.

In cases where a FSC isn't generating an appreciable surplus, the CFA still serves an important function. As a significant stakeholder in the governance of the FSC, individuals and organisations represented by the CFA can shape decisions about the agroecological transition and production, such as requesting specific produce be grown, or not grown, in coming years. Through their participation, members of the CFA will also come to understand the planning and land management needs of council farms, opening space for dialogue about how other large landowning anchor institutions, such as the NHS, may repurpose their land to support food sovereignty.

National Federation for Food Sovereignty

Farmworkers, communities, and local authorities can organise right now to use council farms in the ways we have described. Regional agroecological PCPs would demonstrate that another food system is possible. But for agroecological PCPs to drive a transformation of Britain's food system, they need to operate at the national level and beyond. Food production in the UK is heavily dependent on local climatic and soil conditions. Whereas the south-east's warm, dry climate and comparatively flat topography lend it to arable production, the north-west's hillier landscapes, wetter weather, and comparatively lower quality soils lend it to grazing and livestock. Moreover, some parts of the UK's current agricultural land may be put to better use as ecological restoration sites for the protection of endangered species or the rebuilding of critically important habitats. This means that if the UK is to pursue food sovereignty and a diverse diet for all who live here, it will need to plan production nationally rather than at the local level. We therefore propose the establishment of a National Federation for Food Sovereignty to coordinate planning across all FSCs and to connect the UK's agroecological farms to international food sovereignty networks and initiatives.

The federation would feature representatives from at least three distinct groups. First, since sector-wide planning requires a high degree of knowledge about each FSC's agroecological systems and production capacities, a delegate from each FSC would be critical. Second, since the federation will be deciding what the country produces, and hence consumes and trades, it must feature representatives of non-agricultural workers and consumers in the UK and representatives of the international food sovereignty movement. Third, the federation's board would have representation from experts in the fields of climatology, agroecology, nutrition, and conservation.

These experts would help to build a climate-resilient and ecologically reparative agroecological system at scale.

The federation's board is responsible for devising a plan to meet as much of the UK's social, ecological, and production needs as possible through the FSCs, as well as UK production for export. Since representatives of FSCs sit on the federation's boards, these production plans are not delivered in a top-down fashion. Instead, they're co-designed by the associated producers themselves to meet immediate social and ecological needs. Planning production in this way would lead to a more rational use of the UK's council farm estate and potentially help end the current food system's ecologically damaging and wasteful overproduction.

Beyond planning production, the National Federation for Food Sovereignty would also serve as a conduit to disseminate agroecological knowledge and best practice. It should always be remembered that the farmworkers leading the transition towards agroecology on council farms are experts in their own right with a deep knowledge of the landscapes they steward. As farmworkers experiment with their agroecological systems they will discover ways to introduce efficiencies such as increased yields, greater climate resilience, or reduced labour time. As workers at 'agroecological lighthouses', farmworkers would therefore be expected to share their knowledge and expertise freely with one another and with partnering experts and organisations. At the same time, the board's academic experts in fields including agroecology and conservation would be expected to help FSCs achieve their production plans while regenerating ecosystems damaged by centuries of capital's metabolic control. Conservationists and ecologists, for example, could help farmworkers understand the needs of their local wildlife, while soil scientists can help farmworkers understand to what extent their farming practice might be improving soil quality. This free exchange of knowledge and best practice is an important part of the commons. In recognition of this, the federation would coordinate farm visits and knowledge exchanges. In Cuba and elsewhere in Latin America, a similar system known as 'campesino a campesino' has already been used to great effect.[62]

TOWARDS AGROECOLOGICAL FOOD SOVEREIGNTY

When we walk into the fruit and vegetable aisle in a supermarket, it seems as if we are presented with an abundance of choice. A rainbow of colours, tastes, and textures. It can be easy to forget that what we see is an extremely narrow range of produce, specially selected not for their nutritional value, taste, or even their popularity, but because they are high-yielding, transport well, and generally return a profit (supermarkets frequently lose money on fruits like bananas but this is another story). It's on these terms that cloudberries don't make the cut. Their rich cultural history is irrelevant. Their unique taste is beyond the point. The same applies to many other delicious and culturally significant foods such as lingonberries, jelly palms, mayhaws, pawpaws, baru nuts, blackcaps, jicama, and mulberries. Even fruits and vegetables that we can easily find in supermarkets are just a fraction of those we could experience.

As is so often the case under capitalism, then, lurking behind the appearance of abundance is an artificially imposed scarcity. Worse, it's a scarcity that robs people and planet of the ecological conditions we need to live and flourish in radical abundance. In this chapter, we've tried to model what an institutional framework capable of delivering a transition towards a new food system could look like in detail. This has necessarily meant getting into the weeds. As we have throughout the book, rather than jumping over the problem of transition to imagine postcapitalist futures, we have sought to dwell in the messy practicalities of transition, seeking out institutional forms and opportunities. The result is a wager on council farms as a conjunctural opportunity to shift the UK's food system away from conventional farming practices towards agroecological food sovereignty.

We understand this vision brings its challenges. Unlike Brazil's MST, England does not have a mass of landless workers clamouring for land access and agrarian reform. For a transition towards agroecological food sovereignty to succeed, it must respond to the conjuncture within which it finds itself, including appropriate social movements, classes, and institutional configurations. In the UK, for example, it would have to draw together struggles led by urban and rural workers. This would necessarily include current and aspiring landless agricultural workers, as well as small-scale and tenant farmworkers who are willing to separate the idea of secure land occupancy from the fetishisation of private property, or become so through their engagement. The transition must also draw on energy from trade unions such as the Bakers, Food and Allied Workers' Union, which mobilises workers in the food processing and distribution sectors. And it would need to galvanise and assist urban workers struggling with the high price of good-quality food. This includes the Right to Food Campaign, which fights to 'ensure all people regardless of their gender, race, immigration status or age are able to access food in a dignified way.'[63] The transition we envision may also be animated by the cooperative movement and community-supported agricultural schemes, though these would need to come to recognise that collectively owned private property is no solution to capital's metabolic control. Finally, the transition would have to be internationalist in orientation. It must listen to, and learn from, movements like the MST, as well as Cuba's impressive advances in agroecological production, Kerala's people's planning initiative, Venezuela's system of communes, and advances made by La Via Campesina the world over.

It is only by bringing these various elements of the UK's and the world's working classes together that a transition towards agroecological food sovereignty for all becomes possible. Yet as we've hoped to show here, it's not enough to simply bring these forces together. We desperately need institutional forms, like PCPs, that can create the space for workers to exercise popular protagonism across the food system, from the sites of production to consumption. Only then can the associated producers say that they're on the path towards radical abundance.

9
Conclusion: Futures

This is a book about how to win a world of radical abundance. We began with a broad-sweep analysis of how global capitalism makes the lives of the world's working classes harder, shorter, and generally more miserable than they ought to be. Though not all workers suffer the effects of capital's violent dialectics of bullshit abundance and artificial scarcity equally, we have all suffered from them. This shared experience is the basis for shared struggle and as Marta Harnecker says, 'realising that there are many of us who are in the same struggle is what makes us strong'.[1]

Even so, there's no doubt that winning a green and democratic future for all will be an uphill battle. The world's capitalist classes have had decades to address the world's escalating ecological crises, yet under their watch global heating is getting worse, global biodiversity is in free fall, and what were once called 'extreme weather events' are now the new normal. Meanwhile, billions of people do without the things they and their loved ones need to flourish and live dignified lives. As the primary beneficiaries of capital's metabolic control, the world's capitalist classes have studiously avoided tackling the root cause of these issues: the capital system itself. Instead, they have pursued so-called 'green capitalist transitions' of various kinds that tinker with the system and often empower the very actors that caused the world's crises to lead the way in addressing them: the capitalist state, the fossil fuel industry, banks, and financial institutions.

Consciously or not, this worldview sees transition as a technical problem, a challenge akin to unplugging the capitalist world-system from one set of physical and energetic inputs and plugging it into another. In some circles today, there are sincere overtures about ensuring this is done in a just manner — about making sure that workers in carbon-intensive industries are not just thrown onto the scrapheap, or that those in the periphery aren't further impoverished and exploited to facilitate a technical recomposition in the core. There is also good evidence that it is possible to expand production of renewable energy, ban the use of harmful phosphates, rebuild national habitats, and limit collective meat consumption, all of which are necessary in their own right. The problem is that capital has already proven itself incapable of doing any of these things within a reasonable timeframe. The greatest evidence for this is that, in many ways, it is already too late. The effects of inaction are already here for all to see.

The problem isn't that capital's metabolic regime is being managed 'badly' by its 'personifications', resulting in investment in the wrong inputs or manufacturing of the wrong outputs (though this does often happen), but that capital is itself a *fundamentally uncontrollable social relation* that defies being managed in any way that might undermine and constrain its expansion-oriented dynamics. The capitalist strategy of transition is therefore more properly called an *anti-transition*. It is an attempt to ward off a very different kind of transition, the need for which becomes clearer by the day.

The transition we've argued for in this book is one that wrests control of our collective reproduction from capital and puts it in the hands of the associated producers. Without this kind of transition, the microplastics coursing through our bloodstreams, the endless traffic we sit in to get to work, or the poorly built household appliances we keep having to replace will be the least of our worries. As we discuss in Chapter Two, there are many others who understand that capital itself is the problem and that we will need ecosocialist planning of production if we are to travel in another direction. To reiterate István Mészáros, 'the sustainability of a global order of socio-metabolic reproduction is inconceivable without an adequate planning system, administered on the basis of substantive democracy by freely associated producers.'[2]

At least on an abstract level, we know where we need to get to: a society in which the 'associated producers... govern the human metabolism with nature in a rational way, bringing it under their collective control' and 'accomplishing it with the least expenditure of energy and in conditions most worthy and appropriate for their human nature.'[3] Today, we must add to this formulation from Marx that the associated producers must also plan their collective reproduction within biophysical limits so the conditions for human and non-human flourishing are protected for generations to come.[4] It is this, and not a greenwashed bourgeois electoral system, that we have in mind when we talk about a green democratic future. And while it is certainly important to imagine blueprints and schematics of what such democratic planning systems might look like,[5] we must be clear that this isn't the same as developing a strategy of transition. The problem of transition isn't about imagining a different future, or imagining how democratic planning might work in principle, but of figuring out how we can act in the present to bring a different future and system of democratic planning into being.

We have emphasised that there are two non-negotiable, invariant, features of any anti-capitalist transition worthy of the name: popular protagonism and contested reproduction. Popular protagonism names the process of building the working classes' collective capacities to act in common, but it means this in a very specific sense. Popular protagonism isn't expressed when people come together to demand that the capitalist state act to remedy a situation: global heating, poor public transportation, or economic inequality. It is expressed when the working classes take themselves as the agents of their own destiny, when they organise together to plan their collective reproduction, to shape their own common future. This can only happen through what Che Guevara calls the 'institutionalisation of the revolution'. Institutions must be built — communes, parties, and so on — that denaturalise capital's metabolic control and naturalise new forms of collective consciousness.

Contested reproduction, meanwhile, involves introducing situations where the new communal system of metabolic control comes into contact with, undermines, and challenges capital's metabolic control. In a scenario of contested reproduction, each metabolic system vies with the other for dominance and limits its operation. Capital's law of value, which produces for accumulation's sake, actively undermines efforts to produce for immediate need or live outside of the capital-wage relation. Spaces of communal metabolic control, on the other hand, seek to discipline and diminish capital's effects, fostering new ways to reproduce ourselves and new forms of political consciousness. In Evgenii Preobrazhensky's words, the goal is the 'ousting of other economic forms [capital], the subordination of these forms to the new form, and their gradual elimination'. Popular protagonism and contested reproduction are the building blocks of a new system of metabolic control, but the process of transition itself is always open, provisional, and contested. There is nothing guaranteed in politics. Everything hinges on the balance of forces, on the specific composition of the classes pitched against one another in practice.

FROM A THEORY TO A PRACTICE OF TRANSITION

This is all fairly easy to say in the abstract, but things get murkier when we try to understand how social struggles have put these ideas into practice. As we mentioned in the introduction, part of the function of a 'real utopian sociology' is to study initiatives that are unfolding in circumstances that may be quite different from our own, to understand what forms contested reproduction is taking and what expressions of popular protagonism are proving successful. The goal here isn't to look for modes of organising that can simply be replicated without recognition of the different contextual factors that simultaneously shape them and condition their potential relative effects. It is impossible to produce a facsimile of what has been achieved in Venezuela in the United States, or to transpose the successes of Jackson Mississippi to Berlin without alteration. Rather, the aim is to learn from these experiences in order to think about the kinds of political wagers that may work in our own contexts.

As we argued in Chapter Four, these wagers must be based on an ongoing conjunctural analysis of how capital's contradictory tendencies are manifesting themselves across time and space. Writing from the United Kingdom in late 2024, we have proposed that the rise of the derisking state and disaster nationalism mark a sea change in how the imperial core is responding to two of the world's most pressing crisis tendencies: secular stagnation and the world's compounding ecological crises. We believe this shift matters because it opens new strategic opportunities to foster popular protagonism and contested reproduction. For decades, we were told that it was inadvisable for the capitalist state to meddle in markets, and that the solution to all of our ills would even be found in the construction of *more* markets. Private ownership and the 'invisible hand' of competition would, as if by magic, correct temporary market inefficiencies, produce affordable transportation networks, cheaper water and energy bills, bring down the price of renewables, and so much else besides.

The rise of the derisking state with its interest in state industrial strategy — in other words, economic planning — and Trump's aggressively interventionary tariffs put paid to this idea. By derisking certain projects and industries, the state is actively meddling in markets to channel capital in a chosen direction. By imposing tariffs to protect US industry from international competition, Trump is similarly constructing markets in the interest of private capital. These tendencies repoliticise the state and economy in distinct ways. Pressure can be applied to notionally liberal and progressive governments, initially to specific parts of the government apparatus, to derisk the commons rather than private capital. If they won't support this agenda, they must be forced to do so by whatever means necessary. In disaster nationalist contexts, a more insurgent politics will be needed. Since Trump, for example, has abandoned the idea of a green transition of any kind, it's paramount that the working class seize control over our collective reproduction and the economic sectors we depend on so that we can care for and protect one another on a heating planet.

This is where public-common partnerships enter the scene. PCPs are not a far-out idea. In principle, any national or local government that cares about democracy, workers rights, and community empowerment could support their expansion in the here and now. The 'only' reasons they wouldn't are political and ideological; they believe that the private sector, rather than workers and their communities, should own, govern, and control the things we all need to live rich and fulfilling lives. They believe in bullshit abundance and artificial scarcity. Even unsympathetic (albeit not outright hostile) public bodies can be compelled into supporting the formation of PCPs through mass mobilisation and concerted strategies. This is one of the greatest strengths of PCPs. They're an institutional form that is realisable within the very real constraints of our current realities, and yet their logic points towards the expansion of a communal social metabolism with the power to contest capital's metabolic control. Because of this, they're well placed to push against the fundamental principles of capitalist common sense, to expose as ideological what the derisking state presents as apolitical and pragmatic.

Just as there's no reason why a state can't support the founding of PCPs today, there's no reason why workers and communities can't organise to establish them. PCPs are not conditional on some prior phase of organising — there's no need to elect a sympathetic local councillor or national government — nor are they a strategy that is entirely about what we might achieve in our spare time. Since they are, fundamentally, a struggle over production, they can be incorporated into workplace and trade union struggles. This means they avoid the risk of becoming a subcultural political practice that creates insular spaces of economic otherness, little flotillas of 'ethical' alternatives whose internal logic never points towards a conflict with capital's metabolic control. For these reasons, we think PCPs — and institutions like them that combine the expansion of popular protagonism and contested reproduction — are a worthwhile wager, an appropriate strategy of transition for our conjuncture.

WINNING A GREEN AND DEMOCRATIC FUTURE

This brings us to what is perhaps the most obvious question for a book subtitled 'How to win a green democratic future'. Readers might expect a book subtitled in this way to focus on the very specific question of how to rapidly and democratically phase out fossil fuels. What combination of direct action, populist electoral victories, monkeywrenching, trade union organising, divestment campaigns, replacement renewable infrastructure, and whatever else might add up to break the hold that fossil capital has on the reproduction of our societies? Our initial answer is that we shouldn't stop doing any of these things. What matters is the theory of transition these tactics are in aid of. Olúfẹ́mi O. Táíwò, for instance, argues that whatever tactics are used, 'nothing less than the total defeat of the organised political interests of oil, gas, and coal producers is necessary to make any other climate justice goals even a remote possibility.' He therefore proposes a 'two-step politics' in which we 'first dethrone fossil capital; then transform the world'.[6] Our wager is different. The world can, and indeed must, be transformed as we dismantle the fossil fuel industry's political influence and infrastructure. To win a green and democratic future we must end not only 'fossil capital'[7] — capital invested in or managed by the fossil fuel industry — but capital itself.

As counterintuitive as it might appear, the prospects of a green and democratic future aren't decided by how quickly we can replace fossil fuels with more sustainable energy sources. This of course matters, but the question of how quickly we can decarbonise society depends on a more fundamental set of questions: What is the energy we produced used for? Whose interests does its production serve? Who gets to decide what kinds of energy infrastructures are built, where, and how? In other words, *what regime of metabolic control does our energy system help to reproduce?*

As long as our social metabolism is mediated by capital, as long as the reason why energy is generated and energy-intensive technology is deployed, is to generate the greatest profits, then there can be no end to capital's violent impact on human and non-human nature. As long as human ingenuity is subservient to — and constrained by — the imperative to accumulate, then every relative efficiency gain and every replacement energy source will achieve nothing but an acceleration of the demand for more bullshit abundance.[8] More energy, more biological material, more land, more rare earth metals, more sand, more pesticides, more microplastics, more space, more fresh water, more human time, more lives, more deforestation, more extinction, more bullshit, more scarcity. This is the case no matter how 'green' the global energy mix becomes.[9] Because of this, dethroning fossil capital isn't something that can be done before or after we transform the world. In fact, dethroning just 'fossil capital' isn't the idea at all. The goal must be to dismantle capital's metabolic control in and through the process of transition.

This is a monumental task, and we do not pretend that PCPs can achieve it on their own. This means some caveats are needed about what we hope this book and PCPs can offer to the transition. There are four that come to mind. The first is this: we are not suggesting that everyone stop the organising they may already be doing and build PCPs. PCPs don't need to be, and shouldn't be, the only strategy that people turn to. Rather, we think PCPs could support and amplify other initiatives, whether these be electoral strategies, local environmental campaigns, trade union struggles, social movement mobilisation, or revolutionary party-building. PCPs can support these struggles because they are an institutional form that brings together popular protagonism and contested reproduction.

It's because PCPs combine the invariant features of transition that we think they are a worthy conjunctural wager. On the one hand, building a new communal social metabolism is needed to sustain expressions of popular protagonism, because without the collective power to act, we will be overwhelmed by the forces of capital On the other, it's through participation in sites of contested reproduction that people holding relatively different (but non-antagonistic) class interests might begin to compose a collective subject of social transformation. As these mutually reinforcing processes take hold and expand, increasingly ambitious expressions of popular protagonism may lead to an ever more extensive communal social metabolism, which in turn enables ever more ambitious forms of popular protagonism. This process, which we've called the self-expansion of the commons, is at the heart of PCPs and adds an important missing piece to other ways of struggling for a green and democratic future. We think this is especially important in our time of cascading social and ecological catastrophes. To flourish, the working classes must take control of the means of their collective reproduction and democratically govern them in their collective interest.

Our second caveat: a strength of PCPs is that they're a strategy of struggle that is achievable within the limits of what is currently politically possible, and yet their power to set in motion the self-expansion of the commons points beyond the present. We say this to emphasise that PCPs should be understood as *transitional* organisations, and not as the blueprints of some utopian ecosocialist future. PCPs embrace the messy, provisional, and contingent character of transition — the process of trying to make what now seems impossible possible. As the boundaries of political possibility are transformed through the process of transition, different institutions for communal metabolic control may emerge and PCPs may be adapted or mutate to take on new functions. In Chapter Eight we began to model how this could happen by introducing the prospect of national food planning through PCPs.

Third, we reiterate that PCPs are an institutional form that we hope can take root, and flourish, in a particular moment and in particular places. They're a *conjunctural* intervention. The question of how far they can travel beyond the geographies and conjuncture we've studied is an open question, but what is certain is that PCPs aren't appropriate for all geographies and all conjunctures. For this reason, it's important to stress that while PCPs express the invariant features of transition, they aren't the only institutions that can do this. In other times and places, it may well be that different institutional forms are more appropriate. In such cases, we hope this book has modelled a certain kind of political practice: that of designing and testing the institutions needed to build a world of radical abundance for all.

Finally, this book argues for the patient work of building institutions — and lots of them. This isn't a strategy that promises a quick and decisive victory. Nor does it pretend that an ecosocialist future is waiting just over the horizon. With the increasing intensity of global heating-induced extreme weather events, and with confirmation the world breached 1.5C warming for a full year between February 2023 and January 2024, there will be those who say we don't have time for a strategy that requires patience. In the first instance, our response is to ask what other choice we have. If one agrees with the premise that we must free ourselves from capital's metabolic control to save human and non-human nature from untold destruction, let alone to have a chance at a green and democratic future, we have no option but to do what we can in the here and now. It is at once *too late* to build a new social metabolism and *exactly the right time* to start. In this climatically unstable world, where it is increasingly clear that capital is willing to let people die so that capital might survive, it is critical that we find ways to collectively provide and care for one another. PCPs are one form that this could take. We should also never forget that we are in a time of dramatic social and ecological upheaval and that in times like these, as Michael Lebowitz points out, 'small events may produce major effects'.[10] The course of history is non-linear. What may have seemed impossible one day can suddenly appear inevitable. We build institutions of common democratic control in the hope that their expansion becomes just such an inevitability.

TOWARDS A WORLD OF RADICAL ABUNDANCE

In 1911, the American poet and novelist James Oppenheim wrote the now infamous poem 'Bread and Roses', inspired by the women's suffrage activist Helen Todd. Working as a factory inspector for the State of Illinois, Todd spent her days listening to women's accounts of low pay, inequality, and the drudgery of their work. Along with four other women from the Chicago Women's Club, an association of wealthy middle-class women that had recently established some of the first kindergartens in Chicago, Todd began organising Illinois automobile workers for women's right to vote in the summer of 1910. Inspired by a discussion she'd had with a young woman the night before giving a speech, Todd pronounced that the women's 'vote will go toward helping forward the time when life's Bread, which is home, shelter and security, and the Roses of life, music, education, nature, and books, shall be the heritage of every child that is born in the country'. More than 70 years after the Seneca Falls Convention declared women's universal suffrage as its goal, the seemingly impossible became inevitable, and in 1920 Congress passed the Nineteenth Amendment to the US Constitution.

From its immortalisation in the name of the 1912 Lawrence textile strike and songs on Iowa's factory picket lines in the 1930s, to its 1969 reimagination as a 'fist and a rose' by the French graphic artist Marc Bonnet, its symbolic representation in the logo of the Democratic Socialists of America, and its anthemic rendition in *Pride* — a 2014 film about queer activists who raised money to help families affected by the British miners' strike — Todd's words went on to inspire generations of socialists. The image of Bread and Roses has come to represent the hope for a world in which we have what we need not just to survive, but to flourish. In many ways, our use of 'radical abundance' is much the same. It is a hope that moves us without filling in the details. Only a theory and strategy of transition can give this hope definite shape and direction. Only attention to the messy realities of transition can get us from where we are now to where we know that we need to be.

Notes

Chapter One

1. Enyoh et al., 2023
2. Wang et al., 2023
3. Prata et al., 2021
4. Lerner, 2019
5. Liboiron, 2021
6. Carrington, 2024
7. Da Costa Vieira, 2024
8. Corless & Haynes, 2024
9. Inrix, 2024
10. TUC, 2019
11. Schwartz, 2009
12. Krachler & Greer, 2015
13. Hickel, 2020, Saito, 2024
14. Vangay et al., 2018
15. Shi, 2019
16. Agus et al., 2016
17. Statovci et al., 2017
18. Skypala & Vlieg-Boerstra, 2014
19. Parada-Cabaleiro et al., 2024
20. Serrà et al., 2012
21. Percino et al., 2014
22. Brotherton, 2023
23. Greenfield, 2024
24. Food and Agriculture Organization, 2020
25. Fitzherbert et al., 2008
26. Aguirre-Gutiérrez et al., 2023
27. Parnreiter et al., 2024
28. Smith, 2016
29. Patnaik & Patnaik, 2021
30. Ajl, 2023
31. Tilzey, 2024
32. Dorninger et al., 2021
33. Marx, 2004, p. 799
34. Pinker, 2018, p. 107

35. Sullivan & Hickel, 2023
36. Sullivan & Hickel, 2023
37. Graeber & Wengrow, 2022, p. 20
38. Graeber & Wengrow, 2022, p. 536
39. Keynes, 2008
40. International Labour Organization, 2023
41. Graeber, 2018, p. xvii; p. 8
42. Klein & Thompson, 2025
43. Suits, 2014, p. 43
44. Mészáros, 2010, p. 768
45. Hickel, 2019, p. 62
46. Saito, 2024
47. O'Neill et al., 2018
48. Harnecker, 2015
49. Baiocchi, 2024
50. Wright, 2010, p. 151
51. Gilbert, 2023

Chapter Two

1. Clarke, 2016; Mészáros, 2022
2. Heron, 2024
3. Deutsche Bank Research, 2020
4. Bushby, 2022
5. Tooze, 2022
6. World Economic Forum, 2024, p. 6–7
7. IPBES, 2019, p. 37
8. IPCC, 2023, p. 61
9. Anderson, 2023
10. Parisi et al., 2022
11. Cantone et al., 2021
12. Ajl, 2021
13. Pedregal & Lukić, 2024
14. Perry, 2020
15. Lenin, 1920a
16. Rice et al., 2021; Heron 2024
17. Linera, 2013
18. Garo, 2023, p. 238
19. Endnotes, 2008; Monticelli, 2024
20. Holloway, 2010
21. Bernes, 2018
22. Endnotes, 2008

23. Clover, 2017
24. Bernes, 2018, p. 364
25. Toscano, 2011, p. 94
26. Dean, 2025
27. Toscano, 2011, p. 97
28. Trainer, 2011
29. Trainer, 2020
30. Mészáros, 2022
31. Aronoff et al., 2019; Chomsky & Pollin, 2020
32. The Red Nation, 2021
33. Barlow et al., 2022
34. Vettese & Pendergrass, 2022
35. Bastani, 2020
36. Vettese & Pendergrass, 2022, p. 18
37. Vettese & Pendergrass, 2022, p. 12
38. Vettese & Pendergrass, 2022, p. 17
39. Aronoff et al., 2019, p. 6–7
40. Aronoff et al., 2019, p. 7
41. Foster, 2008
42. Lebowitz, 2020, p. 131
43. Harootunian, 2015
44. Bordiga, 1954
45. Mészáros, 2010
46. Marx, 2005, p. 101
47. Mészáros, 2010
48. Moin, 2024
49. Moore, 2015
50. Marx, 2004, p. 283
51. Smith, 2020
52. Mészáros, 2010, p. 17
53. Marx, 2004, p. 290
54. Mészáros, 2010, p. 139
55. Mészáros, 2010, p. 139
56. Graeber & Wengrow, 2022
57. Mészáros, 2010, p. 802–3
58. Mészáros, 2010, p. 981
59. Mészáros, 2010, p. 792
60. Mészáros, 2010, p. 980
61. Marx, 2024, p. 303. For this quote, we draw from Paul Reitter's translation of *Capital: Volume 1*. In general throughout this book, we use the Penguin edition translated by Ben Fowkes. In this case, however, Fowkes' translation doesn't capture Marx's argument that capital stands outside and above the worker as an alienated power.

62. Mészáros, 2010, p. 981
63. Mészáros, 2010, p. 980
64. Marx & Engels, 2009, p. 125
65. Mészáros, 2010, p. 980
66. Marx & Engels, 2009, p. 36
67. Marx, 2004, p. 739
68. Luxemburg, 2007, p. 80
69. Marx, 1993, p. 571
70. Luxemburg, 2007, p. 80–1
71. Mészáros, 2010, p. 138
72. Mészáros, 2010, p. 792
73. Mészáros, 2010, p. 802
74. Marx, 2004, p. 959
75. Mészáros, 2010, p. 939
76. Marx, 1853
77. Harnecker, 2015, p. 194
78. Harnecker, 2015, p. 177
79. Marx, 1864
80. Marx, 2004, p. 899
81. Lebowitz, 2020
82. Althusser, 2014, p. 156
83. Albert, 2023, p. 16
84. Lebowitz, 2020, p. 156
85. Lebowitz, 2020, p. 165
86. Guevara, 1965
87. Harnecker, 2015, p. 69
88. Lebowitz, 2009
89. Bevins, 2023, p. 192, p. 60
90. Mészáros, 2010, p. 792
91. Marx & Engels, 2017, p. 81
92. Lebowitz, 2009, p. 8
93. Lebowitz, 2009, p.8
94. Preobrazhensky, 1965, p. 77
95. Preobrazhensky, 1980, p. 173
96. Preobrazhensky, 1980, p. 59
97. Preobrazhensky, 1980, pp. 58–9
98. Marx, 1871
99. Marx, 1871
100. Marx, 1871
101. Chávez & Harnecker, 2005, p. 72
102. Mészáros, 2010, p. 939–40
103. Lenin, 1920a

Chapter Three

1. Rustin, 2010
2. Holloway, 2002
3. Lebowitz, 2020, p. 165
4. Marx, 2004, p. 742
5. Gerbaudo, 2012; Mason, 2012; Mattoni & Porta, 2015
6. Ross, 2013; Latif, 2022
7. Hardt & Negri, 2017
8. Dean, 2016
9. Bevins, 2023
10. Sitrin, 2006
11. Monticelli, 2024
12. The Zapatista's declarations of the Lacandon Jungle are available here: http://enlacezapatista.ezln.org.mx/
13. Greenberg, 2013
14. Carney, 2011
15. Mészáros, 2010
16. Carlsson, 2008
17. Karolidis & Karcich, 2023
18. Labour Party, 2017
19. Mouffe, 2018
20. Mouffe, 2022, p. 5
21. Fraser, 2019, p. 24
22. Gerbaudo, 2019, p. 93, 178
23. Deleuze & Guattari, 2006
24. Harnecker, 2015, p. 69
25. For a Basque analysis of how the 'transformative economy' is distinct from concepts such as social economy or solidarity economy, see Talaios Koop, 2023.
26. Hiritik-at, 2022, p. 44
27. Lurralde Askea, 2024, p. 5. Our translation
28. Talaios Koop, 2023
29. Egia, 2025
30. Hiritik-at, 2022, p. 43
31. Hiritik-at, 2022, p. 46
32. Personal communication
33. Birch & Ward, 2022
34. Gabor & Kohl, 2022
35. Hamann & Türkmen, 2020
36. Kusiak, 2024
37. Malcolm X Grassroots Movement, n.d.

38. Franklin, 2009
39. Akuno & Meyer, 2023, p. 130–11
40. Kush refers to the Kush region, 18 contiguous Black-majority counties that span both sides of the lower Mississippi river, starting in Memphis, Tennessee to New Orleans, Louisiana. The overwhelming concentration of this district is in the Mississippi Delta, an area that is larger than Belgium.
41. Akuno et al., 2017
42. Akuno & Meyer, 2023, p. 23
43. Akuno, 2012
44. Akuno & Meyer, 2023, p. 90
45. Akuno & Meyer, 2023, p. 90
46. Nossiter, 1982
47. Menon, 2011
48. Isaac, 2022, p. 55
49. Isaac, 2022, p. 59
50. Patnaik, 1995, p. 37
51. Namboodiripad, 2010
52. Governance Knowledge Centre, 2011
53. Government of Kerala, 2022, p.13
54. Isaac & Franke, 2021
55. Isaac, 2022, p. 82
56. Isaac, 2022, p. 88
57. Kumar, 2007
58. Chavez, 2015
59. Foster, 2015
60. Gilbert, 2023
61. Azzellini, 2013
62. Azzellini, 2023
63. Foster, 2022
64. Union Comunera, 2023
65. Podur & Emersberger, 2021
66. Harnecker, 2015, p. 69
67. See Russell & Bianchi, 2026
68. Maher, 2013, p. 236
69. Maher, 2013, p. 240

Chapter Four

1. Heron, 2024
2. Gupta et al., 2024
3. Hall et al., 1978, p. viii

4. Hall, 2021a, p. 65
5. Gilbert, 2019, p. 15
6. Seymour, 2024
7. Klein & Thompson, 2025
8. Wright, 2023
9. Pineault, 2022
10. Roberts, 2023
11. Summers, 2013
12. Jackson, 2019. There are 38 member countries of the Organisation for Economic Co-operation and Development (OECD). OECD membership is often used to indicate countries with 'developed' rather than 'developing' 'free-market' economies.
13. World Inequality Lab, 2022
14. The Equality Trust, 2019
15. Riddell et al., 2024
16. Pickett & Wilkinson, 2010
17. Pickett, 2024
18. Piketty, 2014
19. Piketty, 2014, p. 447
20. Christophers, 2022, p. xviii
21. Christophers, 2022, p. xxiii–xxiv
22. Christophers, 2022, p. 421
23. Davies, 2019
24. Milburn, 2019
25. Adkins et al., 2020
26. We Own It, 2012
27. Christophers, 2023, p. 37
28. Christophers, 2023, p. 80
29. Christophers, 2023, p. 38–9
30. Fisher, 2018
31. Bessner, 2024
32. Kirk, 2022
33. Reclaim Finance, 2022
34. Malm & Carton, 2024
35. A Minsky moment refers to a financial collapse triggered by the realisation that investors have misanalysed risk, like the one that occurred in 2008. The economist Hyman Minsky traced such events to a tendency within capitalism for borrowing and investment to become more speculative as an economic cycle progresses.
36. Bryant, 2019
37. Lakhani, 2023
38. Christophers, 2024, p. 225–6

39. Wolf, 2021
40. O'Connor, 1991, p. 108
41. The nine earth-system processes are climate change, ocean acidification, stratospheric ozone depletion, geochemical flows (specifically the nitrogen and phosphorus cycles), global freshwater use, change in land use, the rate of biodiversity loss, atmospheric aerosol loading, and chemical pollution. Raworth, 2017
42. Fink, 2024
43. Gabor, 2023, p. 1
44. J. Sullivan, 2023
45. Gabor, 2023, p. 2
46. Elrod, 2024
47. Maye & Mazewski, 2023
48. National Wealth Fund Taskforce, 2024
49. Pendleton, 2018
50. Matthijs & Blyth, 2024
51. Labour Party, 2024
52. Gabor, 2023, p. 4
53. Gabor, 2023, p. 4
54. Benanav, 2023
55. Klein & Thompson 2025, p. 71
56. Slobodian, 2020
57. Weber, 2025
58. Brusseler, 2024
59. Cooper, 2025
60. Cooper, 2025
61. Toscano, 2023, p. 149

Chapter Five

1. Hall, 2017, p. 235–6
2. Hall, 2017, p. 236
3. Hall, 2017, p. 237
4. Hall, 2017, p. 232
5. Ostrom, 2015; Wall, 2017
6. Chi, 2020
7. Baiocchi & Ganuza, 2014
8. Bua & Bussu, 2023
9. Jessop, 2016
10. Flanders, 2012
11. Preobrazhensky, 1965, p. 77
12. Russell & Milburn, 2019

13. Azzellini, 2015
14. Wright, 2010
15. Gilbert, 2023
16. Talaios Koop, 2023, p. 111
17. Mies, 1998; Salleh, 2017; Barca, 2022
18. Harnecker, 2015, p. 94
19. Althusser, 2014, p. 156
20. Barca, 2019, p. 208

Chapter Six

1. Singh & Siahpush, 2013
2. Smith, 2020
3. Rozena, 2023
4. Joint Center for Housing Studies of Harvard University, 2024
5. Richardson, 2023
6. Llaneras & Andrino, 2021
7. Timperley, 2020
8. Ryan-Collins, 2018, p. 4
9. Milburn, 2021
10. Klein & Thompson, 2025
11. Christophers, 2018
12. Howell, 2023
13. Trends are different in the US where house sizes had been increasing since the 1970s, but the size of new build properties has shrunk by 9 percent since a 2015 peak. See Delouya, 2024
14. Watling & Breach, 2023, p. 23
15. Timperley, 2020, p. 98
16. Wainwright, 2023
17. Timperley, 2020, p. 22
18. Howell, 2023
19. Wainwright, 2023
20. Gabor & Kohl, 2022, p. 10
21. Kusiak, 2021
22. Skelton, 1923
23. Ryan-Collins, 2018, p. 29
24. Diner & Wright, 2024, p. 17
25. Rhodes, 2015
26. D'Arcy & Gardiner, 2017, p. 42
27. Timperley, 2020, p. 231
28. Milburn, 2019
29. Ogden & Phillips, 2024

30. Billingham et al., 2023, p. 6
31. Simpson & Kollewe, 2024
32. Aref-Adib et al., 2024
33. Neate & Mathiason, 2018
34. Ryan-Collins, 2018, p. 33
35. Ryan-Collins, 2018, p. 35
36. Haringey Council, 2004
37. UNOHC, 2017
38. Unit 38 Architects & Wards Corner Community Plan, 2019
39. Formal communication from Grainger PLC
40. Heron et al., 2021
41. Hall, 2021b p. 171
42. Williams & Gilbert, 2022, p. 146
43. Przeworski, 1986, p. 92
44. Przeworski, 1986, p. 72
45. Przeworski, 1986, p. 74
46. See Wetherell, 2016
47. Ferreri & Vidal, 2026

Chapter Seven

1. Sommerstein, 2016
2. NICE, 2019
3. González, 2024
4. Kroen, 2024
5. Berlanga et al., 2013
6. Gilio-Whitaker, 2015
7. AUTM.net, 2020
8. Taylor, 2021
9. Paun et al., 2024
10. Adler-Bolton & Vierkant, 2022
11. Wouters, 2020
12. Corporate Europe Observatory, 2021
13. Investigate Europe, 2024
14. Corporate Europe Observatory, 2022
15. Dearden, 2023, p. xii
16. MSF, 2024
17. Campbell, 2024
18. Oxfam, 2021
19. Dearden, 2023, p. 100–101
20. Marriott & Maitland, 2021
21. Barnéoud, 2022

22. Bajaj et al., 2022
23. Our World in Data, 2024
24. Prescire Int., 2014
25. Ledley et al., 2020
26. Fernandez & Klinge, 2020
27. Angelis et al., 2023
28. European Commission, 2019
29. Arnold et al., 2020
30. Benhabib et al., 2020
31. Chaffin, 2023
32. WEMOS Foundation, 2014
33. Koller, 2020
34. Devine, 2010
35. Azzellini, 2015
36. Benford & Snow, 2000
37. Belkhir & Elmeligi, 2019
38. Sammut Bartolo et al., 2021
39. Adler-Bolton & Vierkant, 2022

Chapter Eight

1. Joks, 2022
2. De Luca & Norum, 2011
3. Nilsen, 2005
4. Doonan, 2018
5. Holt-Giménez, 2017
6. Perfecto et al., 2019
7. Ross, 2015
8. Edelman, 2017
9. Albo, 2007
10. Ahmed, 2022
11. Wing et al., 2021
12. Ortiz-Bobea et al., 2021
13. Ray et al., 2019
14. Food and Agriculture Organization, 2023
15. Jung & Hayes, 2023
16. Galler, 2023
17. Patnaik & Moyo, 2011
18. Mahmood et al., 2020
19. Crippa et al., 2021
20. Poore & Nemecek, 2018
21. Clark et al., 2020

22. Weis, 2007
23. United Nations Environment Programme, 2021
24. Food and Agriculture Organization, 2021
25. Brotherton, 2023
26. Wood, 2016
27. Weber, 2022
28. ETC Group, 2022
29. Borg & Policante, 2022
30. Patnaik & Patnaik, 2021
31. Otter, 2023
32. Ross, 1998
33. Sustain, 2022
34. Shaw & Wilson, 2019; Giles & Stead, 2022; Stone, 2022
35. Yeros, 2023
36. Gliessman, 2018
37. Rosset et al., 2011
38. Mier y Terán Giménez Cacho et al., 2018
39. Poux & Aubert, 2018
40. Bezner Kerr et al., 2021
41. Altieri et al., 2015
42. Giraldo & Rosset, 2017, p. 56
43. Nyéléni Declaration, cited in Patel, 2009, p. 666
44. van der Ploeg, 2014
45. Nicas & Arréllaga, 2023
46. Branford & Rocha, 2002
47. Friends of MST, n.d.
48. Empson, 2018
49. Ilbery, 2009
50. Graham et al., 2019
51. Christophers, 2018
52. Wild, 2021
53. Woolley & Scott, 2024
54. Nicholls & Altieri, 2018
55. Graham et al., 2019; Willis et al., 2022
56. Chakori & Hopkinson, 2024
57. Magrini et al., 2019
58. Marx, 1875
59. Galt et al., 2015
60. Galt, 2013
61. Patel & Moore, 2017
62. Rosset et al., 2011
63. Sustain, n.d.

Chapter Nine

1. Harnecker, 2015, p. 194
2. Mészáros, 2014, p. 167
3. Marx, 2004, p. 959
4. See Löwy, 2015
5. There is a growing and important literature on this subject: Devine, 2010; Vettese & Pendergrass, 2022; Benanav, 2022; Sorg, 2022; Thompson & Nishat-Botero, 2023; Durand et al., 2023; Foster, 2023
6. Táíwò, 2024
7. Malm, 2016
8. For work on the rebound effect of efficiency improvements, see Alcott et al., 2012
9. Hamouchene & Sandwell, 2023; Dunlap, 2024; Lang et al., 2024
10. Lebowitz, 2020, p. 179

Bibliography

Adkins, L., Cooper, M., & Konings, M. (2020). *The Asset Economy*. John Wiley & Sons.

Adler-Bolton, B., & Vierkant, A. (2022). *Health Communism: A Surplus Manifesto*. Verso Books.

Aguirre-Gutiérrez, J., Stevens, N., & Berenguer, E. (2023). Valuing the Functionality of Tropical Ecosystems Beyond Carbon. *Trends in Ecology & Evolution*, 38(12).

Agus, A., Denizot, J., Thévenot, J., Martinez-Medina, M., Massier, S., Sauvanet, P., Bernalier-Donadille, A., Denis, S., Hofman, P., Bonnet, R., Billard, E., & Barnich, N. (2016). Western Diet Induces a Shift in Microbiota Composition Enhancing Susceptibility to Adherent-Invasive E. Coli Infection and Intestinal Inflammation. *Scientific Reports*, 6(1), 1–14.

Ahmed, K. (2022, March 17). 'Take from the Hungry to Feed the Starving': UN Faces Awful Dilemma. *The Guardian*.

Ajl, M. (2021). *A People's Green New Deal*. Pluto Press.

Ajl, M. (2023). Theories of Political Ecology: Monopoly Capital Against People and the Planet. *Agrarian South: Journal of Political Economy: A Triannual Journal of Agrarian South Network and CARES*, 12(1), 12–50.

Akuno, K. (2012). *The Jackson-Kush Plan: The Struggle for Black Self-Determination and Economic Democracy*.

Akuno, K., & Meyer, M. (2023). *Jackson Rising Redux: Lessons on Building the Future in the Present*. PM Press.

Albert, M. J. (2023). Ecosocialism for Realists: Transitions, Trade-offs, and Authoritarian Dangers. *Capitalism Nature Socialism*, 34(1).

Albo, G. (2007). The Limits of Eco-Localism: Scale, Strategy, Socialism. *Socialist Register*, *43*.

Alcott, B., Giampietro, M., Polimeni, J. M., & Mayumi, K. (2012). *The Jevons Paradox and the Myth of Resource Efficiency Improvements*. Earthscan.

Althusser, L. (2014). *On the Reproduction of Capitalism: Ideology and Ideological State Apparatuses*. Verso Books.

Altieri, M. A., Nicholls, C. I., Henao, A., & Lana, M. A. (2015). Agroecology and the Design of Climate Change-Resilient Farming Systems. *Agronomy for Sustainable Development*, *35*(3), 869–890.

Anderson, K. (2023, March 24). *IPCC's Conservative Nature Masks True Scale of Action Needed to Avert Catastrophic Climate Change*. The Conversation.

Angelis, A., Lomas, J., Woods, B., & Naci, H. (2023). *Promoting Popular Health Through Pharmaceutical Policy: The Role of the UK Voluntary Scheme*. LSE.

Aref-Adib, C., Marshall, J., & Pacitti, C. (2024). *Building Blocks: Assessing the Role of Planning Reform in Meeting the Government's Housing Targets.* Resolution Foundation.

Arnold, D. G., Stewart, O. J., & Beck, T. (2020). Financial Penalties Imposed on Large Pharmaceutical Firms for Illegal Activities. *JAMA*, *324*(19), 1995.

Aronoff, K., Battistoni, A., Cohen, D. A., & Riofrancos, T. (2019). *A Planet to Win: Why We Need a Green New Deal.* Verso Books.

AUTM.net. (2020, July 16). *The Importance of Technology Transfer*. Better World.

Azzellini, D. (2013). The Communal State: Communal Councils, Communes, and Workplace Democracy. *NACLA Report on the Americas*, *46*(2), 25–30.

Azzellini, D. (2015). Contemporary Crisis and Workers' Control. In D. Azzellini (Ed.), *An Alternative Labour History: Worker Control and Workplace Democracy*. Bloomsbury Publishing.

Azzellini, D. (2023). Commune Socialism Self-Management, Popular Power and Autonomy in Venezuela. In H. Veltmeyer & A. Ezquerro-Cañete (Eds.), *From Extractivism to Sustainability: Scenarios and Lessons from Latin America* (259–276). Routledge.

Baiocchi, G. (2024, June 17). *Learning from the Pink Tide*. Boston Review.

Baiocchi, G., & Ganuza, E. (2014). Participatory Budgeting as if Emancipation Mattered. *Politics & Society*, 42(1), 29–50.

Bajaj, S. S., Maki, L., & Stanford, F. C. (2022). Vaccine Apartheid: Global Cooperation and Equity. *The Lancet*, *399*(10334), 1452–1453.

Barca, S. (2019). The Labor(s) of Degrowth. *Capitalism Nature Socialism*, 30(2), 207–216.

Barca, S. (2020). *Forces of Reproduction: Notes for a Counter-Hegemonic Anthropocene*. Cambridge University Press.

Barca, S. (2022). *Workers of the Earth: Labour, Ecology and Reproduction in the Age of Climate Change*. Pluto Books.

Barlow, N., Regen, L., Cadiou, N., Chertkovskaya, E., Hollweg, M., Plank, C., Schulken, M., & Wolf, V. (2022). *Degrowth & Strategy: How to Bring about Social-Ecological Transformation.*

Barnéoud, L. (2022, April 4). The Huge Waste of Expired Covid-19 Vaccines. *Le Monde*.

Bastani, A. (2020). *Fully Automated Luxury Communism: A Manifesto*. Verso Books.

Belkhir, L., & Elmeligi, A. (2019). Carbon Footprint of the Global Pharmaceutical Industry and Relative Impact of its Major Players. *Journal of Cleaner Production*, 214, 185–194.

Benanav, A. (2022). Socialist Investment, Dynamic Planning, and the Politics of Human Need. *Rethinking Marxism*, 34(2), 193–204.

Benanav, A. (2023, September 29). We're All Stagnationists Now. *Jacobin*.

Benford, R. D., & Snow, D. A. (2000). Framing Processes and Social Movements: An Overview and Assessment. *Annual Review of Sociology*, 26, 611–639.

Benhabib, A., Ioughlissen, S., Ratignier-Carbonneil, C., & Maison, P. (2020). The French Reporting System for Drug Shortages: Description and Trends from 2012 to 2018: An Observational Retrospective Study. *BMJ Open*, 10(3).

Berlanga, J., Fernández, J. I., López, E., López, P. A., Río, A. del, Valenzuela, C., Baldomero, J., Muzio, V., Raíces, M., Silva, R., Acevedo, B. E., & Herrera, L. (2013). Heberprot-P: A Novel Product for Treating Advanced Diabetic Foot Ulcer. *MEDICC Review*, 15(1), 11–15.

Bernes, J. (2018). The Belly of the Revolution: Agriculture, Energy, and the Future of Communism. In B. Ryan Bellamy & J. Diamanti (Eds.), *Materialism and the Critique of Energy*, 331–75. MCM' Publishing.

Bessner, D. (2024, May). The Life and Death of Hollywood. *Harper's*.

Bevins, V. (2023). *If We Burn: The Mass Protest Decade and the Missing Revolution*. Hachette UK.

Bezner Kerr, R., Madsen, S., Stüber, M., Liebert, J., Enloe, S., Borghino, N., Parros, P., Mutyambai, D. M., Prudhon, M., & Wezel, A. (2021). Can Agroecology Improve Food Security and Nutrition? A Review. *Global Food Security*, 29, 100540.

Billingham, Z., Frost, S., Swift, R., & Webb, J. (2023). *Parallel Lives*. IPPR.

Birch, K., & Ward, C. (2022). Assetization and the 'New Asset Geographies.' *Dialogues in Human Geography*, 14(1), 9–29.

Bordiga, A. (1954). *The Historical "Invariance" of Marxism*. Libcom.Org.

Borg, E., & Policante, A. (2022). *Mutant Ecologies: Manufacturing Life in the Age of Genomic Capital*. Pluto Press.

Branford, S., & Rocha, J. (2002). *Cutting the Wire: The Story of the Landless Movement in Brazil*. Latin America Bureau (Lab).

Brotherton, P. (2023, September 29). *State of Nature*. Natural England.

Brusseler, M. (2024, July 18). *A Strategic Holding*. Perspectives. Common Wealth.

Bryant, G. (2019, June 10). *Carbon Markets in a Climate-Changing Capitalism*. Progress in Political Economy (PPE).

Bua, A., & Bussu, S. (2023). *Reclaiming Participatory Governance: Social movements and the Reinvention of Democratic Innovation*. Taylor & Francis.

Bushby, H. (2022, November 1). Permacrisis Declared Collins Dictionary Word of the Year. BBC News.

Campbell, D. (2024, May 8). Medicine Shortages in England 'Beyond Critical', Pharmacists Warn. *The Guardian.*

Cantone, B., Antonarakis, A. S., & Antoniades, A. (2021). The Great Stagnation and Environmental Sustainability: A Multidimensional Perspective. *Sustainable Development*, 29(3), 485–503.

Carlsson, C. (2008). *Nowtopia: How Pirate Programmers, Outlaw Bicyclists, and Vacant-lot Gardeners are Inventing the Future Today.*

Carney, J. (2011, October 11). Why Occupy Wall Street Doesn't have a List of Demands. *CNBC.*

Carrington, D. (2024, May 8). World's Top Climate Scientists Expect Global Heating to Blast Past 1.5C Target. *The Guardian.*

Chaffin, Z. (2023, February 5). French Government Launches Plan to Tackle Medicine Shortages. *Le Monde.*

Chakori, S., & Hopkinson, S. (2024). Living in Abundance: Tool Libraries for Convivial Degrowth. In *De Gruyter Handbook of Degrowth*. Walter de Gruyter GmbH & Co KG.

Chávez, H. (2015, April 1). *Strike at the Helm*. MR Online.

Chávez, H., & Harnecker, M. (2005). *Understanding the Venezuelan Revolution: Hugo Chavez Talks to Marta Harnecker*. Monthly Review Press.

Chi, L. K. (2020). Revisiting Collectivism and Rural Governance in China. *Monthly Review*, 35–49.

Chomsky, N., & Pollin, R. (2020). *Climate Crisis and the Global Green New Deal: The Political Economy of Saving the Planet*. Verso Books.

Christophers, B. (2018). *The New Enclosure: The Appropriation of Public Land in Neoliberal Britain*. Verso Books.

Christophers, B. (2022). *Rentier Capitalism: Who Owns the Economy, and Who Pays for It?* Verso Books.

Christophers, B. (2023). *Our Lives in Their Portfolios: Why Asset Managers Own the World*. Verso Books.

Christophers, B. (2024). *The Price is Wrong: Why Capitalism Won't Save the Planet*. Verso Books.

Clark, M. A., Domingo, N. G. G., Colgan, K., Thakrar, S. K., Tilman, D., Lynch, J., Azevedo, I. L., & Hill, J. D. (2020). Global Food System Emissions Could Preclude Achieving the 1.5° and 2°C Climate Change Targets. *Science*, 370(6517), 705–708.

Clarke, S. (2016). *The State Debate*. Springer.

Clover, J. (2017). Transition: End of the Debate. *Amerikastudien / American Studies* 62, no. 4: 539–50.

Cooper, M. (2025, March 18) Trump's Antisocial State. *Dissent.*

Corless, B., & Haynes, T. (2024, March 29). Modern Household Appliances Break More Quickly than Retro Models. *The Telegraph.*

Corporate Europe Observatory. (2021, May 31). *Big Pharma's Lobbying Firepower in Brussels: At Least €36 Million a Year (And Likely Far More)*. Corporate Europe Observatory.

Corporate Europe Observatory. (2022, July 8). *TRIPS 'Waiver Failure': EU Betrayal of Global South on Vaccine Access Obscured by Lack of Transparency*. Corporate Europe Observatory.

Crippa, M., Solazzo, E., Guizzardi, D., Monforti-Ferrario, F., Tubiello, F. N., & Leip, A. (2021). Food Systems are Responsible for a Third of Global Anthropogenic GHG Emissions. *Nature Food*, 2(3), 198–209.

Da Costa Vieira, T. (2024). Beneath the Insuperable Barrier: Accumulation, State Managers and Climate Policy in Britain. *Environmental Politics*, 1–21.

D'Arcy, C., & Gardiner, L. (2017). *The Generation of Wealth: Asset Accumulation Across and Within Cohorts.* Resolution Foundation.

Davies, W. (2019, August 1). *England's New Rentier Alliance*. Political Economy Research Centre.

De Luca, L., & Norum, K. (2011). Scurvy and Cloudberries: A Chapter in the History of Nutritional Sciences. *The Journal of Nutrition, 141*(12), 2101–2105.

Dean, J. (2016). *Crowds and Party*. Verso Books.

Dean, J. (2025). *Capital's Grave: Neofeudalism and the New Class Struggle*. Verso Books.

Dearden, N. (2023). *Pharmanomics: How Big Pharma Destroys Global Health*. Verso Books.

Deleuze, G. Felix, G. (2006). May '68 Did Not Take Place (1984), in *Two Regimes of Madness: Texts and Interviews 1975-1995*. Semiotext(e).

Delouya, S. (2024, August 5). New Homes are Getting Smaller. That Could be Big News for First-Time Buyers. *CNN*.

Deutsche Bank Research. (2020, September 8). *The Age of Disorder — The New Era for Economics, Politics and our Way of Life*. Deutsche Bank Research.

Devine, P. (2010). *Democracy and Economic Planning*. Polity Press.

Diner, A., & Wright, H. (2024). *Reforming Right to Buy*. New Economics Foundation.

Doonan, N. (2018). Wild Cuisine and Canadianness: Creeping Rootstalks and Subterranean Struggle. *Gastronomica*, 18(3), 14–27.

Dorninger, C., Hornborg, A., Abson, D. J., von Wehrden, H., Schaffartzik, A., Giljum, S., Engler, J.-O., Feller, R. L., Hubacek, K., & Wieland, H. (2021). Global Patterns of Ecologically Unequal Exchange: Implications for sustainability in the 21st century. *Ecological Economics*, *179*, 106824.

Dunlap, X. (2024). *This System is Killing Us: Land Grabbing, the Green Economy and Ecological Conflict*. Pluto Press.

Durand, C., Hofferberth, E., & Schmelzer, M. (2023). *Planning Beyond Growth the Case for Economic Democracy Within Ecological Limits*. Elsevier BV.

Edelman, M. (2017). *Critical Perspectives on Food Sovereignty: Global Agrarian Transformations, Volume 2*. Routledge.

Egia, A. (2025). Beyond the New Municipalism: Towards Post-Capitalist Territorial Sovereignty in the Case of Hernani Burujabe. *Antipode*.

Elrod, A. Y. (2024, September 26). *What was Bidenomics?* Phenomenal World.

Empson, M. (2018). *"Kill All the Gentlemen": Class Struggle and Change in the English Countryside*. Bookmarks.

Endnotes. (2008). *Endnotes 1: Preliminary Materials for a Balance Sheet of the 20th Century*. Endnotes.

Enyoh, C. E., Devi, A., Kadono, H., Wang, Q., & Rabin, M. H. (2023). The Plastic Within: Microplastics Invading Human Organs and Bodily Fluids Systems. *Environments, 10*(11).

ETC Group. (2022). *Food Barons: Crisis Profiteering, Digitalization and Shifting Power.*

European Commission. (2019). *Competition Enforcement in the Pharmaceutical Sector (2009-2017): Report from the Commission to the Council and the European Parliament*. European Commission.

Fernandez, R., & Klinge, T. (2020). *Private Gains We Can Ill Afford: The Financialisation of Big Pharma*. Stichting Onderzoek Multinationale Ondernemingen.

Ferreri, M., & Vidal, L. (2026). Evolving Policy Communities for Public-Cooperative Housing Commons in New Municipalist Barcelona. In B. Russell & I. Bianchi (Eds.), *Radical Municipalism: The Politics of the Common and the Democratization of Public Services*. Bristol University Press.

Fink, L. (2024, June 13). *Remarks at the Partnership for Global Infrastructure and Investment*. the G7 Partnership for Global Infrastructure and Investment.

Fisher, M. (2018). *K-Punk: The Collected and Unpublished Writings of Mark Fisher (2004-2016)*. Repeater.

Fitzherbert, E. B., Struebig, M. J., Morel, A., Danielsen, F., Brühl, C. A., Donald, P. F., & Phalan, B. (2008). How Will Oil Palm Expansion Affect Biodiversity? *Trends in Ecology & Evolution, 23*(10), 538–545.

Flanders, L. (2012, April 30). *Talking with Chomsky*. CounterPunch.Org.

Food and Agriculture Organization. (2021, June 11). COP26: *Agricultural Expansion Drives Almost 90 percent of Global Deforestation*. FAO.

Food and Agriculture Organization. (2020). *Global Forest Resources Assessment 2020*. FAO.

Food and Agriculture Organization. (2023). *The State of Food Security and Nutrition in the World 2023*. FAO.

Foster, J. B. (2008, November 1). Ecology and the Transition from Capitalism to Socialism. *Monthly Review*.

Foster, J. B. (2015, April 1). Chávez and the Communal State. *Monthly Review*.

Foster, J. B. (2022, June 1). Mészáros and Chávez: "The Point from Which to Move the World Today." *Monthly Review*.

Foster, J. B. (2023, July 1). Planned Degrowth: Ecosocialism and Sustainable Human Development. *Monthly Review*.

Franklin, K. (2009, September 29). *The New Southern Strategy – The Politics of Self-Determination in the South*. Grassroots Thinking.

Fraser, N. (2019). *The Old is Dying and the New Cannot Be Born: From Progressive Neoliberalism to Trump and Beyond*. Verso Books.

Friends of MST. (n.d.). *Constitutional Authority: Legality of Land Occupations*. Friends of the MST.

Gabor, D. (2023). *The (European) Derisking State*. Center for Open Science.

Gabor, D. (2024, July 2). Labour is Putting its Plans for Britain in the Hands of Private Finance. It Could End Badly. *The Guardian*.

Gabor, D., & Kohl, S. (2022). *My Home is an Asset Class. Housing Financialization in Europe*. The Greens/EFA in the European Parliament.

Galler, G. (2023, July 27). *Food Insecurity Reaches 25 Percent in Parts of the UK*. New Food Magazine.

Galt, R. E. (2013). The Moral Economy is a Double-Edged Sword: Explaining Farmers' Earnings and Self-Exploitation in Community-Supported Agriculture. *Economic Geography*, *89*(4), 341–365.

Galt, R. E., Bradley, K., Christensen, L., Van Soelen Kim, J., & Lobo, R. (2015). Eroding the community in Community Supported Agriculture (CSA): Competition's Effects in Alternative Food Networks in California. *Sociologia Ruralis*, *56*(4), 491–512.

Garo, I. (2023). *Communism and Strategy: Rethinking Political Mediations*. Verso Books.

Gerbaudo, P. (2012). *Tweets and the Streets: Social Media and Contemporary Activism*. Pluto Press.

Gerbaudo, P. (2019). *The Digital Party: Political Organisation and Online Democracy*. Pluto Press.

Gilbert, C. (2023). *Commune Or Nothing! Venezuela's Communal Movement and its Socialist Project*. Monthly Review Press.

Gilbert, J. (2019). This Conjuncture: For Stuart Hall. *New Formations*, *96*(96), 5–37.

Giles, D.B., Stead, V. (2022) Big Data Won't Feed the World: Global Agribusiness, Digital Imperialism, and the Contested Promises of a New Green Revolution. *Dialectical Anthropology*, 46, 37–53.

Gilio-Whitaker, D. (2015, July 14). When Mad Bear Met Fidel: How Castro's Cuba Advanced Native Sovereignty. *ICT News*.

Giraldo, O. F., & Rosset, P. M. (2017). Agroecology as a Territory in Dispute: Between Institutionality and Social Movements. *The Journal of Peasant Studies*, *45*(3), 545–564.

Gliessman, S. (2018). Defining Agroecology. *Agroecology and Sustainable Food Systems*, 42(6), 599–600.

González, C. A. (2024, May 23). *Heberprot-P: The Half-Open Window to the United States*. OnCubaNews English.

Governance Knowledge Centre. (2011). *Participatory Planning to Strengthen Decentralisation*.

Government of Kerala. (2022). *Fourteenth Five Year Plan (2022 - 2027)*. Government of Kerala.

Graeber, D. (2018). *Bullshit Jobs: A Theory*. Penguin UK.

Graeber, D., & Wengrow, D. (2022). *The Dawn of Everything: A New History of Humanity*. Penguin UK.

Graham, K., Shrubsole, G., Wheatley, H., & Swade, K. (2019). *Reviving County Farms*. CPRE: The Countryside Charity.

Greenberg, M. (2013). The Disaster Inside the Disaster. *New Labor Forum*, 23(1), 44–52.

Greenfield, P. (2024, October 10). Collapsing Wildlife Populations Near 'Points of No Return', Report Warns. *The Guardian*.

Guevara, C. (1965). *Socialism and Man in Cuba*. Marxists.Org.

Gupta, J., Bai, X., Liverman, D. M., Rockström, J., Qin, D., Stewart-Koster, B., Rocha, J. C., Jacobson, L., Abrams, J. F., Andersen, L. S., Armstrong McKay, D. I., Bala, G., Bunn, S. E., Ciobanu, D., DeClerck, F., Ebi, K. L., Gifford, L., Gordon, C., Hasan, S., ... Gentile, G. (2024). A Just World on a Safe Planet: A Lancet Planetary Health–Earth Commission Report on Earth-System Boundaries, Translations, and Transformations. *The Lancet Planetary Health*, 8(10), e813–e873.

Hainbat Egile. (2020). *Soberanias*.

Hall, S. (2017). *Selected Political Writings: The Great Moving Right Show and Other Essays*. Duke University Press.

Hall, S. (2021a). Race and "Moral Panics" in Postwar Britain. In *Selected Writings on Race and Difference*. Duke University Press.

Hall, S. (2021b). *The Hard Road to Renewal: Thatcherism and the Crisis of the Left*. Verso Books.

Hall, S., Critcher, C., Jefferson, T., & Roberts, B. (2013). *Policing the Crisis: Mugging, the State, and Law and Order* (2nd ed.). Macmillan Education. (1978)

Hamann, U., & Türkmen, C. (2020). Communities of Struggle: The Making of a Protest Movement Around Housing, Migration and Racism Beyond Identity Politics in Berlin. *Territory, Politics, Governance*, 8(4), 515–531.

Hamouchene, H., & Sandwell, K. (2023). *Dismantling Green Colonialism: Energy and Climate Justice in the Arab Region*. Pluto Press.

Hardt, M., & Negri, A. (2017). *Assembly*. Oxford University Press.

Haringey Council. (2004, January). In *Wards Corner/Seven Sisters Underground Development Brief*.

Harnecker, M. (2015). *A World to Build: New Paths Toward Twenty-First Century Socialism*. Monthly Review Press.

Harnecker, M., & Bartolome, J. (2019). *Planning from Below: A Decentralized Participatory Planning Proposal*. Monthly Review Press.

Harootunian, H. (2015). *Marx after Marx: History and Time in the Expansion of Capitalism*. Columbia University Press.

Heron, K. (2024). Capitalist Catastrophism and Eco-Apartheid. *Geoforum*, 153, 103874.

Heron, K., Milburn, K., & Russell, B. (2021). *Public-Common Partnerships: Democratising Ownership and Urban Development*. Common Wealth.

Hickel, J. (2019). Degrowth: A Theory of Radical Abundance. *Real-World Economics Review*, 87.

Hickel, J. (2020). *Less is More: How Degrowth Will Save the World*. Random House.

Hickel, J., & Kallis, G. (2019). Is Green Growth Possible? *New Political Economy*, 25(4), 469–486.

Hiritik-at. (2022). *Lurralde burujabetza: Utopia Panikikatzen Segitzeko Proposamen Bat*. BDS Koop. [Territorial Sovereignty: A Proposal to Continue Energising Utopia].

Holloway, J. (2002). *Change the World Without Taking Power: The Meaning of Revolution Today*. Pluto Press.

Holloway, J. (2010). *Crack Capitalism*. Pluto Press.

Holt-Giménez, E. (2017). *A Foodie's Guide to Capitalism*. NYU Press.

Howell, S. (2023, December 18). Labour Must Urgently Tackle Land Banking to Have Any Hope of Solving UK's Housing Crisis. *Big Issue*.

Ilbery, B. W. (2009, January 1). *Structural Change and New Entrants in UK Agriculture: Examining the Role of County Farms and the Fresh Start Initiative in Cornwall*. Research Repository.

Inrix. (2024). *2023 INRIX Global Traffic Scorecard with Q1 2024 Update*. Inrix.

International Labour Organization. (2023, July 24). *Statistics on the Informal Economy*. ILOSTAT.

Investigate Europe. (2024, September 16). Drug Firms Finance Europe's Patient Groups with Multi-Million Donations.

IPBES. (2019). *Global Assessment Report on Biodiversity and Ecosystem Services*. IPBES Secretariat. www.ipbes.net/global-assessment

IPCC. (2023). *Climate Change 2023: Synthesis Report. Contribution of Working Groups I, II and III to the Sixth Assessment Report of the Intergovernmental Panel on Climate Change*. IPCC.

Isaac, T. M. T. (2022). *Kerala: Another Possible World*. Leftword.

Isaac, T. M. T., & Franke, R. W. (2021). *People's Planning: Kerala, Local Democracy and Development*. Leftword Books.

Jackson, T. (2019). The Post-Growth Challenge: Secular Stagnation, Inequality and the Limits to Growth. *Ecological Economics*, 156, 236–246.

Jessop, B. (2016). *The State: Past, Present, Future*. Polity Press.

Joint Center for Housing Studies of Harvard University. (2024). *The State of the Nation's Housing 2024*. Harvard University.

Joks, S. (2022). Frustrated Caretakers: Sámi Egg Gatherers Cloudberry Pickers. In S. Valkonen, Á. Aikio, S. Alakorva, & S. Magga (Eds.), *The Sámi World* (150–164). Routledge.

Jung, C., & Hayes, C. (2023, December 7). Inflation, Profits and Market Power: Towards a New Research and Policy Agenda. *IPPR*.

Karolidis, S., & Karcich, T. (2023, June 14). *How Did the Build Public Renewables Act Get Passed?* Socialist Forum.

Keynes, J. M. (2008). Economic Possibilities for Our Grandchildren (1930). In L. Pecchi & G. Piga (Eds.), *Revisiting Keynes* (17–26). The MIT Press.

Kirk, S. (2022, May 20). *On Climate Risk*. FT Live Moral Money Summit.

Klein, E. & Thompson, D. (2025) *Abundance: How We Build a Better Future*. Profile.

Koller, R. (2020, July 21). Saint-Genis-Laval. Famar repris par l'industriel libanais Benta Pharma. [Saint-Genis-Laval. Famar Taken Over by Lebanese Industrialist Benta Pharma], *Tribune de Lyon*.

Krachler, N., & Greer, I. (2015). When Does Marketisation Lead to Privatisation? Profit-Making in English Health Services after the 2012 Health and Social Care Act. *Social Science & Medicine*, 124, 215–223.

Kroen, G. (2024, May 1). Ohio Company Gets Greenlight from FDA to Test Cuban Drug for Diabetic Foot Ulcers. *Cleveland.Com*.

Kumar, Suresh K. (2007) Kerala, India: A Regional Community-Based Palliative Care Model', *Journal of Pain and Symptom Management*, 33(5): 623–627.

Kusiak, J. (2021). Socialization: A Democratic, Affordable, and Lawful Solution to Berlin's Housing Crisis. Rosa Luxemburg Stiftung.

Kusiak, J. (2024). *Radically Legal: Berlin Constitutes the Future*. Cambridge University Press.

Labour Party. (2017). *Alternative Models of Ownership*.

Labour Party (2024, June 13). *Labour's Fiscal Plan.*

Lakhani, N. (2023, September 19). Revealed: Top Carbon Offset Projects May Not Cut Planet-Heating Emissions. *The Guardian*.

Lang, M., Manahan, M. A., & Bringel, Breno. (2024). *The Geopolitics of Green Colonialism: Global Justice and Ecosocial Transitions*. Pluto Press.

Latif, R. (2022). *Tahrir's Youth: Leaders of a Leaderless Revolution*. American University in Cairo Press.

Lebowitz, M. A. (2009, February 1). The Path to Human Development: Capitalism or Socialism? *Monthly Review*.

Lebowitz, M. A. (2020). *Between Capitalism and Community*. Monthly Review Press.

Ledley, F. D., McCoy, S. S., Vaughan, G., & Cleary, E. G. (2020). Profitability of Large Pharmaceutical Companies Compared with Other Large Public Companies. *JAMA*, *323*(9), 834.

Lenin, V. (1920a). *KOMMUNISMUS: Journal of the Communist International for the Countries of South-Eastern Europe (in German), Vienna, no. 1-2 (February 1, 1920) to no. 18 (May 8, 1920)*. Marxists.Org.

Lenin, V. (1920b). *"Left-Wing" Communism: An Infantile Disorder*. Marxists. Org; Progress Publishers.

Lerner, S. (2019, July 20). How the Plastics Industry is Fighting to Keep Polluting the World. *The Intercept*.

Lewontin, R., & Levins, R. (2007). *Biology Under the Influence: Dialectical Essays on the Coevolution of Nature and Society*. Monthly Review Press.

Liboiron, M. (2021). *Pollution is Colonialism*. Duke University Press.

Linera, Á. G. (2013, April 29). *Once Again on So-Called "Extractivism."* MR Online.

Llaneras, K., & Andrino, B. (2021, July 1). Why Young Spaniards are Taking Longer than Other Europeans to Leave Home. *Ediciones EL PAÍS S.L.*

Löwy, M. (2015). *Ecosocialism: A Radical Alternative to Capitalist Catastrophe*. Haymarket Books.

Lurral de Askea. (2024). *Ongi bizitzeko: 100 konpromiso*. [To Live Well: 100 Commitments]. Oiartzun Burujabe.

Luxemburg, R. (2007). *The Essential Rosa Luxemburg: Reform or Revolution and the Mass Strike*. Haymarket Books.

Magrini, M.-B., Martin, G., Magne, M.-A., Duru, M., Couix, N., Hazard, L., & Plumecocq, G. (2019, January 1). *Agroecological Transition from Farms to Territorialised Agri-Food Systems: Issues and Drivers*. Springer International Publishing.

Maher, G. (2013). *We Created Chávez: A People's History of the Venezuelan Revolution*. Duke University Press.

Mahmood, T. A., Arulkumaran, S., & Chervenak, F. A. (2020). *Obesity and Obstetrics*. Elsevier.

Malm, A. (2016). *Fossil Capital: The Rise of Steam Power and the Roots of Global Warming*. Verso Books.

Malm, A., & Carton, W. (2024). *Overshoot: How the World Surrendered to Climate Breakdown*. Verso Books.

Marriott, A., & Maitland, A. (2021, July 29). *The Great Vaccine Robbery: Pharmaceutical Corporations Charge Excessive Prices for COVID-19 Vaccines while Rich Countries Block Faster and Cheaper Route to Global Vaccination.* The People's Vaccine.

Marx, K. (1853). *Revelations Concerning the Communist Trial in Cologne*. Marxists.Org.

Marx, K. (1864). *The International Workingmen's Association, General Rules*. Marxists.Org.

Marx, K. (1871). *The Civil War in France*. Marxists.Org.

Marx, K. (1875). *Critique of the Gotha Programme*. Marxists.Org.

Marx, K. (1993). *Capital: Volume III*. Penguin UK.

Marx, K. (2004). *Capital: Volume I*. Penguin UK.

Marx, K. (2005). *Grundrisse: Foundations of the Critique of Political Economy*. Penguin UK.

Marx, K. (2024). *Capital: Critique of Political Economy, Volume 1*. Princeton University Press.

Marx, K., & Engels, F. (2009). *The Economic and Philosophic Manuscripts of 1844 and the Communist Manifesto*. Prometheus Books.

Marx, K., & Engels, F. (2017). *The Communist Manifesto*. Pluto Press.

Mason, P. (2012). *Why It's Kicking off Everywhere: The New Global Revolutions*. Verso Books.

Matthijs, M., & Blyth, M. (2024, April 30). Don't Bet on a British Revival. *Foreign Affairs*. www.foreignaffairs.com/united-kingdom/dont-bet-british-revival

Mattoni, A., & Porta, D. D. (2015). *Spreading Protest: Social Movements in Times of Crisis*. Ecpr Press.

Maye, A., & Mazewski, M. (2023). *Economic Impacts of the Inflation Reduction Act's Climate and Energy Provisions*. Data For Progress.

Menon, A. S. (2011). *Kerala History and its Makers*. D C Books.

Mészáros, I. (2010). *Beyond Capital: Toward a Theory of Transition*. Monthly Review Press.

Mészáros, I. (2014). *The Necessity of Social Control*. Monthly Review Press.

Mészáros, I. (2022). *Beyond Leviathan: Critique of the State*. NYU Press.

Mier y Terán Giménez Cacho, M., Giraldo, O. F., Aldasoro, M., Morales, H., Ferguson, B. G., Rosset, P., Khadse, A., & Campos, C. (2018). Bringing Agroecology to Scale: Key Drivers and Emblematic Cases. *Agroecology and Sustainable Food Systems*, 42(6), 637–665.

Mies, M. (1998). *Patriarchy and Accumulation on a World Scale: Women in the International Division of Labour*. Palgrave Macmillan.

Milburn, K. (2019). *Generation Left*. Polity.

Milburn, K. (2021). Generation Left after Corbynism. *South Atlantic Quarterly, 120*(4), 892–902.

Moin, B. (2024). Mapping 'Metabolism' in Marx's Capital. *Critique*, *52*(1), 129–138.

Monticelli, L. (2024). *The Future is Now: An Introduction to Prefigurative Politics*. Policy Press.

Moore, J. W. (2015). *Capitalism in the Web of Life: Ecology and the Accumulation of Capital*. Verso Books.

Mouffe, C. (2018). *For a Left Populism*. Verso Books.

Mouffe, C. (2022). *Towards A Green Democratic Revolution: Left Populism and the Power of Affects*. Verso Books.

MSF. (2024, April 25). *MSF Reveals Cost of Landmark TB Clinical Trial in Push for Drug-Development Cost Transparency*. Médecins Sans Frontières (MSF) International.

Namboodiripad, E. M. S. (2010). *History, Society, and Land Relations: Selected Essays*. LeftWord Books.

Neate, R., & Mathiason, N. (2018, September 3). Berkeley Calls Affordable Housing Targets "Unviable" as Chairman Earns £174m. *The Guardian*.

Nicas, J., & Arréllaga, M. M. (2023, April 30). If You Don't Use Your land, These Marxists May Take It. *The New York Times*.

NICE. (2019). *Diabetic Foot Problems: Prevention and Management*. NICE.

Nicholls, C. I., & Altieri, M. A. (2018). Pathways for the Amplification of Agroecology. *Agroecology and Sustainable Food Systems*, 42(10), 1170–1193.

Nilsen, G. S. (2005). Cloudberries—The Northern Gold. *International Journal of Fruit Science*, *5*(2), 45–60.

Nossiter, T. J. (1982). *Communism in Kerala: A Study in Political Adaptation*. University of California Press.

Noys, B. (Ed.), (2012). *Communization and its Discontents: Contestation, Critique, and Contemporary Struggles*. Minor Compositions.

Nunes, R. (2021). *Neither Vertical Nor Horizontal: A Theory of Political Organization*. Verso Books.

O'Connor, J. (1991). On the Two Contradictions of Capitalism. *Capitalism Nature Socialism*, 2(3), 107–109.

O'Neill, D. W., Fanning, A. L., Lamb, W. F., & Steinberger, J. K. (2018). A Good Life for All Within Planetary Boundaries. *Nature Sustainability*, 1(2), 88–95.

Ogden, K., & Phillips, D. (2024). *How Have English Councils' Funding and Spending Changed? 2010 to 2024*. The IFS.

Ortiz-Bobea, A., Ault, T. R., Carrillo, C. M., Chambers, R. G., & Lobell, D. B. (2021). Anthropogenic Climate Change has Slowed Global Agricultural Productivity Growth. *Nature Climate Change*, 11(4), 306–312.

Ostrom, E. (2015). *Governing the Commons: The Evolution of Institutions for Collective Action*. Cambridge University Press.

Otter, C. (2023). *Diet for a Large Planet: Industrial Britain, Food Systems, and World Ecology*. University of Chicago Press.

Our World in Data. (2024). *Cumulative Confirmed COVID-19 Deaths by World Region*. Our World in Data.

Oxfam. (2021, September 2). *COVID Vaccines Create 9 New Billionaires with Combined Wealth Greater than Cost of Vaccinating World's Poorest Countries*. Oxfam International.

Parada-Cabaleiro, E., Mayerl, M., Brandl, S., Skowron, M., Schedl, M., Lex, E., & Zangerle, E. (2024). Song Lyrics have Become Simpler and More Repetitive Over the Last Five decades. *Scientific Reports*, 14(1), 1–13.

Parisi, L., Escribano, P. G., Holthausen, C., Stracca, L., Payerols, C., & Boissinot, J. (2022, November 18). *From "Orderly Transition" to "Hot House World" – How Climate Scenarios Can Facilitate Action*. European Central Bank.

Parnreiter, C., Steinwärder, L., & Kolhoff, K. (2024). Uneven Development Through Profit Repatriation: How Capitalism's Class and Geographical Antagonisms Intertwine. *Antipode*, 56(6), 2343–2367.

Patel, R. (2009). Food Sovereignty. *Journal of Peasant Studies*, 36(3), 663–706.

Patel, R., & Moore, J. W. (2017). *A History of the World in Seven Cheap Things: A Guide to Capitalism, Nature, and the Future of the Planet*. University of California Press.

Patnaik, P. (1995). The International Context and the "Kerala Model." *Social Scientist*, 23(1/3), 37.

Patnaik, U., & Moyo, S. (2011). *The Agrarian Question in the Neoliberal Era: Primitive Accumulation and the Peasantry*. Fahamu/Pambazuka.

Patnaik, U., & Patnaik, P. (2021). *Capital and Imperialism: Theory, History, and the Present*. Monthly Review Press.

Paun, C., Payne, D., Odejimi, T., Schumaker, E., & Reader, R. (2024, June 10). *The Cuban Drug That Could Come to America*. POLITICO.

Pedregal, A., & Lukić, N. (2024). Imperialism, Ecological Imperialism, and Green Imperialism: An Overview. *Journal of Labor and Society*, 27(1), 105–138.

Pendleton, A. (2018) *Carillion's Collapse Matters More Than You Thought*. New Economics Foundation.

Percino, G., Klimek, P., & Thurner, S. (2014). Instrumentational Complexity of Music Genres and Why Simplicity Sells. *PLOS ONE*, 9(12).

Perfecto, I., Vandermeer, J., & Wright, A. (2019). *Nature's Matrix: Linking Agriculture, Biodiversity Conservation and Food Sovereignty*. Routledge.

Perry, K. (2020). *The New 'Bond-Age,' Climate Crisis and the Case for Climate Reparations: Unpicking Old/New Colonialities of Finance for Development Within the SDGs*. Center for Open Science.

Pickett, K. (2024, July 22). *The Spirit Level at 15: The Enduring Impact of Inequality*. White Rose Research Online.

Pickett, K., & Wilkinson, R. (2010). *The Spirit Level: Why Equality is Better for Everyone*. Penguin UK.

Piketty, T. (2014). *Capital in the Twenty-First Century*. Harvard University Press.

Pineault, É. (2022). *A Social Ecology of Capital*. Pluto Press.

Pinker, S. (2018). *Enlightenment Now: The Case for Reason, Science, Humanism, and Progress*. Penguin UK.

Podur, J., & Emersberger, J. (2021). *Extraordinary Threat: The U.S. Empire, the Media, and Twenty Years of Coup Attempts in Venezuela*. NYU Press.

Poore, J., & Nemecek, T. (2018). Reducing Food's Environmental Impacts Through Producers and Consumers. *Science*, 360(6392), 987–992.

Poux, X., & Aubert, P.-M. (2018). An Agroecological Europe in 2050: Multifunctional Agriculture for Healthy Eating. In *IDDRI*.

Powell, A. (2024, April 25). *Economic Update: Inactivity Due to Illness Reaches Record*. House of Commons Library.

Prata, J. C., da Costa, J. P., Lopes, I., Andrady, A. L., Duarte, A. C., & Rocha-Santos, T. (2021). A One Health Perspective of the Impacts of Microplastics on Animal, Human and Environmental Health. *Science of The Total Environment*, *777*, 146094.

Preobrazhensky, E. (1965). *The New Economics*. Oxford University Press.

Preobrazhensky, E. (1980). *The Crisis of Soviet Industrialization: Selected Essays*. Palgrave Macmillan.

Prescire Int. (2014). Drug Developments in 2013: Little Progress, But French Authorities Take a Few Positive Steps to Protect Patients. *Prescrire Int*, *23*(148), 107–110.

Malcolm X Grassroots Movement. (n.d.). *Principles.*

Przeworski, A. (1986). *Capitalism and Social Democracy*. Cambridge University Press.

Raworth, K. (2017). *Doughnut Economics: Seven Ways to Think Like a 21st-Century Economist*. Random House.

Ray, D. K., West, P. C., Clark, M., Gerber, J. S., Prishchepov, A. V., & Chatterjee, S. (2019). Climate Change Has Likely Already Affected Global Food Production. *PLOS ONE*, *14*(5).

Reclaim Finance. (2022). *Banking on Climate Chaos. Fossil Fuel Finance Report 2022*.

Rhodes, D. (2015). The Fall and Rise of the Private Rented Sector in England. *Built Environment, 41*(2), 258–270.

Rice, J. L., Long, J., & Levenda, A. (2021). Against Climate Apartheid: Confronting the Persistent Legacies of Expendability for Climate Justice. *Environment and Planning E: Nature and Space*, 5(2), 625–645.

Richardson, N. (2023, July 26). Housing Purchase Affordability, UK. *Office for National Statistics.*

Riddell, R., Ahmed, N., Maitland, A., Lawson, M., & Taneja, A. (2024). *Inequality Inc. How Corporate Power Divides Our World and the Need for a New Era of Public Action.* Oxfam International.

Roberts, D. (2023, February 22). Hearing from the Author of Biden's Industrial Strategy. *Volts.*

Ross, C. (2013). *The Leaderless Revolution: How Ordinary People will Take Power and Change Politics in the 21st Century.* Penguin.

Ross, E. B. (1998). *The Malthus factor: Poverty, Politics and Population in Capitalist Development.* Zed Books.

Ross, K. (2015). *Communal Luxury: The Political Imaginary of the Paris Commune.* Verso Books.

Rosset, P. M., Sosa, B. M., Jaime, A. M. R., & Lozano, D. R. Á. (2011). The Campesino-to-Campesino Agroecology Movement of ANAP in Cuba: Social Process Methodology in the Construction of Sustainable Peasant Agriculture and Food Sovereignty. *The Journal of Peasant Studies*, 38(1), 161–191.

Rosset, P. M., & Val, V. (2018). The 'Campesino a Campesino' Agroecology Movement in Cuba. In J. Vivero-Pol, T. Ferrando, O. De Schutter & U. Mattei (Eds.), *Routledge Handbook of Food as a Commons* (p. 251–265). Routledge.

Rozena, S. (2023). One Kensington Gardens: Buy-to-Leave Gentrification in the Royal Borough. *Antipode*, 56(3), 1006–1026.

Russell, B., & Bianchi, I. (Eds.). (2026). *Radical Municipalism: The Politics of the Common and the Democratization of Public Services.* Bristol University Press.

Russell, B., & Milburn, K. (2018). What Can an Institution Do? Towards Public-Common Partnerships and a New Common-Sense. *Renewal*, 26(4), 45–55.

Russell, B., & Milburn, K. (2019). *Public-Common Partnerships: Building New Circuits of Collective Ownership.* Common Wealth.

Rustin, M. (2010, May 19). *From the Beginning to the End of Neo-Liberalism in Britain.* openDemocracy.

Ryan-Collins, J. (2018). *Why Can't You Afford a home?* Polity.

Saito, K. (2024). *Slow Down: The Degrowth Manifesto.* Astra Publishing House.

Salleh, A. (2017). *Ecofeminism as Politics: Nature, Marx and the Postmodern.* Zed Books Ltd.

Sammut Bartolo, N., Azzopardi, L. M., & Serracino-Inglott, A. (2021). Pharmaceuticals and the Environment. *Early Human Development*, 155, 105218.

Schwartz, B. (2009). *The Paradox of Choice: Why More is Less,* revised edition. HarperCollins.

Serrà, J., Corral, Á., Boguñá, M., Haro, M., & Arcos, J. Ll. (2012). Measuring the Evolution of Contemporary Western Popular Music. *Scientific Reports*, 2(1), 1–6.

Seymour, R. (2024). *Disaster Nationalism: The Downfall of Liberal Civilization.* Verso.

Shaw, A., & Wilson, K. (2019). The Bill and Melinda Gates Foundation and the Necro-Populationism of 'Climate-Smart' Agriculture. *Gender, Place & Culture*, 27(3), 370–393.

Shi, Z. (2019). Gut Microbiota: An Important Link Between Western Diet and Chronic Diseases. *Nutrients*, 11(10), 2287.

Simpson, J., & Kollewe, J. (2024, October 6). 'It's Decimated': Rayner Faces a Battle to Boost Britain's Social Housing. *The Guardian.*

Singh, G. K., & Siahpush, M. (2013). Widening Rural–Urban Disparities in All-Cause Mortality and Mortality from Major Causes of Death in the USA, 1969–2009. *Journal of Urban Health*, 91(2), 272–292.

Sitrin, M. (2006). *Horizontalism: Voices of Popular Power in Argentina.* AK Press.

Skelton, N. (1923, May 19). Constructive Conservatism IV. Democracy Stabilized. *The Spectator.*

Skypala, I., & Vlieg-Boerstra, B. (2014). Food Intolerance and Allergy. *Current Opinion in Clinical Nutrition and Metabolic Care*, 17(5), 442–447.

Slobodian, Q. (2020) *Globalists: The End of Empire and the Birth of Neoliberalism.* Harvard University Press.

Smith, J. (2016). *Imperialism in the Twenty-First Century: Globalization, Super-Exploitation, and Capitalism's Final Crisis.* NYU Press.

Smith, N. (2020). *Uneven Development: Nature, Capital, and the Production of Space.* Verso Books.

Sommerstein, D. (2016, May 16). *Mohawks Travel to Cuba for Cutting-Edge Diabetes Treatment.* NCPR.

Sorg, C. (2022). Failing to Plan is Planning to Fail: Toward an Expanded Notion of Democratically Planned Postcapitalism. *Critical Sociology*, 49(3), 475–493.

Statovci, D., Aguilera, M., MacSharry, J., & Melgar, S. (2017). The Impact of Western Diet and Nutrients on the Microbiota and Immune Response at Mucosal Interfaces. *Frontiers in Immunology*, 8.

Stone, G.D. (2022). Surveillance Agriculture and Peasant Autonomy. *Journal of Agrarian Change*, 22(3), 608–631.

Suits, B. (2014). *The Grasshopper: Games, Life and Utopia* (3rd ed.), Broadview Press.

Sullivan, D., & Hickel, J. (2023). Capitalism and Extreme Poverty: A Global Analysis of Real wages, Human Height, and Mortality Since the Long 16th Century. *World Development*, 161, 106026.

Sullivan, J. (2023, April 27). *Remarks by National Security Advisor Jake Sullivan on Renewing American Economic Leadership at the Brookings Institution.*

Summers, L. (2013, November 8). *Crises Yesterday and Today*. IMF Fourteenth Annual Research Conference in Honor of Stanley Fischer.

Sustain. (n.d.). *Promote and Support a Right to Food.* Sustain.

Sustain. (2022, December 2). *Unpicking Food Prices: Where Does your Food Pound Go, and Why Do Farmers Get So Little?* Sustain.

Táíwò, O. (2024, June 17). *Climate, State, and Utopia.* Boston Review.

Talaios Koop. (2023). *Sindicalismo y Economía Social Para la Transformación.* [Trade Unionism and the Social Economy for the Transformation]. Fundación Manu Robles-Arangiz Institutua Barrinkua.

Taylor, L. (2021). Why Cuba Developed its own Covid Vaccine—and What Happened Next. *BMJ*, 374(1912), n1912.

The Equality Trust. (2019). *Billionaire Britain.*

The Red Nation. (2021). *The Red Deal: Indigenous Action to Save our Earth.* Common Notions.

Thompson, M., & Nishat-Botero, Y. (2023). Postcapitalist Planning and Urban Revolution. *Competition & Change*, 29(1).

Tilzey, M. (2024). Ill Fares the Land: Confronting Unsustainability in the U.K. Food System Through Political Agroecology and Degrowth. *Land*, 13(5), 594.

Timperley, C. (2020). *Generation Rent: Why You Can't Buy a Home or Even Rent a Good One.* Canbury.

Tooze, A. (2022, October 28). *Welcome to the World of the Polycrisis.* Financial Times.

Toscano, A. (2023). *Terms of Disorder: Keywords for an Interregnum.* Seagull.

Toscano, A. (2012). Now and Never. In B. Noys (Ed). *Communization and Its Discontents: Contestation, Critique, and Contemporary Struggles.* Minor Compositions. 85–104.

Trainer, T. (2011, April 6). *The Transition Towns Movement; Its Huge Significance, and a Friendly Criticism – Feasta.* Feasta.

Trainer, T. (2020). *The Simpler Way: Collected Writings of Ted Trainer* (S. Alexander & J. Rutherford, Eds.). Simplicity Institute.

TUC. (2019, November 15). *Annual Commuting Time is Up 21 Hours Compared to a Decade Ago, Finds TUC.* TUC.

Union Comunera. (2023). *Communard Union: Programmatic Foundations and Statutes 2022*. Progressive International.

Unit 38 Architects & Wards Corner Community Plan. (2019, July). *Wards Corner Community Plan*.

United Nations Environment Programme. (2021). *Our Global Food System is the Primary Driver of Biodiversity Loss*. UN Environment.

UNOHC. (2017, July 26). *London Market Closure Plan Threatens "Dynamic Cultural Centre" - UN Rights Experts [press release]*.

van der Ploeg, J. D. (2014). Peasant-Driven Agricultural Growth and Food Sovereignty. *The Journal of Peasant Studies*, 41(6), 999–1030.

Vangay, P., Johnson, A. J., Ward, T. L., Al-Ghalith, G. A., Shields-Cutler, R. R., Hillmann, B. M., Lucas, S. K., Beura, L. K., Thompson, E. A., Till, L. M., Batres, R., Paw, B., Pergament, S. L., Saenyakul, P., Xiong, M., Kim, A. D., Kim, G., Masopust, D., Martens, E. C., ... Knights, D. (2018). US Immigration Westernizes the Human Gut Microbiome. *Cell*, 175(4), 962-972.e10.

Varvarousis, A., Asara, V., & Akbulut, B. (2021). Commons: A Social Outcome of the Movement of the Squares. *Social Movement Studies*, 20(3), 292–311.

Veltmeyer, H., & Ezquerro-Cañete, A. (2023). *From Extractivism to Sustainability: Scenarios and Lessons from Latin America*. Taylor & Francis.

Vettese, T., & Pendergrass, D. (2022). *Half-Earth Socialism: A Plan to Save the Future from Extinction, Climate Change and Pandemics*. Verso Books.

Wainwright, O. (2023, October 21). Cracked Tiles, Wonky Gutters, Leaning Walls – Why are Britain's New Houses So Rubbish? *The Guardian*.

Wall, D. (2017). *Elinor Ostrom's Rules for Radicals: Cooperative Alternatives Beyond Markets and States*. Pluto Press (UK).

Wang, Y., Okochi, H., Tani, Y., Hayami, H., Minami, Y., Katsumi, N., Takeuchi, M., Sorimachi, A., Fujii, Y., Kajino, M., Adachi, K., Ishihara, Y., Iwamoto, Y., & Niida, Y. (2023). Airborne Hydrophilic Microplastics in Cloud Water at High Altitudes and Their Role in Cloud Formation. *Environmental Chemistry Letters*, 21(6), 3055–3062.

Watling, S., & Breach, A. (2023). *The Housebuilding Crisis: The UK's 4 million Missing Homes*. Centre for Cities.

We Own It. (2012, August 6). *We Need Publicly Owned Care*.

Weber, A. (2022, January 5). *The Big Six to the Big Four: The Rise of the Seed and Agrochemical Oligopoly*. Policy Review @ Berkeley.

Weber, I. (2025, February 28) To Defeat the Far Right, We Must Adopt an Anti-Fascist Economic Policy. *The Nation*.

Weis, A. J. (2007). *The Global Food Economy: The Battle for the Future of Farming*. Zed Books.

WEMOS Foundation. (2014, September 1). *Added Therapeutic Value: European Citizens Should Get Their Money's Worth*.

Wetherell, S. (2016). Duncan Tanner essay prize 2015. *Twentieth Century British History*, 27(2), 266–289.

Wild, D. (2021, September 9). Farming on "Verge of Crisis" Unless More Young People Enter. *FarmingUK*.

Méndez de Andés, A., Hamou, D. & Aparacio, M. (2021). *Códigos comunes urbanos: Herramientas para el devenir-común de las ciudades*. [Urban common codes: Tools for the becoming-common of cities]. Icaria.

Williams, A., & Gilbert, J. (2022). *Hegemony Now: How Big Tech and Wall Street Won the World (And How We Win it Back)*. Verso Books.

Willis, G., Williams, C., Graham, K., & Swade, K. (2022). *Reimagining Council Farms: A Vision For 2040*. New Economics Foundation; Shared Assets; CPRE.

Wing, I. S., De Cian, E., & Mistry, M. N. (2021). Global Vulnerability of Crop Yields to Climate Change. *Journal of Environmental Economics and Management*, 109, 102462.

Wolf, M. (2021, November 23). Dancing on the Edge of Climate Disaster. *Financial Times*.

Wood, R. (2016, August 5). *RoboBees: Autonomous Flying Microrobots*. Wyss Institute.

Woolley, D., & Scott, N. (2024). *Community Models for Farm Ownership*. Stir to Action.

World Economic Forum. (2024, January 10). Global Risks Report 2024. *World Economic Forum*.

World Inequality Lab. (2022). *World Inequality Report 2022*.

Wouters, O. J. (2020). Lobbying Expenditures and Campaign Contributions by the Pharmaceutical and Health Product Industry in the United States, 1999-2018. *JAMA Internal Medicine*, 180(5), 688.

Wright, E. O. (2010). *Envisioning Real Utopias*. Verso Books.

Wright, O. (2023, June 14) No Growth in Average Earnings Since 2005, Data Shows. *The Times*.

Yeros, P. (2023). Generalized Semiproletarianization in Africa. *The Indian Economic Journal*, 71(1), 162–186.

The Pluto Press Newsletter

Hello friend of Pluto!

Want to stay on top of the best radical books we publish?

Then sign up to be the first to hear about our new books, as well as special events, podcasts and videos.

You'll also get 50% off your first order with us when you sign up.

Come and join us!

Go to bit.ly/PlutoNewsletter